Down Under and Up Over – Travels with Narrative Therapy

David Epston

Edited by Barry Bowen

First published in Great Britain in 2008 by AFT
Publishing Ltd, Warrington, England

Cover design and typesetting by Louise Norris

Photography by Mike Gowing

Printed in Great Britain by Antony Rowe,
Chippenham, Wiltshire

ISBN 978-0-9523433-1-8

I would like to dedicate this book to my parents,
Helen and Benjamin Epston,
for inspiring the work that makes up this book

In loving memory of Michael White (1948-2008),
my friend, colleague and 'brother'.

David Epston: Down Under and Up Over:
Travels with Narrative Therapy

Contents

Introduction

Barry Bowen

The sub-title of this book, *travels with narrative therapy*, led me to think about my own Narrative journey, in particular my longstanding interest in David Epston's practice. I then began to wonder about David's journey, from his own early influences to having become a major influence on both Narrative Therapy and family therapy, especially with regards to the UK.

I can't remember how I first heard about David Epston. I also can't remember how I first heard about Salvador Minuchin, Milton Erickson, Bill O'Hanlon, Michael White, or any of the other major influences upon my career as a therapist. As far as David is concerned, I am fairly sure it would have been in either 1989 or 1990, around the time that *Literate Means to Therapeutic Ends* (later republished as *Narrative Means to Therapeutic Ends* in the United States) was published in Australia (White & Epston, 1989). I doubt at that time if any of us were thinking of what later emerged as Narrative Therapy as being a separate entity, but more as another exciting school of family therapy. In the UK, Narrative Therapy has remained a therapeutic approach in its own right and has also merged into the mainstream of family therapy. As a family therapist (or a systemic psychotherapist, to use the newer and wider term) I have felt happy to embrace Narrative Therapy in both ways, although I am aware that this has not always been the case in other countries or in other cultures.

So what do I identify as being basic to my being an Epston-influenced therapist? Four elements come to mind: one is the emphasis upon practice, the second is co-researching the knowledges of the people whom seek our help (1), the third is the use of everyday language, and the fourth is a deep respect for other human beings and the emphasis upon the strengths of others rather than their 'weaknesses'. This, above all, is what drew me to what later became Narrative Therapy in the early days of 1989/1990.

Long before we in the UK had heard of David Epston, he was already known in his native New Zealand and also in Australia as a creative therapist, teacher and writer (e.g. Epston, 1983, 1985, 1986). In his introduction to *Narrative Means to Therapeutic Ends*, Michael White writes about the influence of David's childhood experiences and his former career as an anthropologist on his earlier work, especially as regards his interest in stories and the influence stories have on the way we see both ourselves and others. During the eighties, for example, David co-ordinated the 'Story Corner' section of *the Australian & New Zealand Journal of Family Therapy*. My co-editor Gary Robinson and I unknowingly followed in his footsteps with our 'Therapeutic Stories' column and themed issues in the UK family therapy publication *Context* and the associated short book (e.g. Bowen & Robinson, 1999).

The main influence on my work derived from *Narrative Means to Therapeutic Ends* was the process of co-authoring alternative stories and the importance of the written word. I had long been interested in stories (e.g. Bowen, 1997), due in part to my interest in the work of Milton Erickson (e.g. Haley, 1973). Now, however, Epston and White were suggesting that helping people to find alternatives to the largely negative stories about themselves and celebrating this through the use of letters, certificates and other written documents could open up new long-lasting opportunities for change. In fact, David Epston and Michael White regularly interviewed recipients of such documentation and sought their opinions as to how many meetings a letter was worth. Of the several hundred whose opinion was sought, the average was five meetings.

My work had already taken on a Narrative flavour when I almost simultaneously met two books that both consolidated this change and confirmed me as an Epston-influenced therapist. The first was Michael White's *Selected Papers* (1989) and the second was David Epston's *Collected Papers* (1989).

Michael White's book excited me, and I can remember being particularly enthusiastic about his papers on externalisation, grief and 'fear-busting' (White, 1989); David Epston's book made an equally strong impression.

Collected Papers (unfortunately now out of print) was made up of thirty papers, published between 1983 and 1988, but some of the work recorded dated back as far as 1979. This, then, is an excellent source for David's therapeutic journey during much of the eighties, as recorded in mainly Australian journals. *Collected Papers* therefore served a similar role in the eighties to that served by Part One of this book: to acquaint those of us who live in the upper hemisphere with papers we would otherwise have missed.

These early papers already have that distinctive style of David's, an avoidance of academic aloofness and 'academic-speak' in favour of a naturalistic first-person account of what actually happened. I am sure David's background in anthropology had a part to play, but so did those aspects I referred to above: an emphasis upon practice, co-researching with people, and the use of experience-near language, combined with a deep respect for the potential strengths of fellow human beings. All these are wonderfully demonstrated in what I consider to be the stand-out (and longest) paper in that book: *In memory of Hatu (Hayden) Barlow (1973-1985)*.

At the time I recommended the reading of this paper to almost every professional with whom I came into contact. It was a very moving account of young Maori boy's struggle with terminal cancer and how he achieved greater control over his remaining life. It is not only the story of Hatu's tremendous courage, but of the co-operation and creativity of all involved: Hatu, his family and the various professionals, including David Epston. David encouraged Hatu to 'test' the abilities of family members to stand up to his worries; he used hypnotherapy, story-telling and metaphor to confront his terrifying dreams, eating difficulties and the side-effects of chemotherapy; he used therapeutic letters and a 'stealing test' so that Hatu could regain his reputation as an honest person (something I have now done several times since, often successfully, having found that the skill is often in 'selling' the idea to the parents: the child is usually on board well before them); he also created an anger control programme that involved an imaginary three-headed tiger. The paper ends with two moving tributes to Hatu, one from his social worker and the other from his mother. No one I know has ever read this last section without crying, and at the same time being inspired by this young man. I am pleased that David has decided to open Part One of this book with a version of that chapter.

Another selection of published papers followed these two separate volumes (White, 1989, Epston, 1989) containing contributions from both David and Michael, and with the intriguing title: *Experience, Contradiction, Narrative & Imagination* (Epston & White, 1992). This book contained their important paper: *Consulting your consultants: the documentation of alternative knowledges.* (pp11-16).

For some reason I didn't hear about David's next venture, the book *Narrative Therapy: The Archaeology of Hope* (Monk et al, 1997). Instead, the next book I read was *Catching up with David Epston* (Epston, 1998). This contained material I had first met at a 2 day workshop David presented in Liverpool, my first meeting with David. The cover shows David characteristically sitting astride his beloved bicycle and the subtitle of the book quite tellingly informs us that this is a collection of *practice-based* papers. The period of time the reprinted papers cover is 1991 to 1996.

In 1994, David had visited Liverpool to present a two-day workshop at the request of Barnardo's Family Therapy Team (2). I was there and I remember David taking us through a number of his therapy sessions, using video and overheads of transcripts. He also very generously allowed the workshops (apart from those parts featuring videos of families) to be recorded on video. For a few years, I was the proud owner of a video of David talking about his creative work with 'imaginary friends' (until an errant video recorder chewed it up!). I met this work again, though, as chapter 6 of *Catching up with David Epston* (pp 39-60). The following year I returned to Liverpool with 15 of the original participants to present our own Narrative Therapy work, much of this later being published in *Context*, including my own presentation on Narrative approaches to anger (Bowen, 1996a) and anxiety (Bowen, 1996b).

The introduction to *Catching up with David Epston* contains the phrase *'I have always committed myself to generate practice from the ground-up rather than theory-down'* and emphasises the importance of 'drawing closer' to the experiences of others. These, he says in the introduction, are the common threads running through what at first glance seem to be a disparate selection of papers. Thus, in the book we read about the important influence of David's father upon his later work, re-authoring, internalising and externalising discourses, internalised other questioning, the above-mentioned imaginary friends, anger control, letter writing and rituals of inclusion, communities of concern and other Narrative approaches to eating disorders, co-researching, and externalising problems. There is also a chapter called 'voices' that I'm still trying to fully understand! The chapters are crystal clear and practice-based. Although I take back the crystal clear description as far as 'voices' is concerned!

Internalised other questioning came up again when I met David for the second time in Manchester in 2005, as it was fairly central to one of the workshops he presented. David also presented what he and his co-researchers refer to as anti-anorexia/anti-bulimia, which is the subject of what I consider to be one of the best books on the subject – *Biting the Hand that Starves You: Inspiring Resistance to Anorexia/Bulimia* (Maisel, Epston & Borden, 2004). But I am getting ahead of myself.

After *Catching up with David Epston*, I read *Playful Approaches to Serious Problems* (Freeman, Epston & Lobovits, 1997). This had been published in the USA the previous year, but I didn't manage to get a copy until a couple of years later. David made a direct link to his earlier influences by in part dedicating the book to *'Benny the Peanut Man'*, a reference to his father, a chapter by the same name having appeared in the *'Catching Up'* book. *'Playful Approaches'* was divided into sections entitled Playful Communication, Playful Means, and Playful Stories. My particular favourite was a chapter about children with 'weird and special abilities' (pp 179-192), a topic that had come up during David's Liverpool workshops. He writes in the chapter of meetings with 'weirdly abled' children, young people who had used their imagination in creative ways. Sometimes these children had been described as 'a nerd', 'a day-dreamer', or as 'living in a fantasy world'. Now they came to realise that having an imaginary friend, or turning yourself into an imaginary animal, for example, were in fact highly prized skills not shared by the unfortunate and less weirdly abled. Once again there was a mention of David's father, who was it seems himself weirdly abled, or perhaps just an early Narrative practitioner! The book includes five extended case stories in the 'Playful Stories' section, themselves worth the price of buying the book. Not all of these are by David, but the book as a whole is a good example of the way David co-works with other professionals.

I was aware of David's interest in eating disorders, mostly from visiting his web site (see below) and so I was not surprised to hear that he was visiting Manchester in 2005 to offer three days of workshops, the first of which was to be on that subject. Unfortunately, because of another commitment, I wasn't able to go to the eating disorder workshop, but I did attend days 2 and 3. On both days I somehow ended up joining David for lunch at a nearby café. I was about to start editing a special issue of *Context* on the theme of Narrative Therapy and already had some very good UK practitioners offering contributions. Over lunch I wondered aloud if David would be interested in also offering a contribution. The result was a fascinating paper called *'Putting pressure on yourself to put pressure on the problem'* (Epston, 2006). The subject area of that paper is expanded upon in chapter 7 of this book.

The conversation moved on and David talked about having published papers 'down under' in Australasia that had never found their way to the western hemisphere. He also had some new material, some of which needed a little editing. Would he be interested in a book, I wondered? I was sure AFT Publishing would be keen to publish it and I knew I was more than interested in editing it. We agreed to pursue the idea. David went back to New Zealand and I went back to Hampshire. I negotiated with AFT Publishing and the publishing house Karnac, as we needed a marketer and distributor, while my e-mail in-tray began to fill up with chapters, part-chapters and papers.

It soon became clear that this book, like *Catching up with David Epston*, would be wide-ranging in its subject matter. Part One (Down Under) contains previously published work from different periods of David's writing career, with some changes so as to form a more coherent whole. As always, each chapter reflects David's creativity, and at times those of his co-writers. Thus we read of therapeutic communication via FAX, a weirdly abled young person, a richly emotional 'haunting from the future', temper taming, undergraduate final papers as a rite of passage, and that chapter in memory of a boy with a terminal illness (Hatu) that had made me cry many years before, and which I still believe is the best chapter David has ever written. Then we turn to Part Two (Up Over) and find six examples of David's current work, all of which are printed for the first time. This section is also both varied and creative. Thus we find inventive approaches to chronic bed-wetting, relationships between children and their estranged fathers, court reports, stealing, and sibling conflicts, as well as a long chapter on Anti-Anorexia, a subject close to David's heart.

Some of the e-mails exchanged between David and I also contained little snippets of David's other commitments, his marathon bicycle ride, and the exciting news that in 2007 he had been awarded the 'distinguished contribution to theory and practice of family therapy' by the American Family Therapy Academy (AFTA). Eventually the book became a viable project, David and I became e-mail pen friends, and I've truly enjoyed being part of both.

Barry Bowen
2008

References
Bowen, B. (1996a) 'Externalising anger' in Exploring the Narrative Approach – The Liverpool Invitation, *Context*, 26, 30-33.
Bowen, B. (1996b) 'Zapping anxiety' in Therapeutic Stories, *Context*, 28, 8-11.
Bowen, B. (1997) 'Stories in the context of family therapy' in Dwivedi, K. N. (Ed) *The Therapeutic Use of Stories*, Routledge, London, 171-184.
Bowen, B. & Robinson, G. (Eds) (1999) *Therapeutic Stories*, AFT Publications, Canterbury.
Epston, D. (1983) Cheryl-Anne's new autobiography, *Australian Journal of Family Therapy*, 4,4, 259-261
Epston, D. (1985) The family with the malediction, *Australian & New Zealand Journal of Family Therapy*, 6, 3,175-176
Epston, D. (1986) Counter-dreaming, *Dulwich Centre Newsletter*, February, 10-15
Epston, D. (1989) *Collected Papers*, Dulwich Centre Publications. Adelaide.
Epston, D. & White, M. (1992) *Experience, Contradiction, Narrative & Imagination*, Dulwich Centre Publications, Adelaide.
Epston, D. (1998) *Catching up with David Epston: a collection of Narrative practice-based papers published between 1991 & 1996*. Dulwich Centre Publications, Adelaide.
Epston, D. (2006) 'Putting pressure on yourself to put pressure on the problem', *Context*, 85, 2-5.
Freeman, J., Epston, D. & Lobovits, D. (1997) *Playful Approaches to Serious Problems: Narrative Therapy with Children and their Families*, W.W. Norton & Co, New York.
Hayley, J. (1973) *Uncommon Therapy – The Psychiatric Techniques of Milton H. Erickson*, W.W. Norton & Co., New York.
Maisel, R., Epston, D. & Borden, A. (2004) *Biting the Hand that Starves You: Inspiring Resistance to Anorexia/Bulimia*, W.W. Norton & Co, New York.
Monk, G., Winslade, J., Crockettt, K. & Epston, D. (Eds) (1997) *Narrative Therapy: The Archaeology of Hope*, Jossey-Bass, San Francisco.
White, M. (1989) *Selected Papers*, Dulwich Centre Publications, Adelaide.
White, M, & Epston, D. (1989) *Literate Means to Therapeutic Ends*, Dulwich Centre Publications, Adelaide, republished as (1990) *Narrative Means to Therapeutic Ends*, W.W. Norton & Co, New York.

1) For more on co-research, and much else, see David Epston's website: www.narrativeaproaches.com

2) Pat Gray, Pete Harmsworth, Helen Marks and Ged Smith.

Down Under...

1

In Memory of Hatu (Hayden) Barlow (1973-1985)

Cynthia Barlow, David Epston, Mike Murphy, Lynn O'Flaherty and Louise Webster

Original version published in Family Therapy Case Studies, 1987, 2(2):19-37 and then in Epston, D. (1989) *Collected Papers*, Dulwich Centre Publications

I first met Hayden, a ten-year-old Maori boy, on the 31st May 1983. In his too short life, his accomplishments were of such an order that everyone who knew him remembers him by his teachings ('he taught me so much'). Even before the recurrence of his disease, Hayden, his parents and I had discussed and started work on making his story known to others. For Hayden, with very little assistance, had found a way to replace the suffering most young people experience as an effect of their chemotherapeutic treatment with the delight of movies in his mind. His death made me set aside the project. He lived on in the taped discussions we had together and my memories of him. And I knew if he had survived, he would have wanted to make his discoveries known to other cancer sufferers. I discussed this with the Barlows, and they supported it in principle and contributed to it. For me, I wanted Hayden's wizardry to be available in some form useable to my colleagues. For that reason, I invited Mike Murphy to add commentary from a hypnotic perspective. I also believed that by writing down Hayden's story that I would keep his memory alive.

Dr. Webster introduces Hayden

When I first met Hayden, he had been fighting his cancer for eight years. He was found to have a Wilm's tumour in his left kidney when he was three years old. His kidney was removed and he started chemotherapy. He had a recurrence several months after his surgery and developed a metastasis in his right lung, which was treated by radiotherapy. Hayden continued having chemotherapy which involved frequent blood tests, needles, drips and drugs which made him ill. This regime continued until he was six.

Just before his eleventh birthday, the metastasis in his lung began to grow again and he came into hospital to have the cancer and part of his lung removed. After that, he was to have another year of chemotherapy.

I first met him after his surgery. Every month, his parents would drive him to the hospital from Tauranga, one hundred miles away, for his chemotherapy. At first he seemed unconcerned about the therapy, always smiling and never showing any distress. But slowly over the next few months, he changed. He had a dramatic weight loss, was not eating and looked miserable and unwell. Initially, it was suspected that these were consequences of the disease process but examination did not support this conclusion. I told Hayden I was worried about him but could find no physical cause for his weight loss. I asked him what he thought the problem might be. Hayden pulled the brim of the baseball cap he customarily wore down over his face. All I could see were his tears trickling out from under it. He hated anyone to see him cry. He told me he couldn't eat. Every time he sat down to a meal, he would see needles and drips and feel nauseated, just like he did after chemotherapy. At night, he had nightmares of tombstones with drip bottles and infusion lines running into them. He was dying while doctors and nurses climbed out of the tombstones towards him saying: 'We're going to get you? It's your fault!' Then he would see a truck bearing down on him. Hayden acknowledged that he was afraid of dying. He told me he had 'never made a fuss before' about his chemotherapy but now he felt he couldn't endure it any longer. Although Hayden seemed relieved by telling me of his fears, I knew that this was insufficient for him to recommence his chemotherapy. I told him that his treatments would be waived until he felt reassured about continuing and that a delay would not matter. Hayden requested that I let his parents know what was happening. He had been unable to reveal to them that his usual bravado was just a front. I talked to them with Hayden and with their permission referred them to David Epston at The Leslie Centre.

First Session (David Epston)

Louise Webster rang me requesting that I urgently see the Barlow family. She reassured me that Hayden's sudden weight loss was unrelated to any disease process and told me of her concerns. I agreed to do so if she was willing to accompany them.

Cynthia and Roy Barlow appeared both confused and desperate. Their five-year-old daughter, Rina, was beside herself with excitement as she had just got a white kitten. She was requested to play in the playroom. Hayden was buried beneath his father's bushman's coat (swandri). Cynthia and Roy told me that Hayden was extremely independent and for some time had preferred to manage his hospital treatments on his own. However, he wasn't managing any more and, without asking, I surmised they must have been dreadfully concerned about his unaccountable weight loss; their observations that he had become "pale and miserable" over the past month, and his refusal to undergo any further treatments. Hayden's eyes were downcast but I noticed in my peripheral vision that when I turned towards his parents he would look up towards me. After establishing the parents' degree of concern and confusion, I turned quickly towards him, meeting his gaze for the first time and said: 'Do you think your parents can stand up to your strong feelings?' Hayden was caught off guard and uttered a defensive 'dunno'. 'Well, why don't you put them to the test? They look strong enough to me but you'll never know until you test them!' Before Hayden could come up with an answer, I turned to his parents: 'Do you mind if Hayden tests you to see if you are strong enough to stand up to his worries?' Although uncertain as to the nature of the test, they wholeheartedly agreed to undergo it. It was agreed that his father would go first and that his test would last exactly fifteen minutes. Louise, Cynthia and I retired to another room leaving father and son sitting across from one another with a box of tissues placed midway between them. After exactly 15 minutes, Cynthia joined Roy and Hayden. Louise and I knocked on the door when Cynthia's time was up and in due course were welcomed back into the room. The floor was littered with tissues so I guessed things had worked out as I had hoped. Everyone had composed themselves, looked somewhat relieved and were laughing. Hayden with some pride assured me that his parents could stand up to his strong feelings. I asked Hayden to give

17

me a measure of his worries as opposed to his fun by holding his hands apart to indicate the 'bigness' of each. I carefully took measurements with a tape measure – 50 centimetres of worry and 15 centimetres of fun. Louise reiterated that this month's treatment would be deferred. Instead, I invited them to return the next day to meet together once again.

Second session (next day)

The mood of the family was lighter but they still didn't really know what to expect. I asked if I could meet with Hayden on my own. I told him Louise had informed me of his bad dreams. He told me he dreamt that a medical round of doctors surrounded him and pointed their fingers accusingly at him, shouting: 'That's the one!' They then stood aside for him to see a truck bearing down on him. He would then awake from this nightmare. He went on to me that as a young boy, he had been responsible for the supervision of an intellectually handicapped uncle. Hayden crossed a road ahead of him but his uncle walked in front of an oncoming truck. Hayden recollected: 'He went to hospital but before he died he had drips in him. I just about beat up the lorry driver. I didn't think!' I elicited Hayden's guilt and self-accusation but did not challenge it in any way. I merely accepted his construction of events. I requested his parents to join us and asked their permission for me to hypnotise Hayden. They agreed and sat by my side, looking on with keen anticipation. I guided us all into a trance by inviting Hayden to close his eyes and asked him if he could see a TV screen in his mind and ratified this by the questions: 'Is it black and white or colour? Is it a big one or a little one?' Hayden confirmed it was a large colour TV set in his mind. To ratify the trance behaviour for Hayden and his parents, I had Hayden levitate his hand by having him imagine a balloon being linked to his wrist by a fine string. While his hand was levitated, I told the following story:

A long time ago and in another far away place, I was doing the job I am doing now. A man came to see me. He told me he couldn't eat anymore, and that he used to really like his tucker. 'Why not?' I asked. He told me it was a long story. I told I had plenty of time and he could tell me the whole story if he wished. He said he had to. He had no choice. It had been bothering him for a long time and he had had enough of it. He told me was a truck driver and had killed a man ACCIDENTALLY. And ever since then, he hadn't been able to eat properly. 'How did it happen?' I asked. He told me that he had been driving along when a young boy crossed the road in front of him. Then a bee came from nowhere and stung him in the face. Then he temporarily lost control and ran over a man who had followed the boy. 'Well', I said, 'You can now start eating again. It surely was not your fault. It was the bee's fault'. He replied: 'I know that..... I know that. That's not what I am worried about. I'm worried sick about the boy!' I became confused and asked him why. He said: 'He'll blame himself even though it was the bee's fault!' Now I knew I was getting somewhere. I told him, 'Look, I've been doing this job with children now for nine years and I know what I'm talking about. I want

18

you to know that no boy would believe such a crazy idea!' He immediately brightened up and asked if I was sure about that. 'Sure, I'm sure,' I said. And you know, he went home that day, regained his appetite, and starting eating again. He let me know later that his life had improved in many ways although to this day he doesn't like bees much. But I guess that is easy to understand.

I continued with some trance 'talk' and then asked Hayden what his favourite foods were. After some thought, he said they were Kentucky fried chicken and pizzas. I then mockingly warned him that if he didn't START TO EAT, I would get some drips from the hospital and give them to his parents. They were then to put the pizza on one plate and some drips on another and he would have to choose between them. He said he would definitely choose pizzas over drips. I then said that his parents were to insist that he jump up and down on the drips, saying, 'That isn't food. That's for doctors and my coming right!' Before he was allowed to start on his pizza, he should throw the drips in the rubbish bin. He assured me that this would be no trouble for him. I said, 'At the dinner table, there's only ONE thing you're going to have and that's food'. I gradually re-oriented Hayden who immediately grasped about his head for the imaginary balloon, much to his parents' amusement. We agreed to meet a day before his next treatment in a month's time.

Third Session (one month later)
I began the session by asking Hayden if I could re-assess his fun versus worry ratio. Everything about him and his family told me the result would be a good one. It was: 120 centimetres of fun versus 1 centimetre of worry. When I asked him how this had happened, he told me that finding out that his mother and father 'could stand up to my worries' had helped him 'cut down' on his worrying. 'I tell them my worries. I had tested them. They can take a lot'. Both Roy and Cynthia told me that they had been unaware of the nature of his concerns and felt they had now convinced him that he didn't have to be 'so strong'. They said there had been 'big changes' since our last meeting. Hayden was talking a lot, looking happy, not hiding behind his swandri and eating well. Now his plate was 'always piled up' and despite my concern for him becoming overweight, it was a concern he didn't share. His nightmares had stopped and been replaced 'by good dreams of just nothing'. He no longer saw drips so his parents didn't have to play 'our joke' on him. His colour had now returned to his face and he was able to look at his hair growing back, whereas before he didn't dare to.

When I asked Cynthia what advice she would give to other mothers, she said: 'Talk to him. Ask him all the time what's going on in his head. Cry about it. It's not bad to cry'. Roy's reply to the same question was: 'I'd do the same. I'd get into a room and talk to him. He was a different boy after that'. Hayden's reply was: 'Tell your mother and father and get everything out of your system. Don't bottle it up inside you. After talking to you (David), it just came out. Now I know my mother and father can take my worries. I sleep right away now!'

Cynthia commented that Hayden was no longer frightened of his treatment. In the meantime, I had had discussions with Wilma Schwartz. I was informed that Hayden was one of the worst reactors she had known to the side-effects of the treatment. He would vomit approximately five times in anticipation of the treatment, after which he would persist in dry retching. He required medication and often had to stay overnight in the hospital to be rehydrated. I asked Hayden if this was so and he assured me it was. I asked him if he wanted to learn to control his vomiting. In a matter of fact way, he informed me that he already knew how: 'You just switch yourself off. I know a boy who has a technique to switch himself off'. The parents concurred as they too know of Carl, the boy to whom Hayden was referring. Carl, a fellow patient somewhat older than Hayden, was well-known for his self-taught ability. I said: 'Well, with that in mind, you teach yourself how to switch off and I'll show you how to switch on to movies in your mind. BUT YOU WILL HAVE TO PRACTICE. You want to switch yourself on to movies?' Everyone considered that to be a great idea. I re-guided us into a trance focusing on Hayden. I established that the needle was inserted in the vein in the back of his hand and the sensations associated with it. 'You feel the coolness of the drips. You feel it go all the way up your arm and it stops just past your arm'. Hayden told me that Carl switched off and 'thinks of good things!' I found out that Every Which Way But Loose was his favourite movie and he told me its story. I then gave him a post-hypnotic suggestion, employing the sensation of coldness and/or nausea to 'switch on' the movie of his choice.

I arranged to ring Louise Webster after his treatment (9am-4pm) the next day, but I couldn't wait until it finished. I rang at 2pm to learn that he had indeed 'switched off', avoided vomiting, was deeply relaxed throughout his treatment. He was so relaxed in fact that he wet himself. Next time, I would remind him to go to the toilet BEFORE he 'switched off/switched on'.

Fourth Session (two months later)

There had been some mild distress during the next month's treatment although this probably had something to do with 'a cold'. We met again and the following is a transcript of that session with commentary by Mike Murphy. After this session, Hayden was to never vomit again and endured his treatment with equanimity until the year was up. Although I visited Hayden and his family on several occasions, these were social calls. Things were certainly looking up for Hayden.

Mike Murphy's commentary

David's description of his work with Hayden includes much reference to the use of hypnotic approaches, particularly indirect and Ericksonian hypnosis, reflected in the use of metaphor and indirect suggestion. The basic hypnotic effect used is one of encouraging pleasant and/or distracting associations with some of the unpleasant stimuli Hayden experienced as part of his chemotherapy. Hayden had associated chemotherapy with nausea so that the thought of intravenous drip equipment triggered nausea and eating had become associated with visualising drips and hence also nausea. A relationship between the chemotherapy and the nightmares can be considered as the nightmare included the image of a group of medical practitioners accusing Hayden.

David's metaphor incorporating the truck driver who accidentally killed a man and who subsequently could not eat appears to address the possible issues of self-blame and self-punishment in the form of not eating. As well as providing a story regarding someone who began eating again, and hence a classic form of Ericksonian indirect suggestion, it also provides a new perspective for Hayden to attribute blame for his relative's death, shifting the ultimate responsibility to a bee who stung the driver. It also presents the driver as concerned about, and hence responsible for, the little boy who was with the man who was killed.

The issue of self-control is then introduced with the proposed task of choosing between a plate of Kentucky fried chicken or a plate of intravenous drips. A distinction between drips and food is being drawn but the choice is emphasised by the imagery of Hayden smashing the drips. He has to have chemotherapy but he does not have to 'eat' drips.

In the third session, in which the switching off/switching on metaphor is constructed, David utilises Hayden's account of a fellow sufferer who has learned to switch off. By doing so, he has indirectly suggested that Hayden 'switch off' his experiences of chemotherapy and nausea and 'switch on' a favourite movie in his imagination. Their term 'switching on' is usefully ambiguous in that it has connotations of being the right thing to do. This approach makes use of the hypnotic concept of disassociation, often used for pain management, in which Hayden's attention is 'switched on' to his internal visual and auditory world of remembered or imagined movies. As a result he is less aware of the unpleasant aspects of intravenous drips and nausea.

In the transcript of the fourth session, David makes extensive use of indirect suggestion, particularly presuppositions and binds which presupposes a certain outcome. An example of a presupposing indirect bind is the statement, 'When are you are going to a make a cup of tea?' in which it is presupposed that the listener is going to make a cup of tea but their attention is focussed on 'when'. David uses several suggestions of this form with Hayden, always presupposing Hayden is in charge. Throughout, he suggests metaphors and images to which Hayden responds. Aspects of David's use of indirect suggestions and the utilisation principle are illustrated in the following remarks inserted in the transcript of the fourth session:

DE: *Well Hayden, I just thought we'd start talking about- I'd like to know what's happened to your nightmares?*
Hayden: *They've gone away....they just vanished um ... um because I came to see you.*
DE: *Where do you think they went to? Did they just go down the drain?*
Hayden: *(gleefully) Yeah!!*
DE: *Do you think you ever want them back?*

Hayden: *(assertively) No!*
DE: *Yeah. Do you have any ideas ... why I'm asking is because I am trying to learn about this, right, learning from you then I'll teach you something ... I'm just wondering, do you have any ideas how it happened? I know it happened but I'm trying to learn how it happened. I'm not quite sure myself. I've done it quite a few times but I learned from the kids telling me about it. What do you think happened?*

David is immediately adopting the position that Hayden has achieved getting rid of his nightmares. Hayden is somehow in control. He is challenging Hayden's earlier statement 'because I came to see you'.

Hayden: *It's just....it's just the drips...the needles and all that...*

Hayden sounds as though he has lapsed into an altered state as he recalls the drips. He has difficulty continuing to speak although he sounds comfortable. This could be the post-hypnotic suggestion effect of previous work.

DE: *Yeah......they've disappeared?*
Hayden: *Humph!*
DE: *So your mum and dad didn't have to play that joke on you?*
Hayden: *No....*
DE: *So we saved the hospital having to give you some drips to decide whether you wanted to eat them or not?*
Hayden: *Yep.*
DE: *So you're not having bad dreams?*
Hayden: *No.*
DE: *Are you having good dreams?*

David shifts Hayden's attention from bad dreams to good dreams. Simply eliciting an idea can be regarded as an indirect suggestion, in this case, to have good dreams.

Hayden: *Yep.*
DE: *Can you tell me about some of your good dreams?*
Hayden: *Sometimes I just dream about nothing and sometimes...*
DE: *Is it a happy nothing?*
Hayden: *Yeah, it's just nothing. Sometimes I dream about ... oh, I forget all my dreams. The good ones just somehow slip out of my mind and I can't remember them again.*
DE: *It's easier to remember the bad ones you know. They wake you up. So you've been having some good sleeps?*

The idea of good dreams is broadened and associated with 'good sleeps'.

Hayden: *Mmmm.*

DE: *OK. The other thing I wanted to know is … remember before you found it very difficult to eat?*

Hayden: *Yep.*

DE: *You were off your tucker. Looks like you're gaining a lot of weight?*

Hayden: *Hmmm.*

DE: *Getting stronger?*

The idea of gaining weight is associated with getting stronger, usually an appealing concept for middle childhood boys.

Hayden: *(laughs)*

DE: *What's happened there, do you reckon?*

Hayden: *All the nightmares are gone – that's helped a bit. And now when I eat, I don't feel all those drips.*

DE: *You don't feel the drips?*

Hayden: *I don't see them.*

DE: *Good … good … good.*

Hayden: *And I just eat my tea … breakfast … lunch …*

DE: *And you're having a lot more fun than worries?*

Once again associating a pleasant, positive idea with eating, as distinct from, and a more useful alternative to worrying, feeling nauseous, etc. This is also an indirect suggestion to have fun while eating.

Hayden: *Yep.*

DE: *Are you worrying about the fact that your mother is a bit worried now?*

Hayden: *Yah.*

DE: *What do you think she should do about that?*

David frames worry as her responsibility rather than Hayden's

DE: *Now the other thing I wanted to know was – remember you came to me and I talked to you and the next day, you went into hospital. Not the last time but the time before?*

Hayden: *Yeh.*

DE: *Do you remember what happened? The time you saw the movie and all that...*

Hayden: *Do you want me to tell you about the movie?*

DE: *No, I just want to know what happened...*

Hayden: *It was those bikies and Clyde punched and beat them up.*

DE: *Beat up the bikies? Clyde the gorilla...*

Hayden: Yeah ... and lots of fun...

DE: And tell me how long did the movies last when you were having your treatment?

Hayden: Wouldn't have a clue!

DE: Did you know how long that was?

Mother: A couple of hours.

Hayden: That was a couple of years ago. I saw it – the movie. Ask me another question?

DE: Ask another question ... alright. So you just went out like a light and turned off a switch?

Hayden: Yeah.

DE: Then you turned on the movie?

Hayden: Yep!

DE: Do you want to watch 'The Dukes of Hazzard' this time?

David's question presupposes that Hayden will use the same technique again, but shifts his attention to the choice of 'movies' to watch.

DE: So you're getting like Carl ... switching things off and switching things on. That's really good you can do that!

Emphasises that Hayden is in control.

Hayden: Mmmh.

DE: So if I ever meet a boy who was having bad dreams like you USED to do, what advice would you think I should give that boy? What should he do?

Describes bad dreams as past experience.

Hayden: Of course, he'd have to come to you...

DE: (to mother) He's giving me too much credit. I'm worried about that. You say I did it. YOU DID IT! I just helped. I gave you some ideas. I wasn't there with you. You did it all by yourself with your mum there. You've been doing something about your dreams. I gave you some ideas but you did it. (to mother) Do you agree that he's giving me all the credit? I want him to take it back because YOU did the eating, I didn't do the eating, right? I still weigh the same – you're the guy who's getting fatter, not me. I want to argue with you on that. You've been controlling your food, you've got in charge of your stomach feelings?

Hayden: Mmmh.

DE: Have you wondered about that?

Hayden: No ... oh ...

DE: Like Carl is in charge ... he's in charge. He's the boss of his stomach.

Uses a referential shift to Carl in order to emphasise Hayden is in control.

Hayden: *(laughs)*
DE: *He's turned off his feelings from his stomach. I went and talked to him. I said, 'Carl, how do you do it?' He said, 'I just switch off!' And so have you. You've been switching off ... you've switched on!"*
Mother: *That's what he told me.*
DE: *Well he does. And so have you. You've been switching off but you haven't switched, you have also switched on to the movies. And maybe to the 'Dukes of Hazzard?' OK.*
Hayden: *Yeh! I want you to ask me some more questions...*
DE: *Do you want some more questions? How many times do you think you are going to vomit tomorrow?*

Assessed Hayden's future expectations with respect to vomiting and then suggests ideas to do with less vomiting.

Hayden: *Four.*
DE: *Four? How many times do you want to vomit?*
Hayden: *None.*
DE: *What about if you vomit twice?*
Hayden: *Mmmh ... I would be satisfied.*
DE: *You'd be satisfied? What if you vomit twice and didn't get very upset?*
Hayden: *I'd be happy.*
DE: *You'd be happy? OK. When would you like to vomit? What time do you want to vomit?*
Hayden: *When I get back to the motel.*
DE: *When you get back?*
Hayden: *No, on my way there.*
DE: *On your way there?*
Hayden: *On the way to the motel.*
DE: *On the way to the motel?*
Hayden: *Yeah!*
DE: *Is there any nice place you'd like to go to vomit? Is there a nice tree or somewhere in the park you would like to go?*
Hayden: *No ... I'll just vomit anywhere if I have to.*
DE: *Yeah but why don't you somewhere you'd like to go? Maybe we could find a nice place where no one was looking ... you don't want to do it where people are looking, do you?*
Hayden: *It's hard when you're walking through the park.*
DE: *Why ... are there lots of people there?*
Hayden: *Yeh! They're always jogging past you.*
DE: *Do you think you'd like a secret place to vomit?*

Hayden: In the motel.
DE: I'll tell you _. why don't you wait until you get back to the motel? Do you feel that's a good place to vomit?
Hayden: Yep!
DE: And not in a way that is unpleasant ... maybe next time after that you could do without any vomiting? But maybe you're rushing into it? Because you didn't vomit very much at all last time. (to mother) Right?
Mother: He did the first time but he got sick after the second time.
DE: So he seemed to forget?
Mother: He'd go back to the motel and dry retch.
DE: Right, so maybe this time, you should just vomit twice in a way that isn't too unpleasant. Just the way you want to.

Throughout the above sequence, David is framing or presupposing Hayden as having a choice, being in control. This is very similar to an example Haley (1973) describes of Erickson's work with a man who fainted in public. Erickson kept offering him new alternatives of where to faint, each one requiring a move nearer the goal of the exercise, which was to go to a restaurant. David discusses choices of where to vomit, each one later than the other, and then shifts to the idea of vomiting in a pleasant way. Even if Hayden had not accepted this seemingly remote possibility, he probably would have overlooked any critical assessment of the previous discussion of where to vomit, and hence would be more likely to accept the suggestion.

Hayden: Yah...
DE: You know you can control these things. It takes a lot of strength. Do you think you've got enough strength inside of you to do this?

David links the idea of control to that of strength.

Hayden: Yep!
DE: Sounds like you really meant it. Do you think you've got a tiger inside of you that could take charge of your stomach feelings?
Hayden: Yeh...
DE: Do BATTLE with them?
Hayden: Yeh.
DE: Do you think it's a tiger inside of you (1) or is it something else inside you that will give you strength? What do you think you need inside you to FIGHT back your stomach ... to keep those feelings under your control?
Hayden: What I need in there?
DE: Yah, what do you need to give you strength? I know you're pretty strong on the outside but what about on the inside? I met this one kid who needed a Batman inside him and another who had a tiger. What do you think you need?

Hayden: Oh boy, I need a three-headed tiger.

David has suggested the 'tiger inside' Hayden, which Hayden responds to favourably. Later when offered some choice about what sort of strong ally he might have inside him, it is presupposed that Hayden can and does have some strong ally. He takes David's suggestion regarding a tiger and elaborates it as a three-headed tiger. Hayden's elaboration of this image indicates his engagement with it.

DE: *A three-headed tiger ... OK. Do you think the tiger needs a lot of tiger food?*

David utilises the three-headedness of the tiger by asking about the quantity of food such a three-mouthed creature would require.

Hayden: *Yep, I'll give it to him.*
DE: *Will you give him some tiger food tonight?*

This sentence frames Hayden as in charge of the tiger. The imagery of Hayden feeding the tiger becomes an indirect way of discussing and suggesting aspects of Hayden's eating.

Hayden: *Yep.*
DE: *What kind of tiger food do you think he'll need to be REALLY strong for tomorrow?*
Hayden: *MEAT!*
DE: *Meat. Is that what tigers like?*
Hayden: *Yep.*
DE: *Three-headed tigers! (to mother) You've probably fed a few three-headed tigers in your time. Do you know what they like to make them real strong?*
Mother: *I hope this tiger inside Hayden likes mince because that's what he's getting for tea.*
DE: *Oh they love mince ... they love mince ... Do you know that?*
Hayden: *Why?*
DE: *You know what mince is. Mince is meat cut up into little bits so they don't have to work so hard with their teeth. So those tigers will save their energy on their teeth because it's so soft and easy to chew. You know mince is a lot easier to eat than steak, isn't it?*
Hayden: *Yep.*
DE: *So what else do you think that tiger will be getting to make him strong?*
Mother: *A few veggies and mashed potatoes.*
DE: *Do you think they like that?*
Hayden: *Yup!*
DE: *This tiger is going to have good tucker. I guess he needs a good night's sleep?*

Hayden: *Hmmm.*
DE: *What time do you think you're going to put the three-headed tiger to bed tonight?*

Good food is linked to good sleep, and again Hayden is framed as in charge of the tiger.

Hayden: *After whatever has taken over from "Falcon Crest?"*
DE: *OK. What else do you need for this tiger to be really, really strong tomorrow?*
Hayden: *Faith.*
DE: *Faith? What kind of faith?*
Hayden: *STRONG FAITH!*
DE: *Strong faith. Any ideas you'd like to give the tiger that would help him?*
Hayden: *No.*
DE: *If you were going to give him a talking to about having strong faith before you go to bed, what would you say to him ... this three-headed tiger?*

David uses the idea of the tiger gaining strong faith through Hayden's advice and guidance. Hayden again is presented as in charge and the device of talking to the tiger is an indirect way of having Hayden 'talk to himself' in a positive way.

Hayden: *Kill the yucky feelings.*
DE: *Kill the feelings?*
Hayden: *Yeah!*
DE: *Bite it?*
Hayden: *Eat it!*
DE: *Right ... now you're talking. And do you think that three-headed tiger has enough heads to eat up those yucky feelings? I guess there's quite a lot of those feelings in your stomach.*
Hayden: *It's got some cousins.*
DE: *Some cousins. How many heads have they got?*
Hayden: *About three.*
DE: *Do you think the three-headed tiger could invite them to come along tomorrow?*

David checks the strength of Hayden's ally. Hayden creates a great deal of resources for his tiger – a hopeful indication.

Hayden: *Great! I think you've got a lot of help. Are those tigers friendly to you?*
Hayden: *To me they are.*
DE: *You've tamed them?*
Hayden: *Yeh.*
DE: *Have you ever shown them off to anyone else or do you keep them to yourself?*

Hayden: *To myself.*
DE: *Yeh. They might bite me or your dad but you've tamed them?*
Hayden: *Yeh!*
DE: *Tiger tamer. You're a tiger tamer! You're a pretty interesting boy. Tell me, are you going to give this tiger a talking to tonight?*

Again emphasising Hayden is in charge, and then checking Hayden's auto-suggestion plans for the future.

Hayden: *Yip!*
DE: *What are you going to say to him?*
Hayden: *Kill that yucky feeling that makes me want to vomit.*
DE: *So that tiger has to eat up that yucky feeling?*
Hayden: *TIGERS!*
DE: *Tigers or rather tiger-heads plus cousins.*
Hayden: *Yeh.*
DE: *Are the cousins bigger or smaller than the three-headed tiger?*
Hayden: *Similar to the three-headed tiger.*
DE: *About the same size. Did you get these in Africa?*
Hayden: *Yip…some from Africa. (2)*
DE: *How did you get them to New Zealand?*
Hayden: *(laughing) Smuggled them.*
DE: *Did you? On an airplane or on a boat or did you swim over with them?*
Hayden: *Ran…*
DE: *You ran. How did you run over the water?*
Hayden: *I jogged.*
DE: *You jogged over the water. Wow! That's really good…really good.*
Hayden: *No, I swam on their backs.*
DE: *You swam on their backs?*
Hayden: *And then I ate them.*
DE: *You ate them and now they are inside you and they are going to TAKE CHARGE of your yucky feelings?*
Hayden: *Yip!*
DE: *Do they do what you tell them to do?*
Hayden: *Yip … sometimes.*
DE: *Sometimes they do what you tell them and sometimes they are a bit naughty. If you're a tiger tamer, they should do what you tell them to do.*
Hayden: *Sometimes I don't feed them.*
DE: *Sometimes you don't feed them. I wonder if you weren't feeding them before. That's probably why they weren't so helpful.*
Hayden: *(nods in agreement)*
DE: *Not doing what you wanted them to do. You're going to give them a good meal tonight – mince, mashed potatoes and veggies. Do they eat puddings?*

Hayden: Yah...heaps!

DE: Do they? They're pudding monsters? What sort of puddings to three-headed tigers generally like?

Hayden: Ummm ... chocolate puddings. And some will have to go to the dentist. My ten-headed tiger had to. It ate too much chocolate.

DE: Did you warn him that he should cut down?

Hayden: Yip.

DE: But he didn't listen?

Hayden: No.

DE: So most of the time, they pay attention to you ... sometimes they don't if you don't feed them?

Hayden: Nope.

DE: They generally are happy to do what you ask of them ... like pussycats in their natures.

The remainder of the transcript seems to be largely a bit of fun in which David and Hayden play with the imagery that they have co-created; however, at all times, David is asking questions which assume or presuppose Hayden in control of the tigers and hence by metaphorical implication, in control of his nausea. An extremely nice piece of imagery from Hayden is the idea of eating the tigers in the first place. Eating and control are very closely associated. This also provides an explanation for the previous problem as Hayden had punished his tigers by not feeding them, thus making them weak.

Letters
We exchanged letters:

Dear Hayden,
  Your three-headed tiger and its three cousins sure did a good job on your yucky feelings in your stomach. You obviously are feeding them good tucker that makes them real strong. Or maybe they are copying your strength, especially the way you have taken charge of your nightmares. Please write so I can learn exactly how you switched off like Carl and got your tigers working so hard.
  You surprised me once again! I keep wondering how you will surprise me next time we meet. Have fun practising!
  Your friend,
  David

Dear David,
  My yucky feelings are nowhere to be found. Yes, I'm feeing strong. The tiger is so strong. To turn myself on, I just close my eyes and think about your voice and mum tells me to turn on my TV.
  Hayden

Fifth Session(five months later)

Cynthia tried to make an appointment. Hayden had been found to be involved in a number of incidents of theft from home and shops. We met together and the 'letter' summarises the intervention and its context.

Dear Friends,

Hayden vowed the other day that his dishonesty had gone as far as it was going to go and that he preferred to be honest. He knows now that his dishonesty has made both his mother and father distrustful of him, very angry and unhappy. Maybe his dishonesty was his way of celebrating that his 'treatments' are over. Whatever the reason, Hayden now says it was a mistake. He also vowed that he saw no reason to steal and he knew he could stop it. He shook his mother's hand and said so; he shook mine and said the very same thing. What Hayden is beginning to realise is this: once you are known as a stealer, people don't trust you. It's very hard to prove to people that they can trust you again. Hayden asked me if I could help him with this and I agreed. Cynthia also said she would give him another chance to prove he is worthy of their trust and that of others.

What I suggest is the following:

1. *Have Hayden ring up ten relatives who care about him and tell them he has been dishonest, that he has made a vow to be honest, that his parents are going to give him Honesty Tests. He will ring them after every test to tell them he has passed or failed. This is VERY IMPORTANT!*
2. *Then tell Hayden that within the next two weeks, he will be tested ten times. If he passes all the tests, you will accept him as an Honest Person and celebrate that by an Honesty Party.*
   All those caring relatives should be invited. An Honesty Cake should be baked and Hayden should give everyone a piece, thanking them for their help to become honest and their newfound trust in him.
3. *Tell Hayden too exactly what his punishment will be if he fails a test.*
4. *Make a large cardboard chart and put it over Hayden's bed. It should read:*

TEST: *Proving I'm Worthy of Your Trust*

1.
2.
3.
4.
5.
6.
7.
8.
9.
10.

After each test, have him write up his result: PASS or FAIL. Each of you should write your comments e.g. 'I knew you could do it! Mum.' 'I'm proud of you'! Dad' 'Only four more to go! Mum' 'That was a big one! Dad' etc.

5. Tests:

Under no circumstances is Hayden to know you are setting a test. It wouldn't be a test then. Here's how you do it: Leave small sums of money (vary the amount) in a place that only Hayden could be the thief. Leave him in temptation for approximately a minute and then go and check if he passed or failed. If he passes, congratulate him, fill in his chart, and have him inform his relatives of his successes; if he fails, follow through on your agreed punishment, and have him inform his relatives. Here is an example of how you might set a test: Leave some bags of groceries in the car. Also some change in the dashboard. Ask him to go and get the groceries. When he returns, say: "You've been tested!! Let's go and see if you have passed!' It might be a good idea to set a test at your mother's place when you are visiting, etc. You are going to have to invent situations to test him. Here is another example: When he is visiting your mother, ring her up and ask her to leave some money by the phone. Then ask her to have Hayden talk to you over the phone. Finish your conversation and then ask your mother to check if he passed or failed and ring you back immediately.

I believe that stealing is a bad habit that grows if it is fed by neglect. This programme is a way to challenge the habit and give your son a chance to prove he is worthy of your trust. A parent-child relationship without trust is a sad thing. I believe that Hayden wants to regain your trust and I have no doubt that you both wish to see that happen.

Good luck!

Yours sincerely,

David

Two months later Hayden sent me the following letter:

Dear David:

I have been honest. My mother has been testing me just about every day. The only thing I do wrong is that I like to wander off on my own and sometime I forgot (sic) to come home at the right time.

I try not to have anything to do with my old mates but it is very hard because they go to the same school.

So I passed all my tests! The hardest task was when I got blamed for breaking into a bakery shop. It was broken into Friday, Saturday and Sunday but I proved to everyone, even the people that blamed me, I was inosant (sic). Mum and Dad and me were away those days. So the only reason they blamed me was because I had a bad record. Mum and Dad were so happy for me. Mum said I could have my ear pierced so we went to the chemist. GUESS WHAT? Yes, I have a pierced ear.

Your friend,

Hayden

Intervention (ten months later)

In the previous session Cynthia mentioned to me that Hayden was having difficulties at school and she was worried that he might be expelled. I requested that she have his school teacher write to me. I received a letter two months later detailing non-compliance, disruption, answering back and violent temper tantrums which included attacks on property. The Headmistress felt that the school could no longer sustain 'their approach of sympathy'.

I wrote the following letter:

Dear Miss Cook:

Thank you for your letter of 25/4/84. Just let me say a few things in general about Hayden's condition. You may be aware that he recently finished his chemotherapy and is now only attending Auckland Public Hospital on a three monthly basis for review. There is no reason whatsoever why Hayden shouldn't be treated exactly as you might treat his class mates. As far as his anger problem goes, the control he exhibited in other areas of his life indicates that there is no reason whatsoever for him to have temper tantrums. In our last meeting, Hayden informed me, in fact, he was intending to apply some of these things he had learned to control his anger. I wonder if this has had any effect yet? If it has, clearly the following should be ignored.

HAYDEN'S ANGER CONTROL PROGRAMME

You may not know this but Hayden has a tiger inside of him that has been used in the past to control feelings of nausea caused by his treatment. Previously, he vomited six times or more even before he received the treatment. This can be the case with children under this medical regime. He did this by learning to turn himself off. If he can turn himself off to chemically-induced nausea, he can certainly turn himself off to inappropriate anger.

Here's how he can generalise this learning to another problem:

1. Sit down with him and discuss that if he can learn to turn off his yucky feelings with the help of his three-headed tiger, he can control his anger. And that you intend to help him REMEMBER how he did it.

2. Tell him exactly how you will remind him. In his presence, make four cards with large writing on it. They should read: i) You have a temper tantrum coming on! ii) Remember your TIGER!' iii) TURN OFF your angry feelings; and iiii) TURN ON pleasant feelings.

3. You are to keep these handy (I set) and Hayden is to have another set handy. If necessary, hold up Card 1 and act calm, cool and collected. If he controls himself, congratulate him:

'That TIGER of yours is very strong ... you must be feeding him well!' If he continues, one minute later hold up Card 2, once again acting calm, cool and collected. If he stops, congratulate him (see above) and so on.

4. After four minutes have elapsed, say: 'Go to ... who will put your tiger suit on and give you (x minutes) to practice control on your own'.

5. TIGER SUIT: you might like to make this with Hayden e.g. a paper bag for a tiger head, a tail made of yellow and black wool, and an old shirt spray-painted black and yellow.
6. I will leave 4 and 5 up to your discretion and what is possible in your school. His practice time could in fact be done after school.
7. Optional: If he controls his anger, secretly send him a sweet with a note: 'This is for your TIGER. I know you are feeding him well because he gave you so much strength to stop your anger getting away from you. So here's a treat for your TIGER. I like him very much because now I can be a much friendlier teacher to you because you can control your anger.

Please keep me informed.
Yours sincerely,
David

Hayden's teacher assisted him to control his anger and his school teacher only had to hold up one card on only one occasion.

Follow-up (twelve months later)

DE: You came here and found out some things about your mother and father. Do you remember what it was that you learned about them?

Hayden: They worried a lot. They didn't like me being sad. That's about it, wasn't it?

DE: What you said on the tape was: 'That you learned that they could stand up to your strong worries that you had been keeping inside yourself?' Remember you tested them?

Hayden: Yah, that's right!

DE: And they passed the tests with flying colours. Were you surprised how strong your mother and father were?

Hayden: Yes.

DE: Do you remember where you got the idea you had to do all the worrying on your own? Do you know where you got the idea from? You kept the fact that you were having bad dreams from your mum and dad.

Hayden: I didn't want them to worry.

DE: You didn't want your mum and dad to worry so you did all the worrying by yourself? He's a very strong kid. Remember I tried to convince him he didn't have to be quite so strong?

Mother: NOT QUITE SO STRONG!

DE: He's got a strong mother and a strong father. After you tested them, have you kept up telling them your worries or did you keep them to yourself?

Hayden: (referring to the first option) Yep!

DE: What do you think, Cynthia?

Mother: Yah, most things.

DE: He'd want to keep a few secrets. He wouldn't want to tell you about all the naughty things, but the important things – that's different! Did he start doing that right away, Cynthia?

Mother: Yah, soon as we left here. He had a few more bad dreams but he'd tell us and we'd get up and have a drink of coffee.

DE: Do you remember the dreams you had where everything you were going to eat looked like a drip. You'd start looking at food and you'd see a drip.

Hayden: Mmmh.

DE: That's why you were losing so much weight. You weren't eating very much.

Hayden: It reminded me of a drip.

DE: So IN YOUR MIND it reminded you of a drip?

Hayden: So I just said I was full.

DE: So you tricked your parents. You really didn't tell them what was worrying you. You just said you were full. What did you really think was going on, Cynthia? Did you get really worried?

Hayden: Yah! I did because it started to show in his weight loss. Quite a big weight loss!

DE: Yah! He came back a week later and he had gained five or six pounds.

Hayden: Yah! He ate like a horse that week. And he hasn't stopped. He hasn't lost weight and he's grown taller.

DE: Then it seemed to me you got in charge of your dreams. Then you started to learn to switch off your mind and switch on movies. It seemed to me you were doing quite a bit of practising. You had a three-headed tiger. Remember that?

Hayden: Yah, it could walk across water and it liked chocolate.

DE: And remember one night you fed it a lot of mince and he ate it. Can you tell the boys and girls anything you can remember on how you learned to turn off your feelings – your yucky feelings – and turned on a movie?

Hayden: I just closed my eyes and think of nice, good things and not bad things. I'd just feel funny (shaking his left arm) and go somewhere else. I'd go somewhere else. And the movie would come on.

DE: Can you automatically do it now?

Hayden: I could do it here.

Mother: He can do it anytime ... even with his homework now.

Hayden: I did it last night, didn't I, Mum?

Mother: Yes. Now he can turn himself off to TV and on to his homework, whereas before he'd be looking at the TV. And nothing would be right. (laughing)

DE: Those feelings in your stomach were still happening but he would turn them off. Can you describe for other mothers and fathers whose children might choose to learn what Hayden has learnt, what it looks like?

Mother: Totally relaxed. Before when he got his needles, he'd feel cold and then hot and flushed and vomiting. Once he turned himself off or on, that stopped. As soon as the needle touched his hand, he'd just go out (mother mimics trance behaviour). You could pick up and drop his legs.

Sometimes he even wet. He did that twice. He can turn off and on now whenever he chooses. They didn't have to give more of that stuff to make him drowsy so they could give him his treatment better. Once he learned to turn himself off and on, they didn't have to do that.

Hayden: The last treatment I stayed awake.

Mother: He stayed awake all the way through. Oh, that's another thing...

DE: How did you do that, Hayden?

Hayden: I turned myself off inside but my outside was still awake.

DE: You learned even a better way. You turned your insides off and kept your outsides in full operation.

DE: What would you have done normally in the old days when he'd get upset and vomit a lot?

Mother: Him upset and me upset. It would be a big ordeal. And we'd end up staying the night (in Auckland) because he'd be uncontrollable and I wouldn't be able to drive.

DE: He'd be uncontrollable in terms of his vomiting or his anger?

Mother: His anger!

DE: So the difference for you then was you could feel really confident he was in control of things and you could have some fun going shopping.

Mother: Not only that ... it didn't look like he was in pain. Before it was just throwing up, his breathing ... if you didn't watch him, he'd choke.

DE: You pretty much upset each other in a sense. That would be pretty normal for a mother to get so upset.

Mother: He taught me a lot because I learned to relax too!

DE: Can you tell people about your three-headed tiger?

Hayden: Just a tiger that I made up. A really good tiger ... likes eating now ... didn't used to but it eats lots of things now. It ate up my yucky feelings. It liked them more than anything else.

DE: How did you get the tiger inside of you?

Hayden: Oh I just made it up inside of me. Before it used to lounge around, didn't eat much and made me skinny.

DE: Did you get it to co-operate with you?

Hayden: I GOT IT CRACKING!

The ending

Some months later, it was discovered Hayden had another site for his disease. The family decided against further treatment as his prognosis was poor.

Lynne O'Flaherty knew him well over this time:

When I first met the Barlow family, they appeared to be coping well with this next lot of tests. Having had so many treatments in the past, the whole family were veterans. Hayden, himself, couldn't remember a time when he hadn't been involved with hospitals and their personnel. He was a quietly spoken and pleasant young man who was accustomed to it all and didn't seem worried at all about being back again. I think the family viewed it as just one more hurdle they were going to get over and this enabled Hayden to make his own way.

Routinely, the children are weighed and their height measured. Usually it is seen as insignificant and the children and families rush to get it done, hoping they will be seen sooner if this is out of the way. Hayden's weight loss was visible and he appeared haggard and aged. He was apprehensive about being weighed and so was his mother. She was becoming worried by how little he was eating. This is not uncommon for our clients. I guess the majority of the parents are worried about their children's food intake while on chemotherapy. Some parents allege that their child has eaten almost nothing despite the evidence of satisfactory weight gains. It was not so for Hayden. And it was obvious from his mother's degree of distress and his quiet desperation and persistent weight loss that things were badly amiss. I remember one day – he'd just arrived and he had a bright eyed, haunted look and he admitted to being worried. It was here that Louise (Dr. Webster) came into the picture and you know the rest.

It seemed to me that quite quickly there was a change. He was like a kid with a secret. Hayden was never one to enlarge upon things so we were never to know. But something definitely was changing. After awhile, there was a huge difference. His gentle humour was back. He was so much more confident and self-possessed. And now he was different: more mature, more sure of himself, and there seemed to be an air of confidence about his family.

Even the relapse didn't entirely shake all this. The news that this was the end of hope for his survival was terrible but it didn't seem crushing – not for long anyway. For the period he was home there was a family and neighbourhood support group. Apparently he required and would take a surprisingly small amount of pain relief. His mother told me how he was 'refusing to give in' and was enjoying getting out and about even when it was difficult for him. His mother felt that they all drew strength from Hayden's vision.

It was always terrible for the Oncology Team to have their children die. With many of our children, it doesn't feel quite so terrible. There is a sense that they have died as complete people and not torn apart by what they had to endure. I felt this was so with Hayden.

Cynthia Barlow remembers

Hayden, better known to many as Hatu (or 'man') was born a healthy baby with blue eyes, blond hair. on 22/1/73. His 9lb birth weight was a good start, and he seemed to be developing normally. At the age of 18 months health problems began to appear.

When he began having convulsions, and after numerous attempts to get the doctor on duty, we decided to take Hayden to the Tauranga Hospital Outpatients. Hayden was admitted, countless tests were carried out, and after the removal of a kidney it was discovered that Hayden had cancer (Wilm'sTumour). The shock of knowing our son had cancer was devastating: numbness and confusion took over. Talking about it was too painful; we both blamed ourselves. We questioned everything. Why did this happen? Was it caused by an infection I had overlooked; could it have been a fall he had taken while trying to walk as a baby; was it the amount of x-rays I had while pregnant; or his dad's job working with weed control agents? We asked ourselves and the doctors these questions and many more, but no one had the answers. One thing we knew for sure was that a great task had been laid upon us and, one way or another, we would cope. For us, part of the coping process involved Hayden's second birthday, which he spent in hospital undergoing chemotherapy and radiation treatment. Planning his birthday was all we wanted to think about, and the memories of that day remain in our minds. Cards, flowers, presents and a birthday cake which fed the whole ward arrived at the Waikato Hospital. The biggest surprise was his two wheeler bike his grandmother had bought him. Even after his chemotherapy, which made him violently sick and sleepy, he still had the strength to ride his bike and terrorise the hospital. Our trips to Waikato Hospital were now monthly and being pregnant slowed me down, so Hayden's Dad took time off work to help with all the extra pressures. These we managed to overcome. Once Hayden had received all the treatment Waikato Hospital could give him, he was referred back to Tauranga Hospital for monthly checkups. By this time, he was going into remission. We believed, with all our hearts, that when remission ended Hayden would be cured, but this was not to be. By the time Hayden was five years old he had spent over half of his baby years in and out of hospital.

Having Hayden home meant so much to us, and now fun and laughter filled our house. We watched our son bloom and flourish and the noise of his school friends playing was welcomed. School life and weekends away meant a lot to Hayden, for at least he was really starting to live.

But, like a nightmare, fate was once again against us. For the second time we faced that empty feeling. Hayden now had cancer of the lung, so that long road which we prayed was over, started again. Hayden was transferred to Auckland Hospital and had major lung surgery, followed by more chemotherapy and radiation treatment. By now, he was old enough to understand his illness. This brought a new challenge for us. We had to somehow tell our son the truth as we knew it. During our conversations together, we realised our son was no longer a child, but an adult in a child's body. After numerous trips from Tauranga to Auckland, Hayden again went into remission. And once again our lives were back to normal.

Although we tried not to think about it, Hayden was going through mental and physical stress. We helped him overcome this by buying him a motor bike. His feeling of freedom riding his motor bike helped release the tension within, and enabled him to be himself. Hayden became self-sufficient, handling his own money and business affairs. He sold his 50cc bike and bought a 125cc trail bike which scared the hell out of everyone. The motor bike was bigger than him, but the decision was his, even though he was only ten years old.

Just when we thought everything was stable, we discovered that Hayden had cancer in the leg. The doctors suggested Hayden's leg be amputated, but biopsies showed that Hayden had cancer throughout his body. Amputation or chemotherapy would be useless. Our son was dying with only morphine to stop the pain. We took him home. Because Hayden's leg was so painful, he could no longer start his bike. It was a minor problem. Hayden would get his friend, Mathew, to kick it over and off they would go. After a few months, he couldn't bear to see it sitting in the shed – a motor bike was meant to be ridden. Pain, morphine and weakness made his riding days impossible.

Hayden learned to cope with many emotions and adjusting to changes in his appearance was one of his greatest hurdles. Trying to accept the fact that many things he longed to do would never be. Hayden had a collection of many things that filled his room. One of these was hats and he wore one wherever he went. Although Hayden's life was short, he accomplished a lot more than anyone, even those older than him. He made us realise that life is too short to worry about petty things, but to live life to its fullest. When he died in his father's arms, we no longer feared death either.

The most precious memories of Hayden we hold in our hearts are those last two years.

Hayden was loved and admired by many and those who took the time to listen to him learnt so much. Being a very unselfish and special boy, Hayden had many friends who he shared his thoughts and ideas with. The hardest task for those close to him was not being able to relieve his pain; we could not help him cope with it. The pain and torment Hayden endured no-one will ever know but we can only assume. Hayden has left us with the gift of love, patience and how to endure and understand each other. Through him, we learned closeness and the importance of friends, neighbours and family. This closeness is a life-long bond. Thank you son.

Postscript (1988)

Cynthia and Roy have a new baby now and their daughter, Rina, is growing up. I asked after Rina's white kitten which I had recalled so vividly from the first day I met the family. Cynthia said the cat had become Hayden's pet and had always remained by his side when he was bed-bound. The day Hayden died, the cat disappeared and was never seen again.

References
Haley, J. (1973) *Uncommon Therapy: The Psychiatric Techniques of Milton H. Erickson*, W.W. Norton, New York
White, M. (1984) Pseudo-encopresis: from avalanche to victory, from vicious to virtuous cycles, *Family Systems Medicine*, 2(2), 150-160.

(1) The 'tiger inside you' is taken from White, 1984.
(2) As Hayden believed tigers lived in Africa (they actually live mainly in India and China) we
    must guess that he knew one that was a good swimmer!

2

Annals of the New Dave: status-abled, disabled, or weirdly abled

David Epston, Dean Lobovits & Jennifer Freeman
Introduction by Sharon Murphy

Original version published in Epston, D., Lobovits, D. & Freeman, J., Annals of the 'New Dave', *Gecko – A Journal of Deconstruction and Narrative Ideas*. 3, 1997.

Introduction: The Boy Who Dared To Be Different
Sharon Murphy (Dave's mother)

Dave was different from the day he was born. It wasn't anything anyone could put their finger on but I could SEE he was different. Sure he had two arms, two legs, blonde hair and blue eyes but somehow or other I knew he was different. At school, his class-mates soon noted that he wrote differently. His attempts at writing were always back to front and despite his painstaking efforts looked like chicken scratchings. Predictably his spelling was funny like 'enuf', 'kat' or 'qik'. Dave NEVER passed his spelling. But he seemed happy and cheerful and was always 'doing'. It was as if he was filled with insatiable curiosity. Others would snigger behind his back and occasionally to his face – 'Curiosity killed the cat!' Dave was oblivious because he was happy. Most days he would wander around the playground picking things up to investigate. Teachers complimented him, thinking he was 'tidying up'. But they were not different so failed to realise he was investigating the unknown and learning about it.

One day, he found this beautiful bottle full of the colour blue. He lifted it towards the sun to watch the sparkles dance off the bottle when it tipped all over him. Everyone began to scream - 'Miss, Dave's turned blue!' He was rushed off to the sick bay and I was contacted - 'Hurry please. It's a chemical of some sort. He may have to go to the hospital.' My work colleagues laughed when I told them. 'The Blue Boy. Isn't that a famous painting?" one quipped. I was hurt, as was my daughter seeing my hurt. Couldn't they see that he just wanted to know and now he could be injured?

Many questions were asked by the doctors. The 'blue' was analysed chemically and scrutinised under a microscope. At the same time, Dave was poked and prodded. My fear drained all the colour from my face. Dave wondered what all the fuss was about and tried to tell the doctor about what beautiful sparkles in the sky the bottle made. He also started to enquire how the microscope worked. Could he have a look and "what's that thing around your neck?". Everything turned out alright in the end, but for a while Dave was clearly different on account of his beautiful blue hair.

Dave busied himself from morning to night taking things apart but not quite getting them back together again. He built wonderful, fantastical structures everywhere but forgot to put the tools away. He cooked fabulous concoctions but overlooked them when something else caught his attention. At school, he went from one thing to another. 'He's bright', the teachers said, 'but he never finishes anything'. When I ask him why, he says 'Oh, I know that but I just had to check this out, it's more interesting.' His teachers despaired of coping with him and his work, so full of promise but never completed.

He doesn't have many friends because he is different and they are not, and don't understand him. Dave now knows he is different and copes with it. This is not to say at times he isn't saddened and would prefer to be the same as everyone else and find acceptance.

Dave is going to grow up. He still may not spell and his writing may always be laboured. Sometimes he still may not quite get his clothes right. But I can see Dave working for an advertising agency 'thinking up' ideas all day, wonderful ideas like dancing sparkles in the sky. How would he get such a job, you might ask? They may very well say – 'You're different, Dave. You think in wonderful ways that no one else dares to.' If Dave replied – 'But my spelling!' they might say - "Anyone can spell but not many people are different.' And you, Dave, dare to be different. That takes courage!

First meeting with the "old Dave" and his family

Sharon Murphy sank into the nearest chair in David's office and started drawing deep and audible breaths that indicated utter exhaustion and the cessation of a great effort. Vestiges of her determination to manage the behaviour of her 14 year old son, Dave, lived on in her constant but half-hearted remonstrating with him to desist from his constant flurry of activity.

Jenni, Dave's 13 year old sister, observing that her mother's admonishments had little or no effect, made desperate and reckless attempts to take over from her by insisting that he 'Stop It!' These only seemed to provoke Dave to more excess. Jenni's seething rage was palpable. Such was the frustration of her indignant forays to reign Dave in, that she would be reduced to tears on each and every occasion. However, for Dave, the room seemed a marvellous source of novelties that he had to explore, touch, and touch again.

When there was the first break in these proceedings, David began the conversation by inquiring about Sharon's visible despair. She bravely related to him the intolerable strain she was under as a single parent, as 'bread winner' for her family, and as the manager of Dave's mind and body. She spoke of her "weariness" from having lived "on the edge" since Dave's birth. She declared that this meeting was her "last ditch stand" to avert her own 'nervous breakdown' and to avoid placing both her children in foster care - a prospect which was the opposite of everything she had devoted herself to over the past fourteen years.

When he heard this, Dave ceased his activities for the first time - but only momentarily. Sharon was becoming more and more despondent as she spoke of her plans and Jenni alternated between wrath and crying. To emphasise her point, Sharon gave the example of having to delay toileting herself until after her children's bedtime. This was due to the constant and hazardous fighting between Dave and Jenni. She told how she had been ordered by a government department to closely observe her children at all times to prevent Jenni being injured. She now considered that what was required of her was well beyond both her emotional and physical capacities.

With due respect for Sharon's exhaustion, David invited her to take a break from trying to discipline Dave for the time being. The moment she relaxed her vigilance Dave threw himself to the carpeted floor and began rolling over and over around his room. Despite this, David and Sharon were able to maintain a semblance of a conversation. Jenni, however, continued her expostulations to cease his activity without any success whatsoever.

After a while, David essayed a conversation with Dave, who dutifully responded to his enquiries but not in a manner he was given to expect. Dave's replies were orated with dramatic and rhetorical flourishes and wild metaphorical excursions. Their sense seemed just outside the reach of David's mind but tantalisingly so! It was very frustrating for David to be quite so close (in any particular roll, Dave would often pass within inches of his feet) but be so far away. No matter how hard David tried to catch up to Dave's mind, he was unable to close the gap sufficiently to pull alongside. In spite of this, David determined to do so no matter how long it might take and no matter how far he might have to stretch his mind in doing so.

David thought of an idea that might acknowledge his understanding of Sharon's dejection and total exhaustion. He initiated it by asking her consent for a secret meeting with her children in which the three of them would 'cook up a secret'. David reassured her that although this secret would be kept from her for a specified period of time, it would be revealed to her in its entirety in due course. Sharon quickly consented, appearing somewhat relieved to absent herself from the room.

Mother Appreciation

When the three of them were alone, David asked Dave and Jenni what their thoughts were about the prospect of a foster care placement. They deeply dreaded the prospect but what concerned them even more was the well-being of their mother. David consulted them as to what ideas they had 'up their sleeves' to provide her with some relief. They took his question very seriously and told him they had already begun nightly foot massages for Sharon. To this news David replied, 'What I have in mind is certainly in line with your initiative! What about a Mother Appreciation Party?'

Not surprisingly, they had never heard of such an event. David readily acknowledged that such occasions are relatively rare in anyone's social calendar. They launched into an enquiry about their appreciation of Sharon and their mother's friends' appreciation of her.

For the first time since they arrived, Dave, Jenni, and David were able to collaborate over a shared concern – mother appreciation! The effect was dramatic. Dave was attentive and Jenni regained her good spirits as they agreed to 'plot a surprise Mother Appreciation Party'.

When they reviewed their shared knowledge about parties in general, they realised they had a lot ahead of them such as deciding on the guest list, catering, baking the Mother Appreciation cake and of course, their respective Mother Appreciation speeches. Hearing the last proposal, Jenni's eyebrows spontaneously raised almost to her hair line. They fell back into place when David quickly reassured her that he would be only too glad to assist. 'How?' they asked in unison and he replied, 'Why, I will ask you 'mother-appreciating' questions so you can come up with mother-appreciating answers! And then all you will have left to do is to roll them up into your speech!'

Despite their uneasiness with this project, Dave and Jenni agreed to proceed with the planning one step at a time with the speeches coming last. As a Mother Appreciation Party was a complicated undertaking, they agreed to "scheme together in secret" over the next few meetings and decided against any deadlines. Everyone agreed that when they were ready it would be only too obvious. David now felt able to risk seeking their consent to ask them a very serious question that he had been burning to ask.

A Burning Question

'Before I ask you this question,' David began, 'I want some reassurance from both of you that you will promise not to even consider answering it until you have heard it out to the very end.' If their facial expressions were anything to go by they considered this request somewhat odd, but nonetheless they agreed. 'Well, here goes,' David resumed, 'By any chance, do you think you are weirdly abled?' Before they could respond David leapt to the edge of his chair, holding his palms outwards and admonished,' Hold on ! Hold on! You promised!' Then he continued: 'By that I mean, are you so abled that many adults and kids your ages believe you are WEIRD when in fact you are WEIRDLY abled?' They both looked quite miffed. Jenni piped up: 'What do you mean by that?'

To answer this important question, David read them Emily Betterton's (Freeman, Epston & Lobovits, 1997) published account of 'weirdly abledness' (p179-182). After doing this he took a Lynda Barry cartoon out from his desk entitled Marlys' Guide to Weirdoes (1993). In this cartoon the following guidance is offered: 'Third knowledge is the first time someone calls you a weirdo. You about start crying, or you sock them in the stomach, or you act even more weirdo, or you just sit there and don't do nothing, or you get happy because at least someone is talking to you. But Fourth knowledge is people get fascinated by you. That's why they buy you. But it's not your first pick of a kind of fascination of you. You will pray to God to take it back but God is busy. What is he busy doing? Making more weirdos. He's a weird God.

Fifth knowledge is when sometimes you meet a man or a lady who is a grown up weirdo - the good kind - and they know you. Even if they never saw you before, they know you and say HiHiHi and your whole life can change - even if you know them for only around one week. My brother Freddie who drew the pictures on this has got a teacher like this, Mrs. LeSense. I go with him early to her room every morning and we open the window shades for her. Her face is always happy to see us, I love her. She cured my brother's life. This is a true story.' (1)

Both read their copy of the cartoon in silence. If anything it was like sealing a pact. They both were determined to show it to their mother and their social worker.

A brief summary of the second meeting and accompanying letter

Dave and Jenni were excited to relate the responses of their mother and the social worker to the cartoon. It wasn't long before David turned to Sharon and asked her if she was of the opinion that Dave and Jenni came to their 'weirdly abledness' through 'nature or nurture'? For the first time since David had met her, Sharon then broke into laughter and began to tell stories about various members of the Murphy Family. David led a very detailed enquiry into the history and genealogy of the 'weirdly abled'. It took up the entire meeting and then some.

Dear Dave, Sharon and Jenni,

With all your help, I have started to more fully understand the history and genealogy of the "weirdly abled" in your family and it certainly seems to go a long way back. Dave, you told me that sometimes you're happy with your mind and that sometimes you're not. You said that "unpredictability" was a strong feature of how your mind works. You said, "No one knows what I'm going to do next - it can be good or bad."

What was clear was that you took your place in the family lineage when you stated that "I've got a mind of my own." I certainly agree with you there. You left me with no doubts whatsoever. Sharon and Jenni, you fully concurred.

Dave, you went on to say that over the last two years you "have been teased a lot" and that you have been using confusion tactics on the teasers. However, there are those who understand you and appreciate you as a "weirdly abled" young man - like last year's math teacher, Mr Johnson. You said, "He is the only one who understands me." But Jenni and Sharon disagreed because they thought they had a pretty good understanding of you too. Dave, had you just taken them for granted?

Sharon, you thought Mr Johnson was able to understand because he "has a daughter with ADD" and he has had teaching experience with some twins with ADD. In addition, Sharon, you were of the opinion that "his approach is different - he is interested in the person and doesn't care about spelling." Dave, you added, "He knows I've got a great sense of humour." Do you suspect that in his own way he is "weirdly abled" too, but because he is a teacher he has to tone it down? What do you think?

When I realised that you, Sharon, had also always been "weirdly abled", you spoke of the effects this had had on your life. You told me that you were "an advanced and lateral thinker as a child but that you were ignored a lot as a girl." Instead of acknowledging and cherishing you for you, you told us that some members of your family "didn't know what to do" with you. Sharon, you told me the tragic story of how your mother has "never been" your mother, that you "offended her as a baby" and that you "don't know what it was" that did this. Sharon, do you think, on reflecting, that your mind was too fast for hers? That you, in a manner of speaking, were always ahead of her or out in front of her?

Then I asked you, Sharon, that if you knew what you know now, and could have been there as an adult in your little girl life, what would you have done differently? You said: "I would have put more pressure on my parents to allow me to be with both sets of grandparents. Both sets had expressed a desire to adopt me." Sharon, is that because your grandparents knew that you were "weirdly abled" and not weird? Were they not afraid of you? Were they more encouraging rather than discouraging? You told me how Grandma Peg insisted when you were 8 that you bought Jane Eyre even though people doubted you were capable of it. Do you think she knew you better than anyone else? Sharon, was it because she recognised herself in you that she knew what you knew?

Sharon, you summed up your experience of both sets of grandparents when you said: "They encouraged me". They appreciated your mathematical gifts when they learned that at age eight you could add faster than a cash register. They understood that you were "mathematically abled". Sharon, did you realise quite quickly that you had a fast mind? Do you suspect that people with slower minds than yours resented the quickness of your mind?

Jenni, you agreed with Sharon's opinion of Grandma Peg by saying "she's cool". And Dave you had this to say and from you I would consider it a great compliment: "She has the best sense of humour I've ever heard". Coming from a pretty witty guy, that seems high praise! Sharon, you also commented that Dave has inherited his Grandma's "dramatic nature and humour" and Dave, you put on a pretty good show to demonstrate this and you told us some of her quips. Then Dave, you informed us that your humour was the key to understanding you. And Sharon, from a wider perspective, informed me about the importance of the Murphy sense of humour

Sharon, you then acknowledged that your "weird abilities" have been something of a mixed blessing for you. You were happy to acknowledge that your weird abilities helped your scholastic abilities which were very good - maths in particular. You described yourself as "mathematically gifted". Dave you said that you were "trying to turn my abilities to my school work" but that it wasn't easy for you. Jenni, you seemed to find it relatively easy to do so. You were lucky in this regard I suspect.

We then went on to review what seemed at least in your eyes, Sharon, to be a "miracle". After our last meeting, Jenni and Dave went "two days without fighting". And this was not a mere allegation but testified to by all concerned parties: Dave, Jenni and yourself.

Jenni, you were amazed by this but you said "I was trying to see how long we could go for". Jenni, would you have believed that you could go for one hour without fighting? Dave, when I pressed you for some explanation for this change of fortune you said: "We were working together." Dave, does that mean under normal circumstances you are working against each other? Dave, what did you prefer: working together or against each other? Jenni and Dave, haven't you got enough people against you already? Or do you think I am getting too preachy here? Let me know when we meet again. Jenni, you summed up the two "miracle" days by saying they were "good". Jenni, why do you say that?

Jenni and Dave, you thought you might go a week this time but Dave, you said in a Taurean way that if I told you to be co-operative, that would be like a red rag to you. So I was quite neutral here and kept my opinions to myself. You both insisted that "if we get up to a week, you've got to reward us." I said I would, but in a "weirdly abled" way. So don't expect anything conventional because if you did, you would be a lot less 'weirdly abled' than I believe you all to be.

I agreed with you, Dave and Jenni, that we should set aside half the next meeting to go over the "secret". Once again, Sharon, let me explain that although we do have a

"secret", it will be divulged to you in full in due course. Please be patient with us. There is no malice whatsoever in our "secrecy".
   Yours Respectfully,
   David

Third meeting

By their third meeting, Sharon was of the opinion that "it's touch and go with me to keep going" and "I still need to warn them about foster homes". However, she was glad to report that "they are getting on better and are not at each other with knives and daggers. They are appreciating each other more".

The miracle had now endured for an entire week. The rest of the meeting was taken up conspiring about the imminent Mother Appreciation party.

Fourth meeting

At their fourth meeting a month later, after reviewing recent developments, it was agreed by Dave, Sharon, Jenni and David that a report would be written to the statutory agency that was funding the therapy. This report was required in order for the therapy to continue to receive funding. They all agreed at the outset that the report was something that they would 'all do together'.

This report, or 'counter document' (White & Epston, 1990) not only served as a request for funding, it more importantly verified that Dave and his family were problem solvers. This was the first entry into the file on Dave in particular, and the Murphy family in general, in which they participated as authorities on their own lives. It proudly took its place in their file, which was already the size of a phone book and filled with the documentation of problems.

REPORT AND RECOMMENDATIONS: Child and Young Persons Service of New Zealand
From: David Epston
Re: Progress report with the Murphy family

As agreed, I am providing you with an account of the meetings so far with Dave, his sister, Jennifer (Jenni), and his mother Sharon. It seems to be a particularly timely point for a review of our meetings. We have welcomed the opportunity to provide you with this record of them.

Jenni contends that 'Dave has been a lot better and we don't fight as much'. Before our first meeting, according to Jenni, fighting consumed 50% of the time she and Dave were in each other's presence. Sharon estimated it at 75% of the time and Dave at 100% of the time. Jenni now estimates that the current level of fighting is about 1% of the time. Dave's estimate is 10% and Sharon deemed it to be 'within normal boundaries'.

I have attempted to establish how Jenni and Dave reduced fighting so substantially. Jenni's explanation is: 'I don't choose to pick fights with him. I wanted to see how long we could go without fighting'. Neither Jenni nor Dave were willing to disclose the specifics of what they referred to as 'our strategy' for reducing fighting. However, Dave has stated that 'if we sold our strategy to the United States, we could be millionaires'.

Dave was willing to comment that when he 'saw Jenni trying ... I tried'. He also said: 'I figured out one simple thing - I could be bullied into fighting. I looked at fighting as if it were homework'. Like homework, Dave was very reluctant to do it. Sharon was of the opinion that it had a lot to do with them finding 'that we had to work together because we wanted the 'Mother Appreciation' party'. And they found that co-operation wasn't so bad after all and in fact was quite enjoyable. I suppose any reader might be curious to know what a 'Mother Appreciation' might be and what it might entail.

Well, Dave and Jenni acknowledged that they were very worried for their mother and her psychological well-being. They feared that on the one hand she was nearing a 'breakdown' and on the other that they would be placed in foster homes. Consequently, they decided to take it upon themselves to plan a surprise party for their mother in order to fully appreciate her and so that her friends could also have an opportunity to do the same. This required considerable guile on their part to keep their planning and preparations a surprise, but they were able to pull it off. Although they spent some time with me preparing their respective 'mother appreciation' speeches, embarrassment and shyness got the better of them and they decided against giving their speeches. Nonetheless their mother basked in the appreciation of her.

To summarise, Sharon has assessed that the situation at home is 'a heck of a lot better' and that 'it couldn't have gone on. They would have ended up in foster homes. It was touch and go. I was worried about them 100% of the time. I couldn't leave them for a split second. In fact, I couldn't even get through going to the toilet because I feared for their safety'. Dave agreed that he too was a bit scared that he would harm his sister: 'I didn't know if I could stop it'. Sharon believed that Jenni feared for her safety as she had overheard her daughter saying so.

Dave recommends that the sessions be extended. He said that he 'still has some fits of anger and although I've come a long way, I've still got a long way to go'. He wanted me to add: 'I thank you (the funding agency) for getting us this far and helping me to stop myself from fighting with Jenni'.

This report has been read and signed by Dave, Jenni and Sharon who in signing their names agree both generally and specifically to its content.

After this fourth meeting, no mention of Sharon 'breaking down' and fostering Dave and Jennifer was ever made again.

Fifth meeting

Following their Mother Appreciation Party and the letter to renew the funding, David got very busy knowing Jenni's and Dave's minds at the same time as Dave and Jenni got equally busy knowing their own minds. Admittedly there were surprises for all of them, but all of the surprises turned out quite pleasantly. In spite of other people's opinions about her that would have caused her to doubt herself in the past, Sharon became more and more comfortable trusting in her 'weirdly abled' parenting.

There was one notable occurrence. Dave's knee-tapping was getting faster and faster when David leaned over towards him and placed his hand above his knee. He inquired: 'Can you feel your knee touching my hand?'

Dave replied that he could. David then asked, 'Were you aware that your knee was going up and down before I placed my hand above it?' Dave and David realised for the first time that he didn't.

This seemed significant so David asked some more questions: 'Does your body have a mind of its own? Does it pay you any mind? Does it ignore you? Is this a sign of disrespect?'

Everyone agreed that such a project of inquiry would be a matter of concern for the future of the therapy.

Letter sent to Dave after the fifth meeting

Dear Dave:

I really enjoyed talking to you the other night. It all began when Jenni started the ball rolling by saying: "Dave has made a tremendous effort to keep out of my room. He learned really quickly. He did it because he was being polite. I think Dave is a whole lot nicer". Your mum also agreed that "Dave has made a concerted effort". She told us how relieved she is that she can now stand back from "the edge" that she has been on for so long.

We then all became aware, even you Dave, that it was possible that the self-control you had been exercising could be "the first of the summer wine". When I asked you about this, you had a very good explanation indeed: "Something in my brain knocked something over which changed the gear into behaviour mode". When I asked how long it would last, you thought it might endure for another week or two. However, Sharon recalled one summer in which you went throughout it self-controlling yourself. Can you remember that summer, Dave? Was it a summer to remember? Certainly, it seems so for your mum.

Sharon, you referred to 1989 as "the summer of self-control". Your mum remembers that she did a lot of work with you like gardening. And this seemed to have helped you be in control of your body and mind. We also talked about how when you look after Auntie Sue, you bring yourself under your own self-control. That also connected with "duty day" and the way you looked after the teachers.

Here are some questions that I have for you, Dave:

1. How does physical activity, e.g. gardening, bike riding, lead to you to being self-controlling?

2. How does looking after people lead you to be self-controlling?

Dave, I felt very sorry for you when you told us how at times your mind and body seem to have minds of their own and don't pay you any mind. And at times as you said, "I'm not aware they are doing it". Dave, is it time for this "therapy" of ours to put all our heads and WEIRD ABILITIES together in order to assist you in some weirdly abled way to have more of your mind and body under your self-control???

I hope we will be able to talk together about this next time. I look forward to such a discussion.

Yours sincerely
David

This letter marked a transition. The Murphy family was now engaged on its own 'weirdly abled' terms to address a persistent problem in their lives. It was time for a less 'weirdly abled' therapist to sit back and see what they came up with.

Letter sent to Dave after the sixth meeting
Dear Dave:
You said that the last letter "had a good feeling". I am glad you thought so as I did too. And what was even better was that we continued to have a good conversation yesterday. I hope you felt that I was able to keep up with you at long last, although I may never get an "Irish sense of humour". In that regard, I may be a lost cause.

When I asked if you were able to make your self-control endure, you said that "it had switched on and off during the week". When I inquired as to how you understand what switched self-control off and on, you said that "tiredness and grumpy people switch off self-control" and "happiness and food switch on self-control".

Sharon you added that "a great deal of physical activity" plays an important part in self-controlling ways. Sharon, you observed that when Dave is exercising his self-control, this has the effect of you experiencing him as "a good son and a good friend".

Dave, you seemed pleased to hear your mum say this. You then went on to tell me some things that were pretty new to me: "To a "weirdly abled" person with ADD, the tables are turned. Physical activity will wind up most normal people but in me physical activity will relax me and make me more self-controlling". Can you understand that wasn't immediately comprehensible to me? When I asked how long you had been aware of this, you said that "the theory has been there for the past 2, 3 years but I didn't know it was there."

Dave, do you think we have hit upon something important if you are to have more of a self-controlling life and less of a life controlled by ADD?

Dave, does such a prospect appeal to you? Do you think it would appeal to your mum and Jenni?

Dave, do you think you might develop an anti-ADD practice from the theory that you have had for the past 2,3 years?

Dave, would you do so by some inimitable "weirdly abled" ways and means?

Dave, do you think I think you will come up with some predictable or unpredictable ways of making a self-controlling practice out of your "theory"?

Dave, what bearing might it have on your life if it became a more self-controlled life rather than an ADD-controlled life?

Dave, how would you try out such a practice in your life? Or would you prefer to surrender this life-time to ADD and live your life out according to ADD?

Dave, we then got talking about your self-pride, something ADD has never been able to take away from you. Dave, can you imagine where you would be today if it had? I would hate to think about it. You put your self-pride down to you and your family's "Irish sense of humour". Can you understand now why I have come to respect your "Irish sense of humour" so much more than when I first met you?

Still, you said that you had to quote "build up" your pride in the face of a lot of teasing. You considered that it was very advantageous that you had "a proud mother". When I asked you, Dave, what you were most proud of, you said, "At school, I have overcome the hurdle of teasing".

Sharon, you have undertaken quite a unique form of parenting, one that I expect plays quite a part in Dave's and Jenni's self-pride. You told me, "I have always challenged their minds. I was on my own for so long, I have always treated them as equals". And I understand that many people really don't respect you for having done this. Does that have to do with Dave and Jenni not being deferential to adults? Does that get them into trouble with some adults?

Merry Xmas and can we look forward to a more self-controlling 1996? I trust so.
David

Seventh meeting

At this point, David had thickened an alternative story by enriching its counter-plot ('a self-controlling life') at the expense of the Problem's plot (an ADD-controlled life). Everyone agreed it was time for the next step - to let everyone know about the new direction in which Dave was taking his life. This included those who cared about him (friends, family) and those who had been concerned about him, including the numerous professionals he had met over the course of his life. David interviewed everyone about Dave's claim pertaining to his 'new Dave' with the express purpose of preparing an affidavit for Dave to swear and Sharon and Jenni to testify to as being an accurate and valid alternative version of his life.

The process of creating the affidavit began with David asking questions and then typing in replies, re-reading the text and having the speaker confirm them. Although this may sound laborious, David 'dug up' the history of a 'self-controlling life' and the 'new Dave' constituted through it. Good progress was made by the end of this visit but it looked like several more meetings would be required before the document was ready to be 'sworn'. Dave, Jenni and Sharon took home the first draft (the complete version is included later in this chronicle).

Eighth meeting summary and "consulting your consultants" (2)
Interview segment

This meeting showed the alternative story in the making. Dave continued to unravel his own account of the 'new Dave' and in this way continued to develop a draft of his preferred (auto) biography.

At the same time, in this interview with the Murphy family, David's mind began to show signs of stretching out to meet the concerns and experiences of all of the family members. The conversation nimbly weaved its way between each of their three individual thematic strands. The conversation reflected the family's unique style of communication and as such, it moved quite fast. It is interesting to contrast this interviewing style to the one in the letter following meeting 2 where one theme is externalised and discussed with everyone.

To begin with David took the chance to consult with Dave about what he believed had helped him become a new person: 'Dave, my question is this. Did the fact that you started feeling you were becoming your new person have anything to do with you recognising along with your mum and your sister that you come from a long line of weirdly abled people and that you have a great deal to be very proud of?'

Sharon clarified the question for Dave: 'What he means is did recognising what Grandma Peg is like, and what Nana Holland was like, and what Granddaddy was like, and what Uncle Kevin was like, did that effect your decisions? Did you realise you weren't so strange after all? Did that help you realise that you were you and that you came from a long line of people that were like this?!'

'Yah. . .' Dave replied.

'How did knowing that you come from a long line of talented people lead to you decide to become a 'new Dave'?' David followed.

Dave began by joking: 'Well, I don't exactly want to get myself into the financial poo that most of my relatives have got themselves into'. But then his family pride set in: 'But if they could do what they have done and still come out on top, I COULD DO IT'.

A hopeless case

David then said, 'Can I ask then - before that, did you feel you were a hopeless case?'

Dave shook his head vigorously in agreement.

'You did!?' David exclaimed, 'If I am putting too much question-pressure on you, tell me - it's just that I am interested. This could be pretty important to other people. Who do you think thought you were a 'hopeless case'?'

'Ten or twenty people.'

'What hospitals did you go to or treatments did you receive?'

Dave hesitated for a moment and his mother jumped in to pick up the narrative: 'Psychiatric hospital for 5 months; a residential treatment centre for a year; another residential treatment centre for 9 months. He then lived with his father and had a case worker and then went to live in a foster home for a year. He came back to me at 11.'

'What age was he when you lost him?' David asked her trying to do the math in his head.

'When he was nine, almost ten.' Sharon replied, 'Then he had a psychiatrist and then we had nobody.'

David turned to Dave: 'Did you get the impression that a lot of people thought you were a hopeless case?'

'Yah.' he shouted.

Sharon interjected: 'But most people give me the impression that I am a neurotic old bag that makes a nuisance of herself over nothing.'

'Did anyone take an interest in the fact that you were weirdly abled? Or that Dave was weirdly abled? Or Jenni?' David asked Sharon.

'No. . . no.' Sharon replied.

'They preferred their version of you as a neurotic rather than as a weirdly abled person?'

'They just treated the symptoms.'

The rest of the interview included explorations of the steps Dave had taken in terms of physical exercise - including swimming and starting a lawn mowing business - and discussions about changes to Dave's diet and the effects of these changes on self-control. Importantly, time was also spent talking with Jenni about the effects the changes in the family were having on her life. It was acknowledged that Jenni also needed appreciation for the changes that were taking place. Now that Jenni could stop spending so much of her time worrying about her mother, everyone spoke about whether she would now be able to have a bit more fun.

Letter written to the Murphy family after the eighth meeting

Dear Dave, Jenni and Sharon:

It was really great to catch up with you all in 1996. It made me wonder if 1996 mightn't be a very interesting year for each and everyone of you. And especially for you, Jenni.

Dave, your "new Dave" really has taken off this year, although it's clear that he had made an appearance around December last year. Do you think your "new Dave" is in a partnership with your new self-controlling ways? Why I ask this is:

1) if your Problem was still controlling your body and mind, how could you possibly have initiated a lawn mowing round?

2) if your Problem was still controlling your body and mind, how could you possibly have committed yourself to organised sports and gaining a Duke of Edinburgh medal?

3) if your Problem was still controlling your body and mind, how could you have determined the prospect of a B+ or A in Phys. Ed?

Is the "new Dave" also in partnership with the family tradition of "can do, no matter what"? Did you take hope from the accomplishments of those who came before you in your family? Did the "old Dave" believe he was a hopeless case? Were the Problem and hopelessness partners? Dave, do you wonder what would have become of you if your mum had given up hope in you too? Do you wonder what would have happened if she had believed she was a "neurotic old bag" rather than believing she was a "weirdly abled" parent?"

Sharon, do you think your "weirdly abled" parenting is starting to pay off for you, Dave and Jenni? Are you glad you kept faith in your beliefs despite many others critiquing you? Do you marvel at yourself that you kept your faith in yourself for so long?

Sharon, is it possible that your life is the inspiration for Dave's "new Dave"?

Dave, can you keep an eye out for how your "alertness" has you "learning a lot more"? Do you find such learning to your liking? Have your "weirdly able" ways kept that mind of yours from going rusty? Are food and learning connected some how or other? As I am personally interested, can you keep me in touch with these developments?

Dave, does the "new Dave" like himself more because others are liking him more? Or are other people liking him more because the "new Dave" likes himself more? Or is it a bit of both? That is something else I am personally interested in. For example, how would you explain that your supply of self-confidence has increased by 6 feet. That would be something around a 33% increase from the last time we measured, wouldn't it?

Dave, I wish we had more time to discuss how your newfound self-confidence is having you believe in yourself more and doubt yourself less. I wish I could hear more stories like the one you told us about believing in yourself more on the trains on your way to school.

Dave, I thought it was very nice of you to have the "old Dave" back every so often, especially if things get too dull. However, you may be too busy for that with everything you are getting up to. Do you think we should make a place for the "old Dave" in our meetings? Is it fair to just dump him? After all, he has been with you for a very long time and perhaps that very fact should be acknowledged. What do you think?

Jenni, do you think it is time to pay more attention to you now that Dave is starting to pay attention to himself? Has all the worry that Dave's Problem got you to do meant that you have got out of the practice of having fun? I would guess that fun and worry really don't mix very well. What do you think? Sharon, what do you think? Will 1996 be a year for you all to find your way back to fun?

Yours sincerely,
David

Tenth meeting: the formal signing of the affidavit of "New Dave"

AFFIDAVIT

I started to become a 'new Dave' shortly after I first visited David Epston at The Family Therapy Centre in August. My mother arranged counselling through the New Zealand Child and Young Person's Service (New Lynn). She had been convinced for some time that this was something both I and my family needed. At the time, my family was in crisis and on the point of breaking up.

At the first meeting I saw mum's side of the story and that she was getting too distraught to cope with my Problem. I started thinking about the Problem in a different way. I had already gone through a foster home and the only thing that kept me from going insane was my mother's letters. They arrived as regular as clockwork once a week on Fridays. I looked forward to those letters as they were just from mum. I realised I had taken my mother for granted until I went and lived with my dad. My heart grew fonder for my mum and I sort of missed my sister, Jenni.

So the beginning of my decision to be a 'new Dave' goes back to 1992. But what actually brought me closer to making up my mind was that somehow or other I and my sister, Jenni, worked together secretly to organise a 'Mother Appreciation' party for our beloved mother. This seemed to pave the way for me to be a 'new Dave'.

The first sign of my 'new Dave' was that the persistent fighting between me and Jenni stopped really overnight. I wouldn't have believed such peace between me and Jenni could have been possible. Jenni was just as surprised as I was. This allowed me to believe much more was possible than this. My next step was stopping some annoying habits like going into Jenni's room uninvited. This, I knew, really upset Jenni. My mother believes these changes had a lot to do with the family characteristic of just making up your mind and sticking with it. My mother has told us that without such a personal philosophy she would not have been able to get through her life. When I gave it some thought, I realised I couldn't have put it any better myself. My mother is a very good example of the philosophy. Still, I was taken aback when I broke the 'going-into-Jenni's-room-without-being-invited' habit and I did have doubts that I could do that. But I patted myself on the back mentally when I did. I think too I felt I was becoming a 'new Dave' in the second meeting.

The second meeting was one in which according to my mother, I 'recognised what Grandma Peg is like and what Nana Holland was like and what Granddaddy was like and what Uncle Kevin was like'. She wondered: 'Did you realise that you weren't so strange after all? That you were you? And you came from a long line of people that were like this?' I replied: 'If they could do what they have done and still come out on top, I could do it.' All the people I had been in contact with about my problem gave me the distinct impression that I was a hopeless case. And my mother gained the impression that as she put it, 'I am a neurotic old bag that makes a nuisance of herself.' No one realised that we were 'weirdly abled' and that we deserve to be respected for that. Although not everyone can or will understand us, my mother has become convinced however that although we have 'very different' ways, they have 'worked for us'.

My next step in my 'new Dave' was experimenting with ways to increase the control over my body and mind. First of all, I started up a lawn mowing business and I received some feedback from my customers that my service was tidier than professionals. I joined a swimming team in order to meet some of the requirements for a Bronze Duke of Edinburgh Award. And I even decided to try in Physical Education. I also stuck at watering the garden which took me half an hour every night. My mother commented regarding my lawn mowing that I pay a lot of 'attention to detail'. If I was the 'old Dave', such a business would have just gone down the proverbial drain.

My sister believes there is some substance to my 'new Dave' in that she noted that I now even cut our lawn within 2 hours. Before, my mother or my sister would have always ended up doing it. My sister, Jenni, has been somewhat overshadowed by my 'new Dave' and for that reason my mother and her decided to keep in mind how much she had invested in keeping our family going. My mother decided to pay more attention to her as she, to my way of thinking, was becoming 'jealous'.

My 'new Dave' also experimented with my diet and self-control and has come up with some interesting results. For example, I have started eating a breakfast which has meant I am more alert at school and am learning more. The 'old Dave' would have usually just had a cup of tea and whizzed away. All this 'new Dave' stuff has had quite an effect on my view of myself. Before, I felt kind of like a person with a pimple on their face whom nobody likes. Then it was like this person had gone to the doctors and they put a whole lot of liquid nitrogen on the pimple, it slowly went away and people start liking the person again. David asked me if people are approaching me for my friendship and I said in reply 'Yes. Before I would get one hullo when I walked into the class and that would be from the teacher and would be a general one to everybody. But now I am getting about two or four hullos just to me.'

You are probably wondering what effect my 'new Dave' is having on my mother. She is really enjoying her life. Another good thing is that my sister, Jenni, instead of worrying 75% of her worry about our mother, is in my opinion now only worrying 10% of her worry about mum and 90% about herself. We were all concerned that Jenni doesn't know how to have fun and our therapy wants to see her allow more fun into her life. My mother has also concluded that she has not had any fun in her life.

One of the big things about my 'new Dave' is that I have heaps more self-confidence than when I was the 'old Dave'. For example, I can confidently go out. I always used to be scared poopless about catching the wrong train. Now I am not always doubting myself and I am believing in my own ideas.

I know you won't believe this, as the 'old Dave' never got any better marks than Ds and Es, but so far this year the 'new Dave' is getting lots of As and even an A+ in Maths. All up the 'new Dave' is getting about a B+ average.

My mother now believes that we are a really great family, a lot better than most because we have had to be so close. However, she has made it clear to Jenni and me that she now wants more of a life of her own. Jenni and I are finding this difficult but we do know how much this means to mum. She broke down and cried when she told us about it.

David thought we should provide you with a transcript of an important conversation we had together:

David: 'Did you make any New Year's resolutions for the 'new Dave'? Did you say good-bye to the 'old Dave'? Which Dave are you more at home with now?'

Dave: 'Well, you can't really get rid of the 'old Dave'. The 'old Dave' is still lurking about. The 'old Dave' is really crafty. He is basically a thief.'

David: 'What does the 'new Dave' do when the 'old Dave' sneaks back?'

Dave: 'Sometimes it gets too dull for too long, so I think: 'It is too dull ... I want some excitement!' Then I let the 'old Dave' come back. BUT ONLY FOR A WHILE AND CONTROLLED!'

Sharon: 'What about for five minutes per year?'

My mum wanted to add some stuff to my affidavit:

'The most noticeable thing is the total abstinence of violence. Before it was daily and bad. We have only had two incidents in the last six months and they were not major. Squabbling is in the normal boundaries. Dave now controls himself. We are a close-knit family and my children realise that we have more than an ordinary family has. I no longer have to watch over them all the time. What proves to me that the 'new Dave' is new is that he does things without being asked.'

David Epston contributed to this letter by asking us questions and typing up our answers.

In our opinion the above is a faithful record of events since NZC&YPS started supporting our counselling at The Family Therapy Centre.

Signed by Dave Murphy: ....

Signed by Sharon Murphy (Mother): ....

and Jenni Murphy (sister): ....

Chroniclers' summary

It has been fascinating to witness how each of the members of this family came to use their own authority and pride with the people and institutions they en-counter and to identify the significance that their legacy of 'weirdly abledness' has played and continues to play in their lives. How many families have you met that have a clear sense of possessing a unique spirit, their own brand of humour and 'weirdly abled' ways? Perilously few, we suspect.

Do the 'weirdly abled' merit 'weirdly abled' therapists? Should 'able' therapists consider whether their practices require 'weirdly abled' people to 'fit in' to estab-lished norms? Might it be more ethically responsible to respect the 'weirdly or uniquely abled' for their persistence and courage to 'stand out'?

David and the Murphy's still meet together every so often. The conversations that they share are somewhat different now; there is more appreciation for each other, themselves, and their ways.

At a recent meeting Sharon lamented that due to her being 'different' all her life she has never been understood by anybody. David disagreed and pointed to Dave and Jenny. Since then Sharon has been telling her children about her history. This led Jenni to an enriched 'mother appreciation' and to say, 'She looks worn on the outside but inside of her it's like an antique shop with so many interesting and rich things scattered here and there.'

Jenni has now been admitted into the 'largest group at school' which she proudly calls 'the weirds'.

She serves as philosopher to the group, providing perspective rather than advice. Advocating for 'the weirds' is sometimes a risky undertaking but it is one that Jenni sees as important.

Dave meanwhile has set himself the Herculean task of orienting his interest to the thoughts of others rather than orating his own. He was unabashed about accepting that this could very well be a life-long challenge.

Notes
* For further reference to the idea of weird and special abilities see Freeman et al. (1997), 179-192.
1. This quote has been slightly adapted for ease of understanding in this different context.
2. For further information on the "*Consulting Your Consultants Interview*" see Epston & White (1995).

References
Barry, L. (1993) *Marlys' Guide to Weirdos*. Funny Times, April.
Epston, D. & White, M. (1995) 'Consulting your consultants: a means to the co-construction of alternative knowledges' in Friedman, S. (Ed) *The Reflecting Team in Action: Collaborative Practice in Family Therapy*, Guilford, New York.
Freeman, J.C., Epston, D. & Lobovits, D. H. (1997) *Playful Approaches to Serious Problems: Narrative Therapy with Children and their Families*, Norton, New York.
White, M. & Epston, D. (1990) *Narrative Means to Therapeutic Ends*, Norton, New York.

3

Mad Fax Sunday: are some virtual communities more real than virtual?

Kerry Lane, David Epston & Sue Winter

Original version published in Lane, K., Epston, D. and Winter, S., Mad Fax Sunday: Are some virtual communities more real than virtual? *Gecko – A Journal of Deconstruction and Narrative Ideas*, 1, 1998.

The following chapter tells the story of a therapist (KL) who was stuck, overwhelmed and isolated by a problem that seemed to defy therapeutic techniques and skills and personal commitment and determination. On the verge of giving up I reached out to access my support network. Because no other alternative seemed available at the time, this reaching out took place by fax. However, what started out as a choice of last resort revealed a range of therapeutic possibilities that we believe deserve to be shared with a wider audience.

We are submitting this chapter both as a critique of isolating and exclusionary effects of many conventional mental health practices, and as an addition to the literature on reflecting teams, audiences and communities of concern. In this instance, although necessity was the mother of its invention, it has prompted the authors to consider alternative practices to those formed on the bases of 'privacy' and 'confidentiality'. It demonstrates ways that reflection and solidarity can be achieved by unconventional means, e.g. fax, letter, telephone, producing some of the same effects as set-piece reflecting team practices. None of the authors has any particular fondness for contemporary technology but this did not stop us from exploring it given the circumstances. What urgency pressed into using allowed us to consider doing the same under less demanding conditions. Although we hadn't counted on it at the time, the mad fax 'team' offered us all some quite unexpected advantages. Although the critique stands, our main concern in publishing this chapter is for us to consider 'mad taxing', etc. as capable of calling into being 'communities of concern'. Such virtual communities can become very real sites where commitment, solidarity and ingenuity co-mingle.

After all, how many of us have colleagues, supervisors, and mentors, etc. who have access to a fax machine or phone? Do we have to work in isolation, especially against 'huge' and intimidating problems such as the 'self-abuse' that was threatening Sylvia's life? Would such 'communities' counteract the 'wear and tear' of our work which in the end either bums us out or, what's worse, leads to cynical indifference?

My initial reason for contacting David was to enquire about the ritual of inclusion. I had read about it and listened to David discuss it at workshops. I knew it was used when young people had been seriously 'unbelonged' by their families or caregivers I also recalled that it entailed the young person being physically held by their parents until the strength of their love and acceptance overtook the feelings of being 'unbelonged' or 'wild'. Sylvia had been isolated from her family by a tragic set of circumstances rather than 'unbelonged'. I wondered if David had ever used the ritual of inclusion in other ways that might fit this family. I really didn't have any ideas about how this might work. Frankly, I was desperate. 'Self-abuse' had made a comeback into Sylvia's life. The most recent 'self-abuse' episode came very close to costing Sylvia her life. I was so scared that I was ready to give up. I felt I was no match for 'self-abuse', even though there had been a long period where 'self-abuse' had been dormant. The power of the comeback intimidated me.

I wanted to consult with David and mentioned this to the family. I explained that David was a narrative therapist who I respected and trusted. They were only too well aware that I had nowhere to go but reassured me that they were relieved that, unlike their previous experiences at such critical times, I did not attempt to medicate Sylvia or have her admitted to hospital against her will. What was not usual was that we all acknowledged to each other that, although we were lost, we would not lose each other. In fact, we experienced being in league against such a frightening problem at the deepest level, even if it was sheer desperation that united us.

Original Letter written on 19th April 1996

Dear David,
I am writing seeking your advice. I am working with Sylvia, aged sixteen, who is in the midst of a dreadful battle with 'self-abuse'. Although the battle has been going on for some time, lately it has increased in its intensity. Sylvia and I believe that this is due to our having exposed 'self-abuse' increasingly over the past 8 months. We are now much more familiar with its tricks and tactics and, at times, Sylvia feels that she is winning. However, it seems that when we catch a glimpse of a victory ahead, 'self-abuse' goes on to the offensive. This is of course to be expected, however, the battle for her life is becoming very hazardous and Sylvia, her family and I fear that Sylvia may be deceived to her death. This may sound strange so let me explain. I know you are familiar with the camps 'Youth Caucus' that Sharon and I facilitate on the Central Coast. Sylvia was attending her second camp a few weeks ago. She was enjoying the feelings of love and acceptance that she experienced at the camp when 'self-abuse' told her that she didn't deserve these nice feelings or the connections she was making with others. 'Self-abuse' encouraged her to isolate herself (one of its favourite tactics) and, in doing so, she made a small but deep incision into her hand with a razor blade. Sylvia thought this would just inflict the punishment 'self-abuse' said she deserved and that then she would feel better. However, in doing so, the razor severed an artery and this turned into a battle for Sylvia's life. As you can see, ' self-abuse' fights dirty. This incident is one of many and that is why I think we need to call for some reinforcements.

Sylvia, her family and I have traced the beginnings of this war and we all thought we should fill you in on its history. Sylvia disclosed on-going sexual abuse by a neighbour when she was ten. This man had posed as a family friend and had regularly offered to babysit. Despite his pressure to keep quiet, Sylvia drew upon her courage to speak up and the Department Of Community Services were informed. As soon as the so-called 'neighbour' found out about her disclosure, he fled leaving his wife living next door to Sylvia and her family. It seems the 'wife' was very confused about who has responsibility for sexual abuse and she began to intimidate and harass Sylvia and her family. This intimidation persisted for almost two years, increasing in its intensity. Vince and Janice (Sylvia's parents)

63

went to great lengths to protect Sylvia from this intimidation, however it was unrelenting and the family recalls this time in their lives as a 'nightmare'. They tried to transfer to another area but such arrangements take a very long time. Sylvia could no longer stand the intimidation and moved out of home to a youth refuge in another town.

As you are only too well aware, sexual abuse can make children feel extremely isolated, even when things go well after their disclosure. This isolation was intensified for Sylvia because of the further victimisation she experienced at the hands of the 'wife'. Sylvia moved around quite a bit between refuges and friends' homes. 'Self-abuse' entered her life around this time and had her make some very serious suicide attempts over the next few years. She also came into conflict with the law. Unfortunately she was held in custody on a number of occasions, not because her offences warranted this but rather as a means of keeping her 'safe'. She also spent some time in a residential psychiatric unit where she underwent lengthy assessments and attended counselling, none of which she found helpful. To add insult to injury, she, along with another girl, was sexually abused by the coordinator of the refuge. This assault was in January last year when she was fifteen.

During this three-year period, Vince and Janice remained in close contact with Sylvia. By now they had moved house and were determined to remain connected to their daughter. Both Janice and Vince report that they were largely excluded from her life by both the refuge system and in particular the medical system. Each time they were informed Sylvia was injured or had attempted suicide, they responded immediately, only to be told that they could not see her or that the matter was confidential. I wonder if you can imagine the level of frustration they felt? On one occasion, Janice and Vince went to Intensive Care to see Sylvia after being notified she had slashed her wrists and attempted to jump off a cliff. They were refused permission to see her by a social worker who claimed she was medicated.

After a day and a half of further requests and subsequent refusals, they spoke to a doctor who informed them that the social worker had decided that their presence was not in Sylvia's best interests. Rightly or not, Vince was so infuriated he made a lunge towards the social worker concerned. He was restrained, arrested and led away. As you can see, it seemed as if everybody was determined to ensure Sylvia's isolation and her parents' exclusion. I am wondering if they had made some false assumptions on the grounds of Sylvia living away from home and didn't bother to check them out with anyone?

Despite this, Sylvia appeared in court on a minor offence and was required to live at home and be accompanied at all times by a family member in an attempt to reduce the likelihood of her suicide. It was around this time, eight months ago, that Juvenile Justice requested that I work with Sylvia. By the way, it was also her choice to return home. Since then, we have worked closely together to discover the 'truth' about 'self-abuse'. At first I spoke only with Sylvia but we soon agreed that it was necessary to more fully expose 'self-abuse' by inviting Janice and Vince to join us. These family meetings have been enlightening for us all. We have discovered how 'self-abuse' isolates Sylvia and tries to exclude her parents from her life. Neither Sylvia nor I were aware of its means to this end, e.g., she gets so 'snappy' that they are encouraged to allow her to go off on her own.

We shared this knowledge with the teenagers at the camp. They agreed that this was exactly what had happened just prior to Sylvia's brush with 'self-abuse' there. They then decided to forbid 'self-abuse' from isolating her from them. They set up a tag team to accompany her wherever she went, along with the commitment not to be put off by the 'snappy' tactics of 'self-abuse'. Sylvia. was pleased about this as she considered that she needed her support team to be much more assertive with 'self-abuse' in the event of her being unable to assert herself. This was a great success for the remainder of the camp.

However, the battle continues at home with 'self-abuse' taking more and more liberties with her life, e.g., the other night Sylvia was encouraged to cut herself in front of Vince. This was without precedent as 'self-abuse' previously always had to isolate her from her family before taking control of her.

Consequently, we fear for Sylvia's life, and I felt that 'the home team' needed to be more assertive with 'self-abuse' just as the 'camp team' had. I spoke to Steve Armstrong in consultation and he suggested I talk to you about the 'ritual of inclusion'. He was of the opinion that it was very important to let 'self-abuse' know once and for all that its messages that Sylvia 'does not belong' and 'is not accepted' are utterly untrue, and that the 'home team' would be only too willing to prove it beyond reasonable doubt. I explained what I knew of the ritual to Sylvia and her family and they were interested to be better informed. A return to the medical system is not an option they even want to consider. They also agree that it is time for some dramatic action on our part to match that of 'self-abuse'. For this reason, they are willing to try almost anything that might help them save their daughter from 'self-abuse'.

David, I will be showing this letter to Sylvia and her family before I fax it to you. I know you are going to America on Tuesday so I will try to contact you before then seeking your advice.

I hope you are well and happy and I look forward to hearing from you.

Regards, Kerry Lane

Janice, Vince and Sylvia edited the letter on Friday, 19th April, and I promised to try to get the letter to David before he went to America on Tuesday, 23rd April. In line with my promise I went into my office on Sunday 21st April at about 1.30pm and faxed the letter to David's office. I hoped that David would receive the letter prior to leaving for America and might write to us while he was away.

I was rather taken aback when my office phone rang just as I had faxed him and it was David. He told me that by chance he was in his office preparing to go overseas and seeing how urgent the situation was he could not help but respond immediately. Both intensity and speed became the hallmarks of our mad fax Sunday. He suggested we exploit what technology we had - we would link up our two fax machines and I would arrange a phone connection with the family. Fortunately they had two phone lines and agreed for Sylvia to have one of her own and Vince and Janice would share the second line. David then faxed comments and questions through and I would ring the family reading David's fax out loud. A discussion followed between the four of us preparing their comments back and responses to the questions. Then I would hastily type up their comments and fax them back to David who was waiting expectantly for them. This went on for two or three hours. I am convinced that the rapid responding, which at times seemed dizzying to us all, played a large part in such an unusual and generative trans-Tasman conversation.

David's Fax No.1 21st April 1996, 1:59pm

I just arrived to work moments after your fax got through here. And I have just read through once and I must confess to being greatly distressed. But. I thought I should just start writing Sylvia, Vince and Janice. Before I do let me just say this. I know we have never met in person but I want you to know, even from this distance, I very much wish that I could be part of a response team, as it sounds as if every one of you has been abused. Moreover, your family has been abused in so many ways. I think it would only be distressing for me and for all of you to catalogue the abuses, some of them arising out of what I assume to have been 'good intentions' e.g., the conduct of 'helping people' forbidding you to be near to and with Sylvia at her darkest moments. If they knew what Kerry and I know, I feel sure they would offer you abject apologies.

Vince and Janice, have you got the idea that people believed you were to blame? Sylvia, did you get the idea that your mother and father were to blame?

Friends, I am also very interested to know more about your experience. Sylvia, at the camp when the tag team was set up to keep you company when 'self-abuse' was trying to have you all to itself, were you happy that they got more assertive with 'self-abuse' when you no longer could assert yourself? When you think back, did it have anything to do with 'SELF-RESPECT'? Why I ask is that in my experience with 'self-abuse' it can't operate very well in the face of 'SELF-RESPECT'. Have you found that in your experience of 'self-abuse'? When you had your tag team, did they show you RESPECT in any way? And if so, did their RESPECT for you ignite your own SELF-RESPECT? Sylvia, could 'self-abuse' have thrown off their RESPECT for you? In a manner of speaking, did the tag team wrestle 'self-abuse' into defeat, at least for the time being? If you are anything like I am, I know my own SELF-RESPECT can sure come and go.

Get back to me as soon as you can through Kerry. I am very upset and angry reading what has befallen you Sylvia and you, Vince and Janice. I very much want to do something to bring some measure of justice into your lives.

Yours respectfully, David

I phoned the family who answered David's questions from Fax No. I. I then faxed David with their responses.

Reply to Fax No. I

Vince and Janice believed that people did think they were to blame for what was happening to Sylvia. In fact, the 'wife' and the 'abuser' blamed Sylvia for the sexual abuse and they accused Janice and Vince of not being able to control their promiscuous ten-year-old. Also Vince feels that the social workers assumed that he had actually been the perpetrator as they treated him in that way and refused to even speak to him.

Sylvia was always clear that her parents were not to blame but did sense that others were blaming her family.

Sylvia was happy that the 'camp team' became more assertive as she feels 'safer'. She did feel better about herself as a person and this was a result of their caring for her.

David's Fax No.2, April 1996, 2.27pm

Dear Friends:

Vince, Janice and Sylvia, if you were all 100% convinced that you were not to blame and that the perpetrators were to blame, would that cleanse your hearts for what lies ahead of us? Why I ask is that I suspect what lies ahead of us will require us all to be clean of heart. Sylvia, knowing that others blamed your mum and dad, did that in any way make you doubt their love for you? Did you feel less beloved by them?

Sylvia, can you help me understand how the 'camp team' made you feel safe? Was it their confident manner? The way they looked at you? Did anyone have tears in their eyes? Did you suspect they know what 'self-abuse' was about? HOW DID YOU KNOW THEY WERE YOUR TEAMMATES? How did you feel better about yourself when they cared for you? I know it was a result of their caring but how did you feel better? Can you explain that to me in words? I am very interested to understand this better. I don't mean to bug you about it though. What would you say were the reasons for the 'tag teams' defeat of 'self-abuse' even if the defeat did not last your lifetime?

I am really glad to get to know you all and thanks for allowing me into your lives at this time.

Yours respectfully, David

Kerry's reply to Fax No.2

Janice and Vince do feel 100% convinced that they were not to blame.

Sylvia did, at times, doubt their love for her and sometimes still does. This doubt used to be about 65%. Now the doubt is about 20%.

The 'camp team' made Sylvia feel safer because - yes, they seemed confident and they were committed to doing it. Yes Kerry was crying. This was a sign that she cared for me but was a bit worrying. Some of the other kids did know about 'self-abuse' but it wasn't present at the camp for them. I can't explain how their caring made me feel better IT JUST DID!

At the camp, it was purely that people from the 'tag team' were there all the time that 'self-abuse' was defeated. Sylvia feels that there could have been other reasons for the defeat but she can't think at the moment.

Sylvia's aunt and uncle have just arrived for Sunday lunch and therefore it will be hard to continue the discussion but they are keen to hear more from you and feel supported by your interest. Can we resume this by mail or when you get back? Do you think the 'ritual of inclusion' is appropriate?

Any other question you think would be helpful for our enquiries?

David's Fax No.3. 21st April 1996, 3.44pm

I am very relieved to learn that you, Vince and Janice, are 100% convinced you are not to blame. It is good to meet people such as yourselves who can keep their faith in what they know is right and what they know to be wrong. Compare yourselves to the perpetrator and his 'wife'.

Sylvia, it was really interesting to me to learn that you have reduced your doubt in your parents' love for you by 45%. It must have been awful for you when you weren't so sure of their love for you as you are now. When you feel the FORCE of their love, is that a bit like feeling their RESPECT for you. Are love and RESPECT sort of the same to you? Can you ... YET AGAIN ... help me understand why of late you have got back 45% belief in their loving of you? (Sorry to pester you about such things!) Are you doing something different? Are they doing something different? Or are you both doing some different loving things to and for each other? Did 'self-abuse, in a manner of speaking try to talk you out of the fact that you are their beloved daughter? If so, why are you now listening to Vince and Janice's loving of your very own self?

Camp Team Questions

When you say they were 'confident, Sylvia, do you mean they were confident that you are a good person, that you are worthy of their (and anyone else's) respect or that you should live your life through to your old age? Can you guess why they were so committed to be on your 'team'? Does that tell you anything about yourself that 'self-abuse' would disagree with? Sylvia, what do you think Kerry was crying for? Was she crying for your life? Was it a bit worrying to know she would cry for your life? How much do you think she would cry if 'self-abuse' executed you?

Does the caring of other people make you feel better in general? Does 'self-abuse' tell you that you don't deserve to be cared for and that you are worthless? Do you have any sense that 'self-abuse' is a form of abuse? Can you think if there could have been other reasons for the defeat of 'self-abuse' at the camp now that you have had more time to think about it? I admit these questions aren't easy ones! They are about life and death and not many people your age can look 'death' in the eyes and say 'no' to it. Sylvia, I think there is a lot for all of us to learn so I hope you will keep in touch with me.

I fly to North America on Tuesday for about a month and I have provided Kerry with my whereabouts. However, I may not be able to get back to you as quickly as I have today, especially with the different 'times' there. However, until we are back in touch, I hope you will consider me part of your 'life' team. From everything I know about you from Kerry and your parents, there is a lot of life in you.

Best wishes, David

I continued to work intensively with Sylvia and her family. But now we had all regained a good measure of hope and vitality and frequently each and every one of us had good cause to draw upon that.

The most important thing for both the family and me was that David said every one of you has been abused ... 'your family has been abused in so many ways'. That had not been acknowledged by anyone before. The injustices in general and the way they had been treated had never been stated that clearly or quickly before. We all felt validated. The way I recall our conversation was as a response to David's 'I can see what has happened to you here ... it's really clear ... it wasn't your fault'. It was pertinent that he asked whether they thought it was their fault and if Sylvia thought that too. Although it was the first question, it seemed crucial to what was to unfold from that day on. Vince spoke poignantly of his belief that the mental health system deemed him to be his daughter's perpetrator for that was certainly how they treated him. Prior to this, he had spoken in general terms such as 'the system thinks teenagers don't need their parents'. Now he was prepared to assert that 'they ...... I abused my daughter and that's why they have excluded me'.

David's feelings of injustice seemed to match ours. It surprised us all that someone so removed from the situation so instantly recognised the injustices here. After all, the isolation and exclusion of this family had persisted for seven years. His sense of injustice and his urgency were a validation for the family and for me. Up until then, I was the only professional this family had encountered that they felt had acknowledged them, let alone their experiences. So it seemed rather wild coming from a trans-Tasman stranger.

On reflection, I realised how important it was for the family and me to co-write their story in preparation for seeking David's advice. I didn't realise at the time what an exercise in trust this was for Vince and Janice. After all, they had been betrayed and 'ripped off' by the various systems so repeatedly that it must have been very hard to expose themselves yet again to professional assessment and appraisal. I guess part of their willingness to take another risk was the desperation we shared along with their refusal to give up on their daughter. The fact that all these events took place on a Sunday demonstrated that we professionals too valued Sylvia's life and were also determined not to surrender to 'self-abuse'. They commented that they had never felt that sort of commitment from professionals before.

David didn't ask different things really. He just was more detailed in his enquiries. And, in doing so, more information than had been previously elicited became available for our considerations. This new information kept us going for several weeks. I guess when it's a matter of life-or-death, you seem to skim over detail looking for something very large to hold on to. Or at least I did. It was wonderful to be reminded of the particulars and the significance of them. With the wisdom of hindsight I now realise I was being taken over by 'self-abuse' as well. It seemed at the time that nothing else was important because it loomed so large over each and every one of us. Returning our focus to the detail of our achievements renewed our commitments to each other. It was a great relief to be honest. Once again, we were addressing 'self-abuse' without allowing it to dominate us. David never lost his intensity throughout the whole afternoon and, as time went by, our motivation to continue to deal with this 'huge' problem was revived. Here was someone who didn't sound defeated nor did he consider this a lost cause. We all regained both our hope and commitment for Sylvia to live on in her life.

Perhaps part of the magic was that David was a stranger, heard when I read his faxes over the phone, but unseen. Sylvia who had been so isolated and distanced by 'self-abuse' was quite perplexed that there was someone who just dived into the deep end of events in her life, seemed unafraid and certainly wasn't writing her off. Not only that but 'self-abuse" had no opportunity to isolate her from David. He wasn't a physical presence. Under normal circumstances, I would have predicted she would have spent a fair bit of time giving him 'stay away from me' signals in order to remain isolated. Here, she didn't have to push him away because he was already away. To some extent, there was no way for 'self-abuse' to isolate her; these mad fax interactions didn't allow for that. The spontaneity of David's spirit, somewhat disembodied, was a new experience for all of us, including 'self-abuse'.

Six months later we agreed to write to David to give him an update.
Follow-up Letter, 10th October 1996

Dear David:
I just wanted to give you an update on Sylvia. She is just doing FANTASTICALLY!! She has been 'self-abuse' free for twenty-five weeks now. She is in her second term at TAFE doing her Year 10 Certificate and is doing really well. She has just been to our September camp and this was her second 'self-abuse' free camp. Not only that but Sylvia participated in all the 'trust' exercises, which she has never done before and was nominated in a small group to report back to the large group. She did it with ease. This was a first for her and was some thing she never thought was possible.

Janice and Vince have noticed an amazing difference in Sylvia as well and say that she is mixing well with the young people at TAFE. They are feeling much more relaxed and confident when Sylvia leaves the house to go out with her friends.

Naturally we are all thrilled and greatly relieved at this turnaround and are beginning to feel some confidence that 'self-abuse' may be finding the going too tough. It may even be giving up. Sylvia reports that there are times 'when it still attempts to make a comeback'. However, she is much more aware of its tactics and is no longer taken by surprise. In fact, she can even now plan ahead.

So, in closing, I am happy to report that 'self-abuse' is the weakest it has been in the last six years and we all have a feeling of being united, strong and confident. Naturally we remain suspicious and ready to fight again if necessary. At the moment, it looks like another win for the 'good guys'.

Hope you are well and happy,
Kerry

Reply letter from David, 24 October 1996

Dear Kerry,

I really appreciate hearing back from you, updating me on Sylvia. It is just so great to learn that she has been 'self-abuse' free now for 25 weeks and that she has returned to school at TAFE and doing well. I guess I am not really surprised when I consider how much abilities and talents must have been held back by 'self-abuse' practices. Does her doing well have anything to do with 'self-appreciation' guiding her in her life? I would be interested to know. Please pass on my delight in learning that Vince and Janice can breath a bit easier now. They must be extraordinary people to have kept alive their hope for Sylvia, given what they have endured over the years along with the injustices connected to that.

It makes my day to know that connecting up with everyone in the somewhat odd way we did in those chance circumstances may have loosened a brick in the wall. I would like to think that for all of us at that time, when the going got tough, we all got going.

Feel free to pass this letter on to Vince, Janice and Sylvia. I wish you all well, although I would doubt that there won't be the odd comeback up ahead. But hopefully, it will be so different now and, from my experience, each day without self-abuse allows self-appreciation and self-love to form us and our relationships. I was very glad to have shared that day in your lives and thank you, in particular, Kerry, for thinking of me in the first instance and finding me in my office and you, by chance, in yours on a weekend. Perhaps, as I like to think, it was all meant to be.

Best wishes to you all,
David

On 4th July 1997 David was conducting a workshop on the Central Coast in Australia and asked if it might be possible for him to meet with Sylvia, Janice and Vince just to say Hi! They readily agreed. When David and I arrived at the home we were greeted by Vince, Janice, Sylvia and her brother Gary (20) and three young people who were on Sylvia's 'camp' support team. There was no opportunity for shyness or embarrassment as the occasion was taken over by the outrageous wit and jollity of the young people present. How marvellous it was for everyone to attend and celebrate Sylvia's life. And, despite her shyness at all the fuss, she physically remained at the very 'heart' of her 'community' with her family, myself, David and 'friends' surrounding her. And, for the best part of the evening, Sylvia wore a wry grin all over her face.

We never spoke of the ritual of inclusion again. I chuckling about it because I think we did one of our own without realising. David responded to my feelings of isolation and despair rather than to my request for information. This experience has highlighted for us the importance of support teams for therapists. Not the traditional support teams of drugs and institutionalisation that can increase isolation, but support teams of concerned and committed people. A 'community of concern' that promotes connection and solidarity. Modern technology allows us to contact and be contacted by fax, phone or email anywhere in the world. We use such technologies to increase our efficiency; why not do the same to access and increase our support teams?

4

Taming the Terrier

David Epston

Original version published in Epston, D, Taming the Terrier, nnn
(Narrative Network News), 27 November 2003, pp14-17

Ronny came into my premises somewhat reluctantly and shamefaced. I guess he knew something was up, something he preferred not to come up. His mother and father were somewhat more resolute but his mother, Sarah, looked uneasy in my presence. I introduced myself and sought for them to introduce themselves. Ronny was nine according to his birth certificate, but when asked, 'What age do you want me to think of you as – nine, ten or eleven?' he preferred to be thought of as a ten year old and that I ask him ten year old questions. I didn't proceed from here in the conventional manner. Instead, I proposed the following to Ronny: 'If I were you, I wouldn't want to meet a middle-aged stranger like myself through a Problem. Do you mind if I get to know you through what your mum and dad think is wonderful about you?' He looked perplexed but at the same time happily consented to this arrangement. I turned to his parents adding, 'If we know what is so wonderful about Ronny, we will have some idea what he might put against the Problem, whatever the Problem may turn out to be.' I suspect his parents hadn't prepared themselves for such a line of enquiry and quite understandably were tongue-tied. I turned to Sarah and added, 'What wonderful things are there about Ronny that indicate to you that you are the good mother you seek to be?' Turning to his father, Jim, I asked something along the same lines.

We all learned that Ronny possessed 'a wonderful sense of humour' that was both 'somewhat original' and 'some copied' like knock-knock jokes. I asserted that to be able to amuse adults, a person Ronny's age would have to have 'a way with words'. They both nodded in agreement and went on to tell me that 'he is very thoughtful with words' and gave me some clever examples of 'double entendres' that resided in their family history. We explored further the nature of his 'wit' and it extended to 'repartee' and his capacity to 'hang out with his parents' and enjoy the company of adults. And they had more to add about his 'way with words'. 'He is sharp with words. Subtle and dry but he can also be farcical.'

That led me to further enquiries around, 'how does Ronny's mind operate?' They described his mind as 'enquiring'. He was curious about a great many things ... and his interests could come out of the 'left-field' and surprise them. When I explored the 'genealogy' of this way he used his mind, it turned out to be a good match 'for our style of interaction'. Jim was a researcher in his professional life and at home Ronny joined him in 'researching' various of their shared interests.

Quite apart from the workings of his wit and mind, both parents spoke with considerable pride that 'he is passionate about sport and in particular cricket'. They laughed aloud remembering that the first word he spoke was 'ball'. But what impressed them most about Ronny was the fact that in soccer he was renowned for his 'tenacious tackling'. Even though he was slight in build, he 'has no fear of the size of the person'. Furthermore, I was informed that Ronny would become even more determined when an opponent out-tricked him and got past him. This would inflame his determination to catch his opponent up. In fact, he had won an award in his club for this aspect of his play. When I asked if he had a 'nick-name' in his club, we all laughed when Jim told me 'Foxy', after the persistence of a fox terrier. By now, everyone, including myself, was looking a lot more comfortable in what for them were strange surroundings and an endeavour (therapy) they had never undertaken before.

I turned full-face to Ronny and asked him what he might like to put his wit, his 'way with words' and his fierce determination not to be outdone to. He pinpointed his 'temper'. We all joined in a discussion as to whether this 'temper' was 'a justifiable moral outrage at some injustices in his life' or was it more like 'tantrumming'. Ronny took the lead in proposing it was more like tantrumming and his parents strongly supported this. We all canvassed a few recent episodes of his 'temper'. They were instances where Sarah had requested him to either do something like 'clean his room' or desist from something like 'pestering his sister (aged five)'. When I asked Ronny if this tantrumming was something he wanted to stick with, he assured me that this was not the case. Further enquiries as to the effects of the tantrumming on his estimate of his maturity (determined by age) clearly indicated that the tantrumming was 'growing him down' and his tantrums were now almost three years behind his 'wit', 'way with words' and his 'passionate sportsmanship'. To my questions as to the 'fairness' and 'rightness' of tantrumming 'growing him down', he strongly disapproved of this and argued that it was 'fading'. Sarah joined the conversation here and disagreed. In fact, she now seemed able to assert her concerns that she was beginning to fear for the future, given she expected his tantrumming to increase as he got 'bigger and stronger'.

Jim said, although he didn't have the same problems with tantrumming, he was there to support Sarah. In discussion, this might just have been the luck of the draw because Jim couldn't be certain that if he had to require Ronny to clean his room and wash the dishes, he might well have found himself on the wrong side of a tantrum. Enquiries to Sarah around the effects of the tantrumming on her and their mother-son relationship spelled out quite a rift.

Sarah was starting to 'walk on egg shells' and 'pussy-foot' around Ronny. To my question, 'Is the tantrumming starting to drive a wedge between you and Ronny, and between the kind of mother/son relationship you desire?' she ruefully acknowledged that such a process was in place. Ronny hadn't been aware of this and said that his preference was for a 'close son/mother relationship', one in which they could be at their ease with one another and be loving rather than 'stand offish' or 'keeping their distance'. Just to be sure, I checked with Ronny: 'Can you see any disadvantages for you if your tantrumming stopped and never happened again?' He took this seriously, if his pondering meant anything. I proposed a few matters for him to consider - such as 'your mother may not pussyfoot around you anymore?' and 'fear may no longer have her shy away from making requests of you?' Ronny, on balance, considered cessation of the tantrumming worthwhile.

'Ronny', I said, 'I would be willing to give your mum and dad a double your money back guarantee if you were willing to trust me enough to consent to a 'temper tantrum approach' of mine. I went over to my book shelf and took down a copy of *Experience, Contradiction, Narrative and Imagination* (Epston &

White,1992), and referred them to the outcome study in the chapter *Temper tantrum parties: losing face, going off your face or saving face*. Since the study included many other therapists, I mentioned my own outcomes as one hundred per cent successful (1), although admitting that Ronny might be the first to fail in 'taming his temper'. Ronny didn't look too worried by that. Jim joined the conversation and said that from his experience of Ronny, he would always want to know ahead of time what he was in for. 'Ronny is just that kind of kid!' I admitted that this would be the first time, but I accepted this about Ronny and would wait until everything was disclosed to him before seeking his consent.

Everyone than turned to me to proceed. 'First of all, Ronny, if you were going to have a party and you could only have one kind of food, would it be a sweet or a savoury?' Ronny was taken aback by where this was all going so I added a few possibilities, 'Damon, who was twelve at the time, chose a chocolate cake? Isobel, who was fifteen, chose pumpkin pie. Jason, who was thirteen, wanted cornish pasties'. To my surprise, Ronny selected sushi as his food of choice. I turned to his parents and asked if Ronny was a 'foodie' too in addition to some of his other virtues. 'Secondly, Ronny, when you are playing soccer, does the tantrumming ever take you over at a practice or during a match?' He looked bemused by such a question and dismissed it out of hand, 'Of course not!' I responded enthusiastically, assuring everyone that I would be now willing to extend my money back guarantee to a 'triple' rather than a 'double'.

I asked Sarah if she thought she could sense a temper tantrum coming on. She didn't contemplate any difficulties with that. 'Sarah and Jim, could you prepare some cards, one set that you carry on your person and another set that you keep in a handy place like the mantle-piece or on the fridge. The first card should read in large writing, 'Ronny, I think you have a temper tantrum coming on!' I then proposed that should she detect the beginnings of a tantrumming, she should merely hand Ronny the first card, turn her back and depart and return to a safe place, timing sixty seconds on her watch. She should then check to see if the tantrumming was proceeding as usual or if Ronny had 'tamed' it. If it was the latter, she was to congratulate him for this and to take some notes to tell Jim when he returned home from work that night. However, if the tantrumming was proceeding as usual, she was to hand him the second card which would read, 'Pre-recording Warning 1', turn her back and depart and return after another minute had elapsed and once again check. Congrats and note-taking was in order if Ronny had 'tamed' the tantrum even at this stage. However, if the tantrumming was proceeding as usual, she was to hand him Card Three which would read, 'Prerecording No. 2' and do what she had done before, once again returning in a minute to review the situation. Congrats and note-taking if Ronny had 'tamed' the tantrumming. If not, there would be handing over of the fourth and final card which would read, 'Final Warning - Recording will start in 60 second's time!' This time she should go and prepare the audio tape recorder they had on hand (or a video-camera if they had access to that), keep a safe distance and just record the tantrum.

I then proceeded, 'Who are your three best soccer mates, Ronny?' 'Tim, Terry and Derrick!' he told me proudly. Directing my comments to everyone, I said, 'Thirdly, go home tonight and Ronny, it would be far more convincing if you wrote the letter yourself but if you find it too difficult, your parents could do it for you. The letter might read something like this:

Dear Tim, Terry or Derrick,
I would like to invite you to my home on .. (leave a blank because you very likely won't have to fill it) at .. (leave a blank because you very likely won't have to decide what time the party begins) .. to a Sushi and Temper Tantrum Party. You may not know this but my tantrumming has been growing me down at home to a seven year old level. I have consulted David Epston, a narrative therapist, along with my mum and dad and it seems that adults can't help me. But I know you can because when we are team-mates both in training and during a match, my temper never takes me over, even when we get goals scored against us. So I know that when you see or hear the tantrumming, you will come up with some good ideas to help me 'tame' it. I know I can depend on you the same way you can depend on me to tackle like a fox terrier and never let the team down.
Your friend, Ronny

Ronny's and my eyes met. He took a deep breath and said unequivocally, 'This will work!' Well, I know Ronny had a reputation for his wit, but I wonder if he and his parents and a relative stranger had ever laughed quite so loudly or for so long before. 'Ronny, in that case, would you might doing something for me and any other young person whose tantrumming was growing them down?' Before he agreed, he wanted to know all the details. 'Well, Ronny, of all the other young men and women who 'tamed' their tempers, none of them to my knowledge were researchers.' Jim mentioned at this point that in fact Ronny had experience as an unpaid 'researcher' in a study. I asked Ronny if he might be willing to watch his 'tantrumming' in the very act of 'taming' it, and either really remember it or take down some notes. As our time was up, I just wanted to say that his research could play a part in assisting other young men and women to 'grow up' to their age, and even past their age, if they were anything like Ronny. I agreed to send him some research questions by post. We agreed to meet back in a month's time to audio tape his 'temper tantrum knowledge' for others to learn from.

Below is the letter with the research questions I forwarded to him by post:

Dear Ronny,
I really liked meeting you the other evening. You really reminded me of myself as I was called something similar to a 'fox terrier' when I played sports. Like you, I refused to give up, even if someone got past me. In fact, that would make me more determined. Do you find that? Since I have never had the good fortune to meet a

77

young person your age who had experience as a research assistant, the 'temper tantrum party' idea, although successful over the years, has never been researched. I was wondering if you might consider some of the following 'research questions', while you grow yourself out of the Problem. After all, I thought it was unfair that a Problem would grow you down to seven when in fact everything else about you suggested you were more ten or eleven.

So here goes:
1) *RONNY, WHEN THE TEMPER STARTED COMING ON AND YOUR MOTHER GAVE YOU THE FIRST CARD, WHAT DID YOU DO IN YOUR MIND TO STOP IT FROM TAKING YOU OVER AND HUMILIATING YOU?*
2) *RONNY, THE SECOND TIME YOUR TEMPER STARTED COMING ON AND ANY FURTHER TIMES, DID YOU FIND IT EASIER TO DO WHATEVER IT WAS YOU DID IN THE FIRST PLACE?*
3) *RONNY, DO YOU THINK IT WOULD HAVE BEEN POSSIBLE TO DO WHAT YOU DID IN THE FIRST PLACE IF YOU DIDN'T HAVE THE PROSPECT OF THE 'SUSHI AND TEMPER TANTRUM PARTY' IN YOUR MIND?*
4) *RONNY, WHY WAS IT POSSIBLE FOR YOU TO DECLARE IN FRONT OF YOUR MUM AND DAD THAT YOU KNEW 'THAT WOULD WORK'? WHAT MADE YOU SO SURE?*
5) *RONNY, THE FACT THAT YOU HAVE BEEN ABLE TO TAME YOUR TEMPER JUST LIKE THAT, HAS THAT MADE YOU FEEL YOUR AGE OR EVEN MORE GROWN UP THAN YOUR AGE FOR EXAMPLE, A TEN OR ELEVEN YEAR OLD NINE YEAR OLD?*
6) *RONNY, IF AN EIGHT OR NINE YEAR OLD BOY CAME TO YOU AND SAID, 'RONNY, HELP ME! I CANNOT CONTROL MY TEMPER! I HATE IT? BUT THERE IS NOTHING I CAN DO ABOUT IT .. IT JUST HAPPENS!' WHAT ADVICE WOULD YOU GIVE HIM?*
7) *RONNY, IN GENERAL, WHAT IS YOUR OPINION NOW OF 'TEMPER TANTRUMMING'?*

Ronny, I thank you so much for you help. After all, would you believe about fifteen per cent of the young people I meet are being 'grown down' by their temper tantrumming?

Yours in co-research,
David Epston, Visiting Professor,
School of Community Studies, Unitec Institute of Technology

Ronny returned with his mother in a month's time, despite the fact that he was suffering a cold and was a little lacklustre. Still, he was determined to report on his research. With great pleasure, Sarah announced a 'one hundred per cent improvement' and related that to there being 'more of his willingness to listen' and her conviction that 'he is taking control'. Ronny thought there had been a fifty to sixty per cent improvement, and it was all because 'I didn't want that (the sushi and temper tantrum party) to happen.' Although that had only been three first cards, Sarah had observed on every occasion that 'he was composed and

78

there was no grimacing'. What reassured her most about his capability to 'tame his temper' was watching his response to being issued the very first card. 'The first time I could see him take control of himself. It was amazing . . . such a huge relief. I was very proud of him and proud of ourselves that we did something about it.' Apparently they had been thinking about a referral over the past year.

Ronny wasn't 'really proud but I don't think it was nothing'. When I asked if he thought the 'party' idea would have worked as well when he was eight rather than nine, he told me that 'I think so but I'm not one hundred per cent sure'. Ronny thought that his temper may very well have come under his control without the 'party' proposal but it would have taken another two years' time.

His mother reported 'sixty per cent more co-operation' and how such co-operation benefited their mother-son relationship: 'It is easier for me to ask him to do things when I know he isn't going to be unhappy to do it ... I no longer have any fear (of escalating conflict)'. She mentioned since he tamed his temper, 'We have more time to negotiate and bargain and he doesn't get so indignant. And he sticks to his side of any bargain'.

Ronny assured me that he had 'grown himself' not only back to his age but ahead to that of an eleven year old. When I enquired as to why he had done this he said 'I like it. It just makes me feel more grown up'. And Sarah agreed that now they were able to have 'more grown-up conversations' in 'an improved atmosphere'. When I asked Ronny to consult to another young boy, he produced laughter all round yet again by his remark, 'I would ask him what his favourite food was'. Ronny did express concern that his temper could make a come-back but his mother thought that was very unlikely. He summed it all up: 'If you try, you can stop it!'

Note
(1) RESULTS (p 68)
Never Occurred Again 60 45
Dramatically Diminished 56 42
Substantially Diminished 10 8
Diminished 2 2
No Change 2 2
Increased 1 1

Reference
Epston, D. 'Temper tantrum parties: saving face, losing face, or going off your face!' in Epston D and White M (1992) *Experience, Contradiction, Narrative and Imagination*, Dulwich Centre Publications, Adelaide, pp 37-74.

5

On becoming a Just Practitioner: experimenting with the final paper of an undergraduate programme as a rite of passage

David Epston, Gavin Rennie & Ksenija Napan 1

Original version published in Epston, D., Rennie, G., and Napan, K. On becoming a just practitioner: Experimenting with the final paper of an undergraduate programme as a rite of passage, Aotearoa New Zealand *Social Work Review*, Vol. 16-4, Summer 2004, pp.38-49.

"You are so young, so much before all beginning, and I would like to beg you, dear sir, as well as I can, to have patience with everything unresolved in your heart and to try to love the questions themselves as if they were locked rooms or books written in very foreign language. Don't search for the answers, which could not be given to you now, because you would not be able to live them. And the point is, to live everything, live the questions now."

Rainer Maria Rilke (1993) Letters to a Young Poet
From letter four, July 16, 1903

Purpose and Intent

The purpose of designing the paper 'Just Practice' was to invite and inspire the graduating class of the Bachelor of Social Practice programme to incorporate social justice concerns into their practice as they begin to enter their work places. It was expected that students would define their social justice intentions, purposes, aims and contexts for their practices in light of the retrospective accounts of those who had gone before them and had been acknowledged for their own 'just practice'. This was made possible by providing opportunities to bring the graduating class into close acquaintanceship with the 'lore' of just practitioners.

By the final year of the programme students have been exposed to a number of theories, worldviews, approaches and perspectives. We wanted them to expand on these various ways of practicing and to develop a well integrated approach encompassing who they are, what they do and how they want to contribute towards a just society. We invited our students to go beyond the circumscribed bounds of radical texts by drawing close to the histories of the just practices of their seniors. We hoped that they might leave them with some stories and memories of their tellers that would imbue their everyday professional lives with 'just practice'.

We accepted the notion of practice not only as a 'series of planned interventions' but also as 'a human action and a process wherein we are both shaped by the prevailing social order and are active participants in the creation of that order' (Finn and Jacobson, 2003). Our intention was to provide a liminal space for reflection where students would be able to explore their personal understanding of justice and the possible ways of realising that through their future professional practice as counsellors, social workers or community developers. In addition, we wished to collaborate with students by 'walking the talk' of 'just practice' throughout the course.

We also wanted to make the course as 'alive' as possible. To this end, we decided to invite social practitioners in the widest possible sense – not only counsellors, community developers and social workers, but also practitioners coming from a wide range of backgrounds and various professions, to share their experiences of practicing justly in unjust contexts, to speak to their passions, and about their challenges, trials and tribulations. This invitation also conveniently allowed us to formally recognise the contributions of their efforts, which are rarely acknowledged and sometimes disdained.

The context

The origins of the degree programme rested in a conviction that the term social practice was both novel and helpful. This term made it possible to implicate all three fields of practice, namely social work, counselling and community development and blur the disciplinary boundaries that separated them. In planning the programme, there was an avowed intention to subordinate these professional endeavours to a larger purpose and that purpose was defined as *social practice*, implicating key themes of social context and social justice. However, each professional discipline was bound to distinguish itself sufficiently so that students could fulfil any requirements for professional memberships, e.g. Aotearoa New Zealand Association of Social Workers (ANZASW), New Zealand Association of Counsellors (NZAC) or sufficient community development practice to enable students to seek employment in positions designated by that term of employment. Accordingly, at the beginning of Year 2, students must indicate which major they wish to undertake. The counselling major included three field specific papers, while the social work and community development majors require two papers designed for them alone.

As students pursue their chosen field of practice, the class starts to fragment along disciplinary lines, at times leading to boundary skirmishing as the commonalities of social practice start fading from the minds of the students. The shape of the counselling third year is somewhat different from that of the other strands and it seems that the fact of being thrown in the deep end on their placements fostered a level of intimacy more intense than in the other two strands. We noticed a tendency for counselling students to detach themselves somewhat from the programme's ideal of producing a social practitioner.

In addition, we were aware that in creating an embryonic professional identity, student practitioners tend to focus more on the differences than the similarities among the different majors. We still hoped that the counselling students would revive their appreciation of the wider social contexts and that social work and community development students would more readily ground social structures in personal agency. We believed that we could achieve that by promoting a lively exchange of ideas amongst the students as well as inviting distinguished practitioners from a wide range of social practice settings to share their experiences of social justice.

Concerns and thinking behind the emergence of a new paper

We intended to find a vehicle that would both bring and bind together the specific knowledges the students had gained in their separate fields of practice. The question we faced was *"How can we reconvene the three fields of practice in the third year of the degree programme and under what banner?"* In discussion, it was easy for us to conclude that social justice was a theme that could serve us well here for the reason that it was social justice that convened the staff as well, despite their respective trainings and professional commitments. Social justice had long been a core value of the School of Community Studies. The question we were left with was *"What would be the means by which we could join up the three fields of practice to this purpose?"* We envisioned the theme of social justice braiding the three strands of practice into a rope that would secure each strand equally well and be far stronger and more durable than any of the strands on their own.

Another consideration was that in the past there had been no climax to the completion of the programme. While we provided students with "breathing space" to complete final assignments, it was very difficult for students to sustain interest in the penultimate papers, possibly due to their heavy workloads. Many third year classes were poorly attended, and those who did attend seemed fatigued and just going through the motions. The mood of the classes was desultory, much like dinner guests on the fifth course pleading for no more dessert.

We had to figure out how to excite our students at this significant time in their undergraduate education in a way that renewed their vitality and enthusiasm for that which lay ahead – the assumption of their professional identities and the commencement of their professional careers. We designed the Just Practice paper to reach out to the students in ways that intellectual debate *about* justice could not. Our intention was to depart from textbook generalisations by creating a context in which students could reflect on and 'breath life into' any number of theoretical notions. We invited students to meet, dialogue with, and be touched and inspired by devoted practitioners and to reconsider accordingly their current understandings of social justice as a 'practice'. We thought it important for them to know, feel, think and do social justice when they graduated. We believed that if we were to 'walk our talk', then it was incumbent on us, as teachers, to make this paper 'just' to its core, which required us to address these concerns in a deliberate and thoughtful manner. We chose the 'rite of passage' as a metaphor to guide and innovate our pedagogy, as it was rich in suggestion for our intentions and purposes.

The Rite of Passage

Essentially, van Gennep, as quoted in Epston and White (1995), asserted that the rite of passage is a universal phenomenon for facilitating transitions in social life, from one status or identity to another. He proposed a processual model of this rite, consisting of the stages of *separation, liminality, and reincorporation*. In traditional cultures, the initiation of each of these stages is marked by ceremony. For example, at the separation stage people are detached from familiar roles, statuses, and locations, and they enter an unfamiliar social world in which most of the taken-for-granted ways of going about life are suspended. The *liminal space*, which constitutes the second stage of a rite of passage, is betwixt and

84

between known worlds and is characterised by experiences of disorganisation and confusion, by a spirit of exploration, and by a heightened sense of possibility. The third stage, reincorporation, brings closure to the ritual passage and assists people in relocating themselves in the social order of the familiar world, but at a different position. The new position is characteristically accompanied by new roles, responsibilities and freedoms. Traditionally, the arrival at this point is augmented by claims and declarations that the person has successfully negotiated a transition, and this is legitimated by acknowledgement within the person's own community.

Accordingly, the just practice paper was not conceived of as the 'final paper" marking the 'end of the road' for the degree studies but rather as a liminal space – 'a twixt and between' undergraduate professional training and professional practice. Even though we were unable to go away to a unique geographical space, the students themselves transformed the mundanities of their familiar classroom into a 'ritual space' in ways that never ceased to amaze us.

Selection of those to be presented with the award of 'Just Practitioner'

We decided to invite guest speakers who were noted by their colleagues or communities for their commitment to social justice. They were provided with guiding questions to orient their presentation to the class and told that students would be given an opportunity to dialogue with them to further explore their concerns around personal ethics and social justice.

We were aware that so many social justice practitioners are unacknowledged in the professions as well as in their work places. Mavericks are not always welcome. Also, many of these practitioners were not people who made their professional way through the more obvious forums of acknowledgement, e.g. conference presentations, journal article writing, or committee work. From our experience, the 'heart and soul' of just practice is practice itself and for this reason 'just practitioners' often do not have the time, energy or writing skills for documenting their experiences, practices and learnings. We also recognised that often the controversial or confidential nature of their work prevents publication of any kind. A number of these extraordinary practitioners had demonstrated courage, exposing themselves to criticism from their profession, at times suffering for that. It interested us to establish an alternative forum of acknowledgement and an opportunity for students to be infused by the stories and lore of such people about why and how they have lived their work lives as 'Just Practitioners'. Given that this rite of passage was to be enacted on campus and under the aegis of a tertiary educational institution, we still wondered if we could pull it off.

At first, we tried to match speakers to particular constituencies among the students. We had representatives from different ethnicities, fields of practice, genders, religious and sexual orientations. We also looked beyond the traditional boundaries of social work/counselling/community development to include social practitioners working in other fields, some of whom were unconventional or radical - a Green Party MP who was a community activist, a progressive Christian clergyperson advocating for gay rights, a community psychiatrist advocating for deinstitutionalisation, a gay disability activist performing as a stand up 'sit down' comedian.

We were seeking those who might be considered to have stood outside conventional practice and who might be better known as political activists, whatever their professional training. We did however have a preference for those who started such activist careers as social workers, counsellors or community developers. What was foremost in our minds was finding exemplars serving social justice concerns in their work lives.

The process of inviting Just Practitioners

We pursued a deliberate process of inviting *just practitioners* 'to engage with our students'. We asked staff, colleagues and students to nominate candidates with a short description of why they considered the practitioner was eligible for nomination. The candidate would then be called and informed of what was entailed in its receipt. If the offer of the award was accepted, this letter would follow.

Dear x,

Following the conversation we had recently over the phone, my colleagues and I are writing to invite you to accept our acknowledgement of you as a 'distinguished social practitioner'.

We consider that your practice over the years has shown a commitment to social justice and that your passion and ingenuity have produced what we are referring to as 'Just Practice'. We mean by that a social practice that is engendered by social justice concerns.

We would like to celebrate the award of this distinction in a rather uncommon manner. We are inviting you to speak to our graduating class, whose programme (Bachelor of Social Practice) culminates in a semester long paper entitled 'Just Practice'. During this paper we expect our students to articulate and confirm their own passions and commitments to social justice concerns and look into their futures as practitioners. This is easier said than done – there is often far more talk than walk.

Concurrently with our students forming their own commitments, we invite you to share with them retrospective accounts of the history of your own 'just practice'. While they look forward, we would ask you to look back over your career.

The following questions might serve you in such an endeavour:
- *Looking back over your career and your life, are there any stories that now come to mind that help you understand and now tell you the reasons for your 'just practice"?*
- *What made you concern yourself about 'just practice' as an essential part of your practice?*
- *How did you sustain your passion in the face of your trials and tribulations?*
- *What were your highlights? Your lowlights?*

- *Who or what kept you true to your calling?*
- *What advice would you have wished someone had given you when you were just starting out in your career, fired by your concerns for justice?*
- *What practice wisdoms, even in hindsight, would you wish to bequeath to those who are just about to begin their careers?*

We would like to invite you to spend a morning with the class on_____ and address the questions above. We hope they will have assisted you with your preparations. These 'orienting' questions will be reasonable facsimiles of the questions the graduating students will be entertaining in their own discussions

The format for the day would be:

9.00 – 10.15   Your address
10.15 – 11.00   Students formulate questions
11.00- 12.00   Questions, reflection and dialogue with students
12.00- 1 pm   Lunch
1.00 – 3.00   Reflection and discussion time for students only

There is an honorarium of $xxx to cover your expenses and at the conclusion of your presentation you will be formally recognised as a Just Practitioner.

If you have any questions or wish to discuss this further to discuss the above before accepting its conditions, please contact the paper co-ordinator. Phone xxx, e-mail xxx.

Yours sincerely,
Course co-ordinator

The storying of Just Practice

The presentations by "just practitioners" were as far from rarefied academic lectures as you could get. They commonly consisted of stories and reminiscences linked one to the other, painful accounts of their trials and tribulations, and deeply considered 'wisdoms' often gained the 'hard way'. The atmosphere was ceremonial and always had a sense of the unexpected and the excitement of the unknown. Each welcoming committee created a different sacred space in the broadest possible sense. The day was opened by a karakia (prayer) or a quote relevant for a specific speaker and a sacred space was created anew on every occasion. The ceremony was reinvented for each speaker by their welcoming committee.

What was quite extraordinary was the degree of intimacy that quickly developed between the speakers, previously unknown to students, and the class itself. What seemed to touch everyone, speakers included, was a palpable sense of mentoring the 'next generation', not by way of the bravura of traditional 'graduation speech-making' but rather a deep retrospective on their own politically active work-lives. Many presenters have expressed delight that they were given cause to reflect on their work lives in a manner that they had not done before.

In spite of the physical environs of a classroom in a tertiary educational institution, a ritual space was created where everyone stood together with the speakers looking backwards over their careers and the students looking forwards to theirs. It was as if each time a torch of social justice was passed to new initiates, and the initiates were participants who resonated with at least some of the stories told in the class. These resonances were not happening only from experienced practitioners to students, but they were obviously mutual and it would be unjust to say that students were the only ones learning. Discovering a just practitioner in a colleague student who has opposing beliefs to your own was probably one of the most powerful learnings for quite a few students.

The morning ends with the award of the designation 'Just Practitioner' together with a 'thank you card' signed by students with some personal comments from each of them.

To prepare the students, they were informed that academic grades were not the primary focus of the paper and that while there were two assignments, there was an expectation that they would be more concerned about creating a socially just practice for themselves. They were also told that what was important was not 'what you know' but 'what you intend to be about' – forming commitments to work towards a just world and "dwelling in possibility" (Dickinson, 1862).

Reviews over the years

We envisaged this paper as being dynamic. This required our commitment to learn from the process of offering of it and to modify it accordingly.

After the first year, we became aware of the significance of students' reflecting on the speakers' presentations. Many buttons were pushed; many hearts were touched. Those students with fundamentalist beliefs, either religious or political, were often challenged the most by the paper. We came to realise that considerable time was required to allow for these reflections to be voiced and processed. For many students, these reflective processes were transformative.

They allowed for open discussion and for mutual appreciation by students of others from various backgrounds who held very different and at times opposing beliefs. In other classroom contexts, we would expect far more contestation. The spell of this rite of passage seemed to allow for more inquiry, more uncertainty, "to live the questions now".

We scheduled full days for student reflection on top of the reflection time that followed each just practitioner address. During the reflection days students were guided by orienting questions such as:

1. *How did what x (a guest speaker) had to tell us resonate with your values and beliefs about just practice?*
2. *What was most challenging in x's talk for you? And why?*
3. *Were your buttons pushed or your heart touched in any way? If so how?*
4. *How was this presentation relevant to your future practice?*
5. *Did you have any learnings that took you by surprise? If so, what were they?*

The purpose of guided reflection was for students to share their responses to guest speakers and also to examine their own ideas of just practice. In addition students worked in their groups, beginning the process of sorting out which particular presentations would have bearing upon their future practice.

In the first year we had encouraged 'just practitioners' to invite their family, friends and colleagues to their award ceremony to share in their honours. We suggested the students do the same when they were doing their presentations on their future just practice before the class. Although very potent for the students concerned, this became practically impossible with the increasing number of students in the class.

We also invited students to negotiate with us how assignments were to be assessed because we believed that that initiative represented a just teaching practice. After these negotiations, most students took more responsibility, giving their best effort in accomplishing all that was required and more.

We noticed, however, that some students preferred to group themselves with likeminded people, almost to the point of excluding others whose beliefs or fields of interests were different from their own. Such groupings had the effect of silencing an honest, fair and challenging exchange of various views and favouring of a preference for feeling comfortable. To encourage greater inclusiveness we decided to impose a group structure to promote the idea of learning from one another's differences. There were to be four in each group and we insisted that there was at least one future social worker, counsellor and community developer in each group and preferably people of different culture, age, gender, sexual orientation and political preference.

Some students initially resisted the introduction of imposed study groups. Two students said they could not work with people in their group because their worldviews were so different, but we persisted. On final analysis the "rebels or fighters for social justice" gratefully admitted that working with people they would never choose to work with was a major learning experience. The outcomes were extremely positive. The imposed structure paradoxically nourished useful dialogue and greater inclusiveness and allowed students to voice their views more clearly in order to present them to their peers with quite different views. The very people who initially opposed such an imposition expressed the greatest levels of satisfaction to staff.

Whereas during the first year of offering the paper students did individual presentations of their intentions to practice justly, we decided to change the assignment to a group presentation the second time around. For the group presentation, students were asked to create a fictional social practice agency where both the policy and practice was guided by their social justice concerns. This assignment required each group to reach a consensus on what would constitute a virtual socially just agency where they all could work in concert. Our aim in requiring this task was to encourage students to collaborate with others, be aware of their own positions and professional disciplines and at the same time learn from dialoguing with other practitioners of fields of practice with their distinctive perspectives. In addition, students were also required to write up their own personal commitments to social justice.

In the second year of the paper, students were given responsibility for the hospitality associated with the award ceremony, including decorating the space as well as welcoming, introducing, and providing refreshments for the speaker. The 'study groups' doubled as welcoming committees, responsible for hosting the day. These activities strongly contributed to the students developing a sense of ownership over the paper and taking charge of their learning. Convening the meeting, establishing its mood, providing food, and so on, allowed students to be far more intimate with the visiting 'just practitioners' than we would have otherwise expected.

Reflections
We were delighted with both the planned and unplanned outcomes of the just practice paper. From the beginning we were aware that we were doing something new, useful and relevant, but we never expected such high quality student work, demonstrated in the depth of discussions and the level of participation. Despite overdue assignments hanging over many of the students' heads like the sword of Damocles, attendance was the highest of any paper in the programme. Students would phone in with apologies when circumstances prevented their attendance. Another encouraging aspect was the consistently high level of student evaluations of the paper. As the course co-ordinator changed from year to year, we attributed the success to the process itself rather than to the charisma of any individual staff member.

Students
I had no idea what to expect, so there was a sense of excitement in the beginning because of the not knowing what was to come. I was not disappointed and the excitement and anticipation were sustained week after week by the speakers' presentations.

I felt allowed to take what I wanted from each speaker and able to leave the rest. This created a kind of cellular memory of things I want to remember. In this way, 'Just Practice' was different from other papers where 'learning outcomes' often dictated what was to be 'learned'. In this paper, I held on to what was special to me and that was the high point for me. This created for me a sense of ownership... a sense I was in control of what I learnt from this paper. It was deep, cellular learning, the stuff I think of everyday and probably always will.

What was of particular value was the idea of that I could make a difference; that as a social worker I am in the business of inspiring people to bring about positive changes in their lives. This remains with me as a filter through which I now view my work with clients.

At a personal level June Kirk-Smith (2) and Ian Lawton (3) moved me to take a more tolerant and balanced view of Christianity. This was totally unanticipated. I acknowledged for the first time that some people in the church have played a significant role in the deconstruction of hierarchies of power which it had been instrumental in creating.

Of all speakers, June Kirk-Smith made a particular impression on me because of her humility. She never used the pronoun "I". She shared with us that she starts each day with a prayer for compassion and wisdom in her work. For her, it seemed like the antidote for burnout.

We survived as a project group, in spite of being so diverse and having different levels of commitment. This enhanced my self-awareness and my understanding of cultural differences regarding hierarchies of importance. I think being put into such project groups is a fascinating bit of social engineering, and certainly for me, it produced unexpected experiences and alliances.

I really enjoyed the de-emphasis on 'academic production', which created for me a sense of freedom, creativity, passion and enjoyment around producing the assignment.

The rituals of beginnings and endings of every class and the beautiful decorations were inspiring. It appealed to my professional love for ritual and ceremony. The speakers were an amazing collection of people. I cannot say that I enjoyed one more than another – each had a pearl to offer, a treasure that I held on to and recall from time to time.

For me 'Just Practice' was a well-earned gift, the reward of three years of personal growth and effort. It seemed like the first steps along the way towards facing practice realities (Wendy Moore, 2002).

Just Practice was different from any other Bachelor of Social Practice Courses. It represented a break from formal academic activities. It embraced a sense of fun, a sense of ceremony in preparing for and welcoming our 'guests', and a sense of equality in that this was not a lecture but rather a gifting from 'one who has gone before'.

When Kiwi Tamasese (4) suggested that we would be the ones creating future 'theories', this allowed me to see beyond the completion of my degree and look to the possibilities that lay ahead. This statement was very influential and contributed to my confidence in becoming the principal researcher of a project undertaken after my finishing my degree. I presented this at the International Narrative Conference in England in July 2003. Warren Lindberg (5) spoke of "handing on the mantle" to the class. Considering this, I was imbued with a confidence not to shy away from the kind of responsibility that such knowledge affords. Christine Herzog (6) said that 'you can step out of the box without anything too bad happening' and knowing this gave me the courage to practice it. I liked what Ian Lawton said about being a human being first and I think that when my personal and professional 'selves' are aligned in ethics then I am at my most 'fully human'.

All of the above were unexpected 'treasures' from the course that have contributed to both my personal and professional life. I believe these speakers 'pushed' me beyond the expectations I would ever have had for myself. Opening such a window of possibility seemed effortless.

This course gave me some ideas of exactly what Just Practice might be about. To be honest, I had never really thought about this before. One always has one's head so stuffed with the academic material during a degree that it was hard to think about how to put this into practice. In this regard, Just Practice was the perfect bridge between completing the degree and establishing my/ourselves in our work.

I think the relaxed nature of the course and the mutual respect that I felt, which was created and held in the room between practitioner and future practitioners, enabled our own ideas of what Just Practice might mean to us to personally to come through. There was something incredibly powerful in listening to the stories of people's lives rather than studying this in academic ways.

There was a good balance between doing a group presentation and a personal piece of writing for assessment. It was good to bounce ideas off each others in the group and come to a consensus as to how we would bring these ideas together to form a cohesive whole.

In the writing and the reflection that this involved, I felt I reviewed my whole life through the lens of Just Practice. Significant events in my life that had previously been 'unfathomable' could now be seen in a different context with new and valued meaning. This was definitely one of the most profound pieces of writing I did during my degree. The powerful stories that I heard gave me a wide range of perspectives on Just Practice. I determined that my 'just practice' would emerge from who I am and choose to be, the values and beliefs I hold at that moment in time and the contexts in which I find myself and how I want to respond to them. (Hazel Thompson, 2002)

Speakers also indicated that their involvement in the paper was an experience that both moved and challenged them. One commented that the preparation challenged him to review aspects of his professional life. Another sent us the following note:

"I simply must send you my heartfelt thanks for allowing me to speak to your students. I felt a deep sense of privilege to do so. The experience for me has been a memorable one. I would be grateful if you could tell the students how impressed I was with them – their attentiveness, their depth, their acceptance of me. I can't tell you what a pleasure it was to read their comments. That is a lovely practice- it certainly meant a lot to me. So often one goes away after giving a talk full of doubt with no idea how it was received. I felt there was a great spirit in the whole department and that for me means good leadership.

Loving greeting,
Pauline O'Regan (7)

Co-ordinators

It was a joyful experience because it joined teaching and learning. Every guest speaker brought something new. Facilitating this paper was for me a privilege and an experience of collegiality with students and guest speakers. It provided a space for discussion and debate of ideas – at times very controversial. We were inspired by exceptional practitioners and our discussions became equally inspiring. This spiritedness is not usually possible because many of the earlier papers I facilitated were content-oriented and content driven. In this paper the context was equally important. The atmosphere was democratising (Ksenija Napan).

It was the best paper yet. It stretched me beyond where I thought I would go. The attendance was the highest compared to any other paper I've co-ordinated. Students would fail to attend only for dire emergencies and they would notify in advance. Several acknowledged that they couldn't take any more, which was intended as praise, not criticism. The atmosphere was extremely lively and excitement permeated the paper. Students took over elaborate decoration sensitive to the speaker – murals which were culturally responsive, symbols, floral arrangements, taped music… all appropriate to each speaker (Gavin Rennie)..

This was the most challenging paper I've ever co-ordinated, but I enjoyed it immensely. It was all about 'walking the talk' and every social justice issue that we addressed was practiced in the classroom. Decisions were made collaboratively and the atmosphere was different to that in any other class. Somehow we all became connected with the common thread of social justice and a whole range of possible views on it. Dialogues, or 'multilogues' in the classroom were deep and meaningful and extremely relevant to social practice (Ksenija Napan).

Students quickly found that this wasn't like any other paper. Assignments were handed in on time and despite the fact this was the final paper in their programme they were of exceptional quality. According to all those involved in marking, many of the students surpassed themselves. The students loved the speakers and the speakers loved the students. The speakers found the students welcoming and hospitable, especially their attempts at symbolising what the speakers represented in terms of their practice. They also mentioned their appreciation for those questions that were really important to them e.g. asking a radical community psychiatrist who had closed down an infamous psychiatric hospital if he had lost many friends? The nature of the students' questions were surprisingly brave as they exposed their own trepidations and fears. (Gavin Rennie and Ksenija Napan)

Bringing Just Practice into being

The 'spirit of social justice' was brought into being in an almost palpable form. Far from textbook definitions, it arose instead out of the stories of those practitioners who had come to 'mentor' their juniors. It was almost as if the seniors were conjuring up that 'spirit' so s/he might pass it on to the initiates who were about to take it up. Social justice was no longer a concept but a kind of lore, which the graduating class avowed an intention to pursue during their working lives. Most speakers told stories more than anything else, many of which were particularly vivid and memorable, touching and laugh provoking, of great deeds alongside risible errors of judgment. Interestingly, many speakers reiterated the point that their "real" learning began after their formal professional training.

Conclusion

We defined 'just practice' as practice that is engendered by social justice concerns. By committing to this definition, we hoped that students in the just practice paper would develop the capacity to see realities from a wide range of viewpoints and to become attentive to client's stories and their ways of experiencing and resisting the injustices in their lives. By listening to and referencing the guest speakers' exemplary lore, students said they were inspired to enter and lead their professional lives for the sake of social justice as they had come to realise it. These newfound or deepened commitments strongly align with the definition of social work formulated by the International Federation of Social Workers (IFSW) and the International Association of Schools of Social Work (IASSW) in 2002 which encompasses themes of social change and social justice:

"The social work profession promotes social change, problem solving in human relationships and the empowerment and liberation of people to enhance well being. Utilising theories of human behaviour and social systems, social work intervenes at the points where people interact with their environment. Principles of human rights and social justice are fundamental to social work" (www.ifsw.org)

Another unplanned but very relevant outcome was that this paper and the ritual associated with it ushered the students into a collegial relationship with their teachers and the speakers as members of the same community, a community of practitioners concerned for social justice.

This collaborative process guided students to make specific commitments for their careers. Voicing these commitments before the assembled class seemed to have a powerful effect and in some instances impelled students to act upon their commitments.

We kept a close tally on what might be referred to as lines of enquiry over the years. The most recurring lines of enquiry were:

1) *How do people with strong commitments to social justice survive in the institutions where they either work or to which they owe an allegiance (e.g. mental health service, statutory child protection service, religious order, church, etc.)?*
2) *What is the price of standing up for a just cause or concern?*
   and
3) *Is it possible to take a stand and not lose a job?*

Students were fascinated with the speakers' responses to their highlights and 'lowlights' and to the 'advice they wish they had received as beginners'.

Students focused on various aspects of their future 'just practice' in their individual assignments culminating in the development of a virtual 'just agency', which they presented to the class as a whole. In a range of scenarios they conveyed the mission and the practices of their virtual agencies. One group exemplified their just practice by interviewing a candidate for a vacancy in their agency. Another group treated with irony practices to which they were opposed. A third used a scenario of a staff meeting to illustrate how their values inhered in their practices.

Providing a space for student imagination to envisage a just workplace enabled us all to reflect on our contributions to creating a just society. Principles and ideas considered in the paper came to life in student presentations and it raised everyone's hopes that if not tomorrow, maybe the day after tomorrow, these virtual agencies would materialise and recruit them and their like – social practitioners committed to social justice.

References
Dickinson, E. (1862) I Dwell in Possibility, *the Complete Poems of Emily Dickinson*, Dickinson, E. (1962), London: Faber and Faber
Epston, D. & White, M. (1995) Termination as a rite of passage: questioning strategies for a therapy of inclusion (pp 339-354) in Neimeyer, R.A and Mahoney, M.J. (Eds), *Constructivism in Psychotherapy*, Washington: American Psychological Association.
Finn, J.L. & Jacobson, M. (2003) Just Practice: steps toward a new social work paradigm, *Journal of Social Work Education*, Vol.39, No.1 Winter.
Rilke, R. M. (1993) *Letters to a Young Poet*, translated by Stephen Mitchell, Shambala, Boston (from Letter Four, July 16, 1903)

1. Gavin Rennie and Ksenija Napan are senior lecturers in the School of Health and Community Studies at Unitec.
2. June Kirk Smith is of the Sacred Heart who has been involved with International work for her Religious Order and has been for many years be involved in social justice groups in Auckland.
3. Ian Lawton was the Vicar of St Matthew in the City Auckland with a particular interest in Liberation Theology.
4. Kiwi Tamasese has been for many years a member of the staff of the Anglican Family Centre in Lower Hutt and a contributor to 'Just Therapy'.
5. Warren Lindberg has been a Teacher and Community worker and was for many years Director of the Aids Foundation.
6. Christine Herzog has been a Town Planner, Community Activist and educator on the Treaty of Waitangi.
7. Pauline O'Regan is a well published author in the area of Building Community. She is a Sister of Mercy who spent the first part of her life in teaching and the second half actively involved in working as a Community Worker.

6

Haunting from the Future: A Congenial Approach to Parent-Children Conflicts

David Epston, Cherelyn Lakusta and Karl Tomm

Original version published as Epston, D., Lakusta, C. and Tomm, K., Haunting from the future: a congenial approach to parent-children conflicts, *The International Journal of Narrative Therapy and Community Work*, 2006, No. 2, pp 61-70.

Reading about "assombrado do futuro" in Richard Zimler's fascinating novel *Angelic Darkness* (1999) and the intriguing prospect of benevolent ghosts haunting from the future was so resonant with an unnamed therapeutic practice of mine that it startled me.

'What's "assombrada do futuro" mean?' I asked.
'What?'
'From the song...She kept singing it over and over.'
'Oh, it's a song she wrote. It means, 'haunted from the future'.
'From the future?' I asked.
'Mara believes in hidden relations between events and people - occult explanations I guess you could say. And she thinks we've got three choices when it comes to ghosts. They're either entities who haunt you because they're fixated on your house, stuck there, so as to speak... that's number one. Or they're repressed moments from your own past come back to get revenge. That's the one favored by psychologists and nineteenth-century novelists. Or they're really from the future. You see? That's what nobody ever seems to consider.'
'No, I don't see,' I said, 'I don't get it at all.'
'Imagine you could go back into the past and help yourself at a difficult moment or someone else.... Wouldn't you do it?'
'I suppose!'
'Well, a ghost is someone from your future come back to help you. A friend. Or maybe even yourself.'
'That's crazy', I said.
    (Zimler, 1999, p. 110)

Unlike the narrator in the above, I did not find it at all 'crazy' but intriguing. It caused me to review the history of a practice I engage with in therapeutic conversations and how it had arisen in particular circumstances out of a necessity that was the mother of its invention.

My first recollection of devising such a 'haunting from the future' was during an urgent consultation at a residential treatment centre called 'Beal Street' in Hingham, Massachusetts. I had been invited by Tim Nichols, the then Director, Cheryl Jacques, the then clinical director, and Sallyann Roth, the then consultant to assist with a rash of 'running aways' by a group of 12-14-year-old female residents. This intrepid group was hanging out in the mean streets of South Boston. Their audacity mixed with their innocence was deemed to be highly dangerous. (1)

I met with four of the 'running away' young women along with the mothers of two of them and all of the staff of Beal Street to co-research their practice of running away.

Recently one of the mothers had taken action to have Sherry, her 12-year-old daughter, incarcerated overnight. This had led to a raging dispute between the two parties. Sherry's mother had lived on these streets when she had been addicted to drugs and was convinced she knew what she was talking about. Her concerns were endorsed by the other mother who had shared similar experiences. Sherry remained standing, glaring at her mother and towering over her seated colleagues. I quickly concluded that most conventional forms of enquiry would be inflammatory. Instead I turned to Lizzie, aged 13, asking her questions to haunt her from the future.

'Lizzie, when you get older and become a loving mother ...'. She looked at me with amazement: 'Me ... a loving mother!'

'Yeah, why shouldn't you become a loving mother of your teenage daughter?'

Her head snapped back and her eyes flashed as if she was envisioning this very prospect. I then went on to ask her what she might have done in Sherry's mother's circumstances. She spoke in a particularly considered manner and provided surprisingly sage counsel. Sherry seemed taken aback when Lizzie counseled even more severe measures than her mother had taken.

I then proceeded to ask her other 'running away' colleagues very similar questions and there was considerable concurrence. This discussion then ranged back over how these two mothers had acted against guilt to take the actions they had taken and were prepared to withstand the consequences of them.

We continued as an agency to co-research 'running away' in the afternoon when Sherry, pushed forward by her colleagues, asked if they might interrupt the discussion. We agreed and Sherry, with some prompting, spoke of her anger at her incarceration but in spite of that, thanked her mother for protecting her wellbeing in this manner. The mothers then thanked the 'running away' co-researchers for vindicating their newfound mothering wisdoms.

Searching my archives, I found some more recent examples, which will give some flavor of similar 'hauntings'.

Garland and Jenny

I met with Garland, a very precocious 13-year-old and her devoted single-parenting mother, Jenny. Apparently, Garland had become desperately concerned that her best girl friend, Alana, had taken a shine to her boyfriend. She was so beside herself that she resolved to settle this matter the best way she knew how – by reading Alana's diary. To do so, she broke into her home knowing that she and her family were away for the weekend.

However, in doing so, she left behind at item of clothing that was both well known and monogrammed, which Alana's parents discovered and easily identified. They did not know quite what to do and instead of laying charges, they rang Jenny and told her of Garland's 'breaking and entering/home invasion' but that no property of theirs was missing. They told Jenny that they would like to leave the matter of how to proceed up to her e.g. either to inform the police that Garland was the culprit, or not.

Jenny learned of Garland's motive for 'breaking and entering' when she spoke to her about the dilemma she faced. Garland, of course, pleaded with her not to disclose her identity to the police and when she saw that her mother remained undecided started to threaten her with dire consequences. Jenny took her own counsel and came to her conclusion to inform the police. They soon arrived and 'read the riot act' with Garland who wept with shame and remorse. The police left after deciding not to lay charges, settling the matter with a warning.

But it was not over. Jenny also required Garland to make a formal apology to Alana and her family and that took some doing. And then what followed was without precedent. Garland took to screaming without cease at her mother for her humiliation and what she considered to be her mother's betrayal of her, especially when the gossip started circulating around her clique. Jenny replied with counter-screaming, detailing both the folly and seriousness of her daughter's actions. This had been going on for some weeks when we met and it continued unabated into our meeting. I was able to intervene long enough to learn what the screaming was all about but no longer.

In desperation, I chose a 'haunting from the future', given that the recent past and present were so vexed. I spoke in a very whimsical tone, one that I imagined a most benevolent 'ghost' might employ rather than that of an interrogating police officer. I tried to make my words come from 'far away' into the present. I chose my time carefully. As it turned out, Jenny had been raised on the same street as my office and she and Garland lived only four blocks away. So I had no doubt they would know the famous coffee shop directly across the road called 'Edge City'.

'Garland, say you were in your 30s, with a daughter of your own, and you had been missing your mum. You thought it might be fun to meet for coffee at Edge City, a place you remembered so well which you had recently driven by and had noted that it was still going after all these years. You remember shaking your head and marveling at that. Jenny, as always you welcomed Garland's phone call but were even more delighted by the prospect of 'catching up' at Edge City. It brought back so many memories for you. You agreed upon a suitable time.'

'Both of you couldn't wait to see each other again, thinking it had just been too long. When you met, you both resolved that you wouldn't let so much time go by again without catching up. You greeted each other with your usual warm hug, ordered a cappuccino, which was up to standard, and immediately got down to the business of talking. To this day, when you speak together, such conversations had echoes of those wonderful times together when you, Jenny, single-parented Garland and you Garland were growing up into the woman you have become. And Garland, at such times, you could recall how all your girl-friends thought you had such a 'cool' mother, one whom you could share everything with and who was as much best friend as mother.'

'Jenny, after you both 'caught' each other up, a thought came to your mind when you chanced to look across to where the Family Therapy Centre had once been. You asked Garland pointing in this direction: 'Darling, do you remember when you were thirteen and we went to that guy over there?' Garland, you turned, looking in the same direction and felt somewhat discomforted remembering
100

what had occasioned that meeting. 'Of course I do! How could I ever forget that?' Jenny, you wanted to press the matter: 'Well, I have wanted to ask you something for a very long time. I have gone over that matter of informing the police time and time again in my mind and I can never satisfy myself if I did the right thing or the wrong thing? What would you have done if you were me?'

Garland, 'haunted by the future' looked towards Judy who by now was withdrawing tissues from her purse to staunch her tears. She took her mother's hands in hers and now spoke in the tone of a mother comforting a distressed child.

'No, mum, you did the right thing telling on me ... I know I was so mad at you and screamed at you for weeks. I even hated you for a while but I guess some of that was because I knew you were right. I thought about how I would have felt if it (the home invasion) had happened to me. I was even glad the Police yelled at me. I just didn't now how serious that was'.

What followed was quite unlike those interactions that preceded it. We all had been literally 'haunted'.

Let me proceed to another example before summarising:

Donna and Jimmy

I was consulting to a family therapy intern (Christine), her supervisor, and a single parent, Donna, aged 22 and her seven-year-old son, Jimmy. Jimmy, by this age, seemed to have done everything wrong anyone his age could have conceivably done wrong. For me, it predicted a great deal of intelligence on his part to have been quite so dedicated in his offending. However he had been lodged in the most 'special school' in his school district with many security measures and Donna had been informed that it was highly unlikely that he would ever be able to return to 'mainstream' education.

In discussion, I soon learned that Donna had said 'no' to Jimmy for the first time a week or two ago.

DE: What is your understanding of how Jimmy developed an immunity to 'no'... and how is it that he can stand it?

D: I think that he is learning there are no options. That a 'no' means 'no!'

DE: Before, did a 'no' have a lot of 'yes' in it?

D: A 'no' had a lot of 'yes' in it or 'maybe-s' in them!

DE: Does this reflect on your confidence or your wisdom that your 'no-s' have fewer 'yes-es' or 'maybe-s' in them?

D: This is very new for me because I am having to use 'no' as a sentence. If I don't, it escalates. I'm now staying calm.

What followed was a very detailed set of enquiries to firstly establish the order of significance of such a departure from their usual way of relating and secondly for some account of why Donna was taking such a radical initiative. Near the end of this meeting we proceeded to be 'haunted by the future'.

DE: Donna, say Jimmy is forming a heterosexual relationship when he is about 20 and it is getting serious. And you and his partner go out together and she says to you: 'I want to thank you for your son! Thank you for what you have done for your son!' What do you think she will thank you for?

D: That's kind of a hard one.

DE: I know... I'm just wondering. What do you think? Woman-to-woman over a coffee and you feel kind of close to her. And their relationship is getting serious. And she says to you: 'Donna or whatever she calls you...'

D: Whatever she calls me....

DE: And she says to you: 'Look, your son is a bit different from a lot of young men I have met in my life and obviously it has something to do with you and your relationship. Because I see it as somewhat different from a lot of other relationships between men and women.' What do you think she will say to you? What do you think she will thank you for?

D: For my conception of him or my ideal of Jimmy ... he would have respect for himself and others. He would respect her on all levels – on a friendship base, on a romantic base. He will be very respectful to her. Maybe she will thank me for his treating her very respectfully and treating her well. Not mean to her but kind to her.

DE: Will you tell her about today? 'Look, it could have gone a different direction but I met my partner, Jack. I met my therapist, Christine. And I met myself – my own cleverness and wisdom. But it could have gone another way.' Donna, do you think the events of today will be on your mind?

D: I would ask her: 'Do you want to know what we went through?'...

DE: (speaking as Donna and presuming the answer has been a 'yes') I could tell you when he was seven. He tantrummed all the time....

D: (takes over from me) I will tell her everything. I keep all of Jimmy's stuff. He wanted to throw all his paperwork away. 'I'm not throwing that stuff away. We keep that. I really want to keep all your papers for when you get married some time. I can give them to you then.'

Donna then went on to tell her about how the events we had been discussing had changed her son's life, her life and their mother-son relationship.

Let me summarise. A 'haunting from the future' is most poignant when the present is particularly vexatious or where parties are passionately committed to their respective position which requires each to either defend it or attack the rectitude of the other and where to relent or even hesitate would risk loss of face.

Aspects of instigating a 'haunting from the future' by friendly ghosts

There are six key aspects to instigating these 'hauntings from the future'.

Firstly, I (DE) abstract myself as best I can from the ambience and its overriding mood of conflict, despair or a sense of impossibility. I do so by reminding myself of the reasons I have for respecting each and every one of the participants and the stories that have endeared them to me. Here I will try to relate myself to them, if I haven't already, to some of their values, beliefs, moral purposes or moral endeavors. Unless I can convince myself of the reasons for my respect of the other, I will not be able to transport myself through time to such a 'future'.

Secondly, I imagine what could be enacted some time in the future if their circumstances allowed for some sort of transformation. I may have to search my catalogue of histories of epiphanic circumstances from my clinical practice, my own life, and stories I have heard from friends and others. Canvassing the literature I have read is one of my most likely sources. However, it is important that such conjectural circumstances are in the realm of benevolent possibility. And for this to be successful, the imagining of the benevolent future depends on the unearthing of a benevolent past. It would very hard, if not impossible, to project oneself into a benevolent future without some knowledge of a benevolent past that had been eclipsed by the current conflict.

Thirdly, I have found that I have to use time generously and add a generation or sometimes two. In Garland and Jenny's 'haunting', I probably added fifteen to twenty years of time and a generation in the sense that Garland was no longer exclusively her mother's daughter but in my fiction the conjectural mother of her own child. A future that 'haunts' has to be the remote future where the possible has free reign.

Fourthly, Although these introductions must of necessity be succinct, they must pack in a counterplot that has yawning gaps for those 'haunted' to fill in with their responses to such searching enquiries. To some extent, these gaps must have an almost irresistible pull into the prospects made possible by the 'haunting from the future'.

Fifthly, when the person enters the 'haunted future', you may need to persist with adjunctive circumstances, e.g. 'the look on her face tells you she is dying to know your answer to her question', or 'she asks you again but this time beseeching you', adding 'Please, I have wondered about this for so long!' to sustain such a 'haunting'. Enquiries as insistent as these allow for the respondent to 'live' into such a future.

And finally, in my explorations of such 'hauntings', I have found that if I feel comfortable with the benevolence of my 'haunting', others do too. At such times, I find that temporarily holding the 'best possible' versions of each and my convictions as to prospects provides a portal for others to pass through as well. On those occasions when I showed any unease, soon all was lost and we returned abruptly to the current conflict with all its vicissitudes.

A family haunting

Another example of therapeutic 'haunting from the future' occurred at the Calgary Family Therapy Centre during a family interview in November 2004. Interestingly, the family subsequently initiated a modified version of the process successfully on their own. The five members of the household included Judy, a native of Portugal, and her four daughters, Jocelyn 18, Lillian 17, Eve 15, and Lola 14.

Judy had separated from the father because of his violence and was raising the four children on her own. Lola in particular had become quite rebellious and proved very difficult to manage.

Cherelyn Lakusta began a therapeutic interview with the five family members while Karl Tomm and David Epston observed behind a one-way mirror (with the family's consent). Judy was a very gentle and soft-spoken woman who struggled to express herself in halting English. In contrast, all four girls had acquired an excellent command of the English language and were very quick-witted. In combination, the girls were a formidable team of fast talkers who did not leave much space for Judy to formulate, let alone articulate a response. Cherelyn decided to privilege Judy's voice by addressing the initial series of questions to her and in so doing try to validate her position as head of the household. Judy proceeded to describe her disappointment in the lack of responsibility and respectfulness of her daughters. She gave examples of them not listening to her guidance or following through on commitments. For instance, she had been led to believe that Lola was honestly trying harder to do better in school this year. However, Judy recently received a phone call from the school indicating that Lola had not even been handing in her assignments.

The emotional tone in this interview was heavier and more subdued than in previous sessions. It turned out that there had been a significant conflictual incident just prior to the interview. Jocelyn had agreed to pick up her mother at the dentist at 3pm but didn't show. Judy had to call home to remind her. The mother was quite upset about this because this meant they were going to be late since they still had to pick up the three other young women and try to make it to the appointment. Jocelyn explained that she had not planned to leave the house until 3pm but had not forgotten. As Judy continued to elaborate on her concerns, her daughters became increasingly defensive and began to protest that their mother's decisions about discipline were unreasonable and/or unwarranted. Eve complained that Judy did not give an adequate explanation for her disciplinary decisions, etc. Lola smiled nervously.

Using a telephone, Karl and David called in with a few suggestions to try to facilitate a shift from critical transactions to more affirming ones. In particular, they suggested Cherelyn ask the sisters what it was that they respected about their mother and some reasons why they could respect her decisions. They had difficulty with this, perhaps because it demanded too big a change in their immediate feelings toward their mother. David and Karl then suggested that they instead try to explain to them, as observers behind the screen, what they could legitimately respect about their mother. This seemed easier and they readily came up with several qualities of their mother that should command David and Karl's respect. These included her personal strength, that she was always there for her children, that she always put them first, and that she was very forgiving. Judy seemed to become tearful in hearing what her daughters were now saying but it didn't last long. The process quickly shifted back to the daughters teaming up to denounce their mother's parenting efforts.

It was at this point in the interview that David proposed an intervention of activating a 'friendly ghost from the future to haunt the girls in the present'. Karl used the telephone again to call in the idea, but Cherelyn decided to come behind the screen to discuss the suggestion more fully. Given its complexity, she preferred to have David deliver the message. Cherelyn then asked the family if David and Karl could join the interview and they agreed.

After the usual greetings, David began as follows:

'Jocelyn, let's imagine you were in your 30s or 40s and you had children of your own. Hopefully you had at least one daughter, and she was about the age that you and your sisters are now. Suppose you were finding that raising a teenager wasn't sheer bliss and this caused you to reflect on your mother raising you at about the same age. And when you thought about it, you felt this pang of regret about what you put your mother through back then. Indeed, you felt it so strongly that you phoned Lillian and told her about it. As strange as this may sound, Lillian, you told Jocelyn that you had been thinking the very same things about your daughter and your mother! You then decided that each of you would take this matter up by phone with Eve and Lola who both said that your mother had been on their minds of late as well! As a result you all decided to convene at Lillian's home and talk about it over coffee. ... When you got there, I think it was you, Lola, who said in jest 'You know, we ought to hold a party in Mom's honour!' Lola, you were quite surprised when everyone enthusiastically agreed with you: 'Yeah, that's what we should do!' But after a while, Jocelyn, you asked: 'But what will we do at the party?' Eve, I think it was you who came up with the idea of a wonderful Portuguese meal. Lillian, you spoke up, not to disagree but to raise a question: 'Hey, we always have meals together. That in itself won't make it special for Mom. Isn't there something that could make it more special?' Then it was you again, Lola, perhaps in jest, saying: 'Why don't we all write her speeches and read them aloud to her to honour her.' Once again everyone jumped on the idea!'

'So here is a little task. Can you take these four pads and pens (we had brought 4 pads and pens with us into the meeting) and write your speeches right now as you might have made them up then? And when you have finished, we can decide when and where you might like to read them to your mother? ... Judy, do you have the patience to wait a few minutes extra for your daughters to write their speeches?'

'Yes, of course.'

All four girls seemed quite amused by this hypothetical situation but took the task very seriously and began writing furiously. Karl added a few suggestions as they were writing: 'You each have probably had some special moments with your mother during those early years that stand out for you, and that you might want to share. Indeed, your sisters might appreciate hearing about them as well. You could even include some comments from people outside the family who have told you stories about your mother that are worth remembering.'

Actually, the girls didn't really need any guidance with their task; they continued to write without interruption. Jocelyn was the first to finish, Eve was second and Lola was third. Lillian, however, kept writing and writing. David invited them to practice delivering their speeches right in the session even though he acknowledged they might not be altogether finished or have their final draft yet. Without hesitation, Jocelyn as the eldest began giving a speech from her point-form notes and did so with considerable poise.

Jocelyn's point-form notes:

When I was a kid I didn't understand why you waited up all night for us.
When I liked a guy you knew wasn't right for me and I got angry for you saying so.
You were loyal, loving, understanding.
When you and I went shopping for my grad dress and you knew how much I wanted it.
The way you treated dad, always did the best you could under the circumstances.
Listened and gave the best advice you thought possible from experience.
You always picked us up anywhere, anytime.
Friends told me how great you were.

Copious tears began to flow down Judy's face. She clearly was deeply moved. David and Karl began to weep as well.

Lola appeared quite excited to deliver her speech next:

Dear Mama,

I wanted to thank you and I'm not just saying thank you for being my mom. I now know what it is like to be a mother and I can honestly say it's not as easy as I thought it would be. I always thought of you as a person I would hope to some day become; you were always there for me from the beginning and we didn't have the greatest life with the divorce and all the fighting. But somehow we made it through when I never thought we would. There was this one time I have remembered all my life. It was when I was in kindergarten and I was learning how to spell my name and I needed your help but you had to do all the housework and I remember you were washing the dishes while teaching me a song on how to spell my name. It is not the fact that you taught me my name, it is that you stuck with me and taught me a lesson to go with my word and still did the things that had to be done. I just wanted to say I love you and thank you. You really don't understand how much you have guided me through life.
Love Lola

Lillian finally finished writing after Lola had completed her speech. However, Eve wanted to go next:

Mom,

I want to thank you for always being there for me since I was a little girl and to this day. The other day as I put my daughter to bed I sat there and I looked at her and thought to myself, I hope I am able to be the mom to her that you were to me. You motivated me to become a better person. I know it wasn't easy to raise Jocelyn, Lillian and Lola. But you were always there, when times were good but also when times were

at their worst. You loved and cared for me and always told me to do my best. The only thing I regret is that as a teenager I wasn't more understanding, and I wasn't always there when you needed me. Growing up, I always looked up to you and hoped that one day I could repay you for all you have done for me and I guess that in some way today is that day. I want you to know that now it is my turn to love you and tell you how much I care. I want you to know that I love you and appreciate you so much. Thank you for being my mom, my friend and my guardian angel.
Love Eve

And finally Lillian delivered her speech:

Mom,
Looking back at when I was a child, I often wondered why you would ask me to do the things that you needed to be done. Why I had to clean or why I couldn't go out. Then there were those times when you'd tell us stories about you as a child, how you always obeyed your mother, and how you and your sisters never fought. Then you'd go on to speak of your 'life experiences' and all I could only say was: 'how lame'. Now as I look at my own children, I think that they must think that of me. I'm glad they think this because I always thought you were so special. I admired every minute that we could sit there and you'd speak and tell me stories and I would say, how did I get so lucky, and at night when we got home from a late night and you would be sitting on the couch and you would welcome us home, although I could tell you were so tired and you needed your rest. Then you'd stay up with us to hear our silly and pointless stories.
I can also remember speaking to my friends after they had met you and they would say: 'Your mom is so cute...I love her'. I guess I always perceived our relationship as different. Your heart controls your mind and your spirit is always present. You have always gone to extremes for your family. I value your character, you always look up and you always put a smile on your face. I loved going for a quick coffee after the chiropractor and I loved your advice. I love you so dearly and I will always cherish you, not only as my mother but also as my best friend and my role model.
Love Lillian

All the speeches were very touching, not only in their content but in the tone in which they were delivered. Indeed, the emotional tone of the interview had been transformed. The pattern of family interaction had shifted, from pervasive negativity with incessant complaints and bickering, to strong positive feelings of appreciation and affection. As therapists we were surprised and in awe with how readily and effortlessly the daughters were able to write and deliver such articulate speeches in recognition of their mother. It was almost as if they were eulogising her in her presence. What became so palpable were the strong bonds they had with their mother and the high regard in which they held her. The session ended with the following question for the four young women: 'How could

107

you use your newfound wisdom from the future to empower yourself to make things better for you and your Mom at home now?'

A month later Cherelyn and Karl met with Judy and the three younger daughters in a follow-up session (the eldest was working). Everyone agreed that there had been a significant positive shift at home following the last session. All of them had become more respectful and responsive to their mother's requests to help out with chores, etc. At the same time, however, they felt that they were at risk of slipping back into old habits of bickering. Karl suggested the possibility of developing a ritual of a 'friendly future family fest' perhaps with a different person as the focus each time. The young women felt they wanted their mother to remain the focus.

Another six weeks later several family members arrived with speeches they had decided on their own to give to Eve, who had gone through a difficult time, and other family members saw as having made the biggest positive changes. Judy herself joined in to read the following:

> *Eve is a very good daughter. I remember when she was a little girl, one day she told me 'Mom I'm very sorry because I can't help you with work, but when I grow up I will help you'. And she did. Of course not every day, but when she's in a good mood. Eve had a bad attitude but I can see a difference, now she is trying very hard to change. I love her and I appreciate her very much.*
> *Thank you, love, Mom*

It seemed as though the culture of the family had changed. They now consciously and deliberately focused on positive aspects of their lives. Even in subsequent sessions, as other problematic issues arose, the disposition to affirm one another continued as a strong ongoing theme.

Some notes on inventions that solicit and cultivate the imagination
For me (DE), inventions like 'the haunting of the future' almost always emerge in the 'heat' of a meeting.(2) What at other times or circumstances might seem audacious, are warranted by the circumstances. Here, in each instance, I was faced with an intractable conflict between young people and their parents that threatened to rupture their relationships.

What has always intrigued me is the solicitation and cultivation of the imagination 'when the going gets tough'. After all, the tendency at such times is to reiterate the known and 'tried and true'. It has often been my experience of practice to meet individuals and families when the 'tried and true' has truly been tried without any apparent 'truth'. To solicit and cultivate your imagination as well as the imaginations of those whom have consulted you with dire concerns, requires some conviction that such a 'site of enquiry' may lead to something or someplace hitherto unknown. In the 'history' of the examples above, and other times I have employed such 'hauntings' in equally fraught situations, we have gained tremendous advantage in reaching such an imagined vantage point in which the comments on the present from the future reveal the 'wisdom of hindsight'.

What has caught my eye (and my interest) are two matters: Firstly, in the case of young people, how prudential their commentaries are. And secondly, when undertaken with the discretion suggested in the above, how enduring these 'hauntings' can be. The imagined future seems to infuse the present with new meanings.

I have reached no conclusions about this, although I am not without speculations. My speculations have to do with the very pleasures of keeping company with our imaginations, especially when they are brought into some sort of imaginative community, if only for a matter of minutes. After all, Collins Concise English Dictionary cites as its third meaning of 'imagination': 'The ability to deal resourcefully with unexpected or unusual problems, circumstances, etc.'

Acknowledgments
I (DE) would like to thank Dorothy Lewis, Aileen Cheshire, Frances Hancock, Peggy Sax and Rick Maisel for their careful and thoughtful readings and comments. Thanks are due to the reviewers who obliged me to go beyond the detail of practice and got me to consider the solicitation and cultivation of the imagination in 'communities' which is so vital to any 'haunting from the future'.

Footnotes
1. Some years later, I was interviewing John in San Rafael, California with my colleague Dr Joel Fay, Community Mental Health Liaison, San Rafael Police. John had been homeless for the previous twenty years following his first psychotic episode in his early twenties and had agreed to discuss his life for the purpose of the 'training' of the policemen/women of California in a mandatory training relating to 'the homeless'. In the course of the interview, he related how notorious the streets of South Boston were and considered them as dangerous as Vietnam battlefields.
2. In this respect, they are somewhat unlike some set piece enquiries that are future-orientated, at the same time as sharing some similarities. See McAdam (2001).

References
Collins Concise English Dictionary, Third Edition (1992) HarperCollins, Glasgow.
McAdam, E. (2001) Talking about the future, in Denborough, D (Ed) Family Therapy: Exploring the Field's Past, Present and Possible Futures. Dulwich Centre Publications, Adelaide,.
Zimler, R. (1999) Angelic Darkness, W.W. Norton & Co, New York.

Up Over...

7

Will you put pressure on yourself to put pressure on your bladder?
An approach to intractable bed-wetting problems

David Epston

Angela's bed-wetting problem appeared to be at the very heart of the Morris family's life. Her mother, Jan, aged 39, was the most ruffled but denied any inconvenience to her of the daily routine of sheet washing because 'Angela can't help it'. Her father, Jim, aged 44, was more disconcerted by the social consequences for Angela of her bed-wetting. Her older sisters, Sharon, aged 13, and Carol, aged 15, fretted over her too. The family, indeed, had 'tried everything possible'. Two hospital admissions confirmed the adequacy of her functional bladder capacity. Two drug trials had been attempted – one had no effect and the other led to 'a personality change' and a relapse on its withdrawal. Angela had successfully slept through all her bed buzzers which roused everyone else.

Everyone seemed so zealous in offering Angela service, advice and commiseration. Angela, aged 11-and-a-half, by comparison, seemed insouciant and unconvinced that the problem belonged to her. She certainly was the least concerned person in the room. When asked what influence the problem was having over Angela's life, her parents and sisters hit upon 50-60%. They had other worries about Angela: 'She likes to be at home all the time . . . she can't cope with being her age . . . she lacks confidence, etc.' In fact, Angela agreed when asked that she had a strong preference for 'youngness' because that would ensure 'my happiness'. Her father reported considerable evidence for her choosing 'youngness'. She played with age-inappropriate toys, rarely left home, didn't want to advance in school and only sought out her parents for company. However, all this was put down to her bed-wetting. Angela, on the other hand, asserted that she had had such a good childhood that she would be sad to leave it behind. Everyone acknowledged that Angela was 'under age for her age'. They explained that their fear of making her 'feel insecure about herself' accounted for their reluctance to bring this to her attention.

The following summary was read to everyone and then sent to them in the form of a letter:

Dear Jan, Jim, Carol, Sharon and Angela,
It's good to discover that Angela has the physical wherewithal – that is, functional bladder capacity – so that she could, with appropriate training and parental coaching, get the better of her bladder over time to make it the same age as she is on the outside. Jim, we agreed with you that such problems as bed-wetting can degrade a young person and stall their growing up. As you mentioned, this seems to be the case for Angela – e.g. preferring children much younger than herself, playing with toys her age-mates have left behind and becoming bound to home and parents.

However, she has made such a good job of a bad lot that we wonder if she hasn't settled for bed-wetting. She appears uncertain whether she should take her growing up to the next stage and for this reason, it came as no surprise to us that she is very reluctant to go to Intermediate School. Understandably, her problem has elicited from her parents and sisters a great deal of caring and concern. We wondered if Angela hadn't become, in a manner of speaking, addicted to a very high dosage of care and is afraid to break from the habit. She may worry that growing up, on a lower dosage, isn't worth bed-wetting plus a high dosage. She seems very satisfied with her lot in life, even though the rest of her family believe she is living less than half the life she might. The sad and difficult thing for parents is that they cannot solve such a problem for their beloved children. Their children must do it for themselves, although that is not to say you cannot provide coaching.

In summary, we are sorry to say that we don't think that Angela is ready to put pressure on herself to put pressure on her bladder. Sadly, we are like you, Jan and Jim – we cannot do her bladder training for her. Only she can! Although she is 'able' in terms of her functional bladder capacity, is she ready????

Angela, it's up to you to make up your mind about growing up. It's a big decision and one that shouldn't be taken lightly. Growing up, admittedly, is both scary and exciting. Staying grown down is neither, as you already know everything there is to know about it. You are 11½, a time when many girls and boys decided to start becoming men and women. You appear to be enjoying your childhood so much that you don't want to leave it behind. We can well understand that because we know if you grow up, you tend to go out and stay at friends' homes; you don't hang around your parents so much; you insist the problem doesn't elicit quite such a high dosage of care and concern; and you stand on your own two feet more. This is a big decision – you need to think carefully about it. We ask you to discuss this with your sisters. They know about it because they have just gotten into their maturity.

When you have made up your mind, phone me and let me know what you have decided. On the other hand, you may just decide to let nature take its course, whenever that is, and by doing so hold on to your childhood for as long as you can.

Yours sincerely,
David Epston

Angela looked relieved by the 'no treatment' option whereas the Morris family assured me that 'we will be back'.

I rang a year later. Mrs Morris was delighted to hear from me as by chance, Angela, three weeks earlier, had decided she wanted to tackle her bed-wetting problem. Mrs Morris advised her to phone me because, as she put it, 'I'm keeping out of it'. I commended her for the confidence she had in Angela and advised her to tell Angela that she was now very likely 'ready'! Angela contacted me that night and sounded very enthusiastic about proceeding against the problem.

We met soon after. Mrs Morris, with a flourish, removed her chair from the circle I had arranged, seating herself at a distance from Angela. She accounted for this by her categorical – 'this is not my problem anymore!' I knew at a glance Angela had done a fair bit of growing up both by her appearance and her manner. There was a lot to support my impression. But despite what we referred to as her 'grow-back', she was still 100% wet by night. However, when I questioned Angela about her new-found friendships and her active participation with her peers, I introduced the 'winning away and losing at home' contradiction. I highlighted the fact that Angela had been dry 100% of the time by night on the twenty-plus occasions she had slept overnight at her girl-friends' homes. In fact, Mr Morris mused that she was hard to keep at home these days.

'How is it that you win away and lose at home when it is well known that most teams win twice as often and lose away about twice as often?'

'Why is that teams, playing before their parents and friends and workmates, not only excel but often surpass themselves?'

'What is it about spectators that encourage their 'team' to play so well?'

'Why do you think it is teams can be so lacklustre and even play beneath their capability when their parents, friends etc., aren't there to cheer them on?'

'What would happen if you invited your girl friends to move in with you and sleep in your room? Do you think you would win against your problem more or less?'

(To parents) 'If she is right about her conviction that she wouldn't wet her bed if her girl friends moved into her room, do you think you might see if her girlfriends' parents would allow you to adopt them? Or do you think it would be simpler for Angela to bring her solution back home?'

I admitted my own curiosity about this state of affairs and by doing so, invited theirs. 'How do you understand this?' I enquired of Jan, Carol, Sharon, Jim and Angela. No one could make any immediate sense of this anomaly and everyone had to admit they were puzzled. Regardless, questions were asked of Angela to specify the measures she had taken, the 'knowledges' she had learned the 'hard way', and the practices she had developed to effect such a 'twenty plus night in a row winning streak'. She was hard put to find any answers, but when we persisted she found she knew a lot more than she had known before the conversation began. I then asked her if she would be willing to consider bringing her 'winning ways back home'. After all, everyone was in agreement that the adoption (of her girlfriends) was out of the question but that bringing her winning ways home would certainly be welcome.

All notions of some sort of 'fixed' physiological and/or psychological causation became untenable in the face of the problem's context-boundedness and Angela's forthright problem-solving know-how that had contributed to her successes 'away' from home. Everyone seemed literally freed to proceed against the problem – Angela as the player and her family as her supporters – as the matter became further ironical by detailed discussion that followed. Angela concluded that she was indeed 'both ready and able'. The only advice Angela was given was to apply her 'away tactics' at home, which she had disclosed to her family who now had been enrolled as her fans and supporters.

I phoned two months later to find that Angela had made no headway whatsoever. Jan had just been discharged from hospital with what she told me were 'unspecified psychosomatic complaints'. She said this had been 'a wake-up call' and she was determined to do things differently from now on. I enquired if she thought Angela was prepared to take extreme measures to put pressure

116

on herself to put pressure on the problem. She said she had to. Apparently Jan's sister had insisted she do something about what she referred to as 'your guilt'. I enquired if such guilt led her to torture her body and soul and we came up with quite a catalogue. I asked in jest: 'How much torture would guilt inflict on you if Angela were to wash her own sheets?' She said that 'would be tough and hard on my conscience' but then hit upon the idea of phoning her sister. She said in jest: 'That would be far more of a torture' than anything guilt could inflict on her. I then found out that Angela would turn thirteen in a matter of five or six weeks.

I phoned Angela and commiserated with her and asked her: 'Would you be willing to put pressure on yourself to pressurise the problem?' She declared she was prepared to do anything that had to be done. I asked her how much money she had in her bank account. Conveniently, her life savings came to $35.00. She agreed to surrender that amount to her mother who consented to spend $1 'madly' each day Angela wet her bed from now on. However, if Angela were to 'win at home', her mother was to return the $1 to her.

I then asked to speak to her mother who was standing by. We conferred and Jan decided that if she found herself at risk of being overcome by 'guilt', she would phone her sister for what she referred to as 'a de-guilting session'.

Much to everyone's surprise, Angela only surrendered around 25% of her life's savings, a small price to pay for starting to 'win at home'. Six months later, Angela contacted me to let me know that she hadn't wet her bed for over a month. We were able to conclude that she was now 'a winner everywhere' and that her problem 'had lost it's place in her life' and that should she wet her bed again, that would be considered an accident rather than a 'problem'.

The 'no treatment today' inspired much of what follows in an approach I have developed more recently for intractable bed-wetters. All had previously undergone conventional medical investigations, drug trials, and behavioural interventions without any enduring relief. Child sexual abuse had been excluded. The young people concerned were in the age range of 9-15 years of age. Some of the parents informed me that they themselves or siblings didn't go dry until late adolescence. In fact, no young person I met in this sample was 'older' than the average age adults of his/her parents' generation 'went dry'. Not surprisingly, their parents were particularly anxious that their child's life was not blighted in the same way theirs or their siblings had been. Other parents expressed a great reluctance to show any response to the problem whatsoever and one had even sought therapy to mute his feelings of disapproval. There was a concern that should they express any disapproval, this could be productive of a 'neurosis; or 'insecurity'.

Either way, these parents were inclined to 'cover over' the problem and quite unwittingly, made it their own by keeping it from their children. 'Guilt', of course, can have the same effect of transferring the problem to the 'guilty' parent. Incidents of bed-wetting then incite self-recriminations and self-reproach. As the parents became more organised around their child's problem, those interventions that are believed to be innocent of the attribution of blame such as medical, surgical or chemotherapeutic or are parent-organised, e.g. behavioural, are readily embraced. Such interventions can have the effect of keeping the cover on the 'cover over'. Such 'cover-overs' extend to entering into secret agreements with their child's friends, their family and family friends to overlook bed-wetting and associated malodours. Family life can increasingly revolve around the problem of bed-wetting, a problem for which the parents assume increasing responsibility and of which the young person can become increasingly oblivious, aside from the obvious discomfort and inconvenience.

Most of the problem's 'pressure' is borne by mothers, many of whom when we embarked upon detailed calculations, had washed over 15,000 sheets, given that in these families there is often more than one practising bed-wetter. Mother-blaming, that widespread explanation for many, if not most, children's problems in professional literatures and folk psychologies can add further 'guilt' to their burdens. And I am guessing that each treatment failure, by implication, makes mother-blame more likely.

The other inspiration for this approach resulted from the serendipitous findings associated with 'externalising conversations' and 'consulting your consultants'. My preference is to think of an 'externalising conversation' as an 'anti-language', a counter-cultural set of discursive practices rather than a technique, tactic or strategy. I have observed for some time now an association between an 'externalised problem' and a sense of personal agency. In the linguistic space 'opened up' between the person/family and the problem, 'insider knowledges' can be found by a method of enquiry that White and I have likened to an archaeology of capabilities and problem-solving 'know-how'. And it is our experience that young people's 'knowledges' are very close to the historical surface and are easily exposed by the 'digging around' of the enquiries. In saying that, it must be noted that the very enquiries 'co-construct' the 'knowledge'. They do not pre-exist such enquiries. But for these 'knowledges' to be experienced as in their possession, some connection must be made between the problem-solving 'know-how' *per se* and a sense of themselves as 'knowledgeable' for an effect to be experienced. Introducing a lexicon of candidate vocabulary such as will-(power), motives such as determination, causes such as pride or 'being your age' is often necessary at this point for such a connection to be made.

I have been exploring for some time now the capability of young people to produce their own problem-solving practices and knowledges. Accordingly, the therapist's task is to assist in the articulation of these knowledges and by doing so, render the young person 'knowledgeable' about his/her own 'knowledgeableness'. How often have young people said, in surprise at themselves – 'I didn't know that I knew!' For those adults committed to the view that children's problems are best resolved by the transfer of adult 'expert' knowledge', this notion of knowledge-generating capabilities may sound strangely romanticising of young people. In response to this, I advance two unrelated propositions: firstly, taking young people seriously is hard for those adults who expect young persons to take them seriously and secondly, much of what I take to be hypnotic phenomena can be considered to be children's play, a play they have prudently learned to keep to themselves or their playmates for fear of ridicule.

In my practice with young people and their problems, some sort of 'capability' is taken for granted and the young person's history of having had some influence on the problem is then staked out for an 'archaeology'. In intractable bed-wetting, the solution is often at most an exquisite elaboration or refinement of 'winning away', even if there has merely been one 'win' in a life-time. With Luke, aged 13, the only incident had occurred when his parents, to their shame, had forgotten to bring along his plastic sheet when their family stayed over as his Uncle and Aunt's home for the weekend. Further enquiry revealed Luke's embryonic capability and negated their understanding of the event as mere chance. This is often represented to the young person and his/her family by way of an audio-taped 'story'. This practice is merely the translation of 'letters as narrative' to another medium that is far more convenient for young people and can managed on their own without required adult accompaniment and at night.

However, 'readiness' determines whether s/he will deploy their 'know-how'. 'Un- readiness' is conceived of as restraining the young person and their family from making their opposition known to the problem. As for the resolution of bed-wetting problems, 'readiness' is vested in those practices associated with agency such as determination, will-(power), or motive. When motives (e.g. 'I want to sleep over at my friend's house') is aligned with a practice (e.g. 'I did it because I didn't want to be embarrassed when I woke up in the morning') both the family and the young person can promote 'readiness' by 'putting pressure on yourself so you can put pressure on the problem'. However, to do so, everyone must be convinced that the young person has the requisite capability. This contradicts all those 'covering over' tactics that have inadvertently removed all the pressure off the bed-wetter and put it on their parents.

By the end of the first session, those families who had been organised around the bed-wetting problem rapidly regroup around the discovered part-solutions and the avowed intention of the young person to take the problem over at home as well as away. The externalising conversation seems to have the effect of separating the young person, their newfound abilities and their 'grownupness' from the inappropriateness of their 'undergrown' bladder. The young person is divided between their capability, their purposes and intentions and the problem which now pertains to 'only a little bit of you'. This allows these families to discharge themselves from the position of a family -with-an-intractable problem to one of encouraging and promoting their young person's acknowledged discoveries. Both the problem and part-solution rest with the young person and all parties to the conversation seemed to enjoy such an outcome.

However, in this approach, the young person designs for and dictates to themselves their own preferred forms of 'pressure'. This exempts the parents or concerned others from supervising the problem. I have found that by this stage most of the young people are rather vengeful and their retribution takes the form of bringing their winning ways home. However, the therapist must have some suggestions 'up their sleeve' from their stock of clinical lore as I doubt if many young people would spontaneously come up with them, if left to their own devices. It is important to keep a 'catalogue' of how other young people have 'pressurised' themselves to 'pressurise' the problem: 'Well, Abby who was 15 and was just 'sick to death' of the problem and thought it would be curtains for her relationship with her new boyfriend surrendered to her mother one item from her make-up collection for each wet bed and that an 80% dry/wet ratio per month would lead to the return of the items her mother was holding in trust for her. Judy, aged nine, slept on the floor in her sleeping bag the next night after she wet the bed to 'put pressure on herself to put pressure back on the problem'. Jimmy, aged 11, said he was so scared he would be found out when they had to change for physical education that he 'put pressure on himself to put pressure on the problem' by running two kilometres every time he wet the bed. As Jimmy said, 'there is nothing I hate more in this world than running'.

The first meeting is usually concluded by my question: 'What did you learn about yourself that came as a surprise to you?' The following is a sample of replies: 'Finding out I could solve this problem by myself' (14-year-old); 'I am a wizard' (11 year old); 'I knew if I could do it at someone else's place, I could do it at home. I didn't link it up. It didn't occur to me' (12-year-old): and 'I just decided that I had been wetting my bed for ten years and that was too long. I've got to stop. I'm on my side now' (11-year-old).

Forewarnings are given that progress is best measured in terms of percentage of dry to wet beds rather than 'winning streaks'. The reason for this is that often young people initiate a lengthy winning streak after the session, one that everyone then tends to use as a base-line for success. 'Complacency' is also discussed and predicted. Parents are asked to come up with a synonym for 'complacency' and come up with 'resting on his laurels', 'overconfidence', 'making it a low priority', 'laid back', etc. I regularly ask for percentage scores to be left on my answer phone daily and if matters are going badly, will suggest another meeting to review the situation. Otherwise, I usually post a 'complacency letter' to the young person when I guess that might be appropriate when 'complacency is very likely to strike': Remember developing 'dryness' will take at least a period of six months, although we discuss the criterion of 21 days in a row as a criterion of 'dryness', although of course that does not rule out the odd accident.

My letter to Abby (aged 14) is an example of such a letter:

Dear Abby,
I thought I had better write you and warn you that it is very likely that about any time now, you will have a little slip-up. This just about happens to everyone so I want to reassure you that it is nothing to worry about. What a slip-up means is that it is

time to meet together and review your knowledge, all the better to make it stronger and put it to good use once again.

If I am wrong about this, I am very sorry. However, from my experience, you are due or even overdue for a slip. If I am right, I am very sorry but it means I will at least get to meet up with you again. And I think I can guarantee you that it will be for the very last time. There always seems to be one slip up just about now or a little while ago.

No matter what, I would like to hear from you one way or another.

Yours Against Complacency,

David

The following is an audio-tape prepared for Hannah, aged 12, who went from dryness on those occasions girl-friends stayed overnight or the family was planning to leave early in the morning for weekends away to full-time dryness over a period of six months. This tape was made after our second meeting:

Hi, Hannah, David speaking. I must confess to having liked you a lot when we met the other day. After we met, I got to thinking how unfair it was that your problem should play such a large part in your life. So I could easily understand what "a pain" it was for you to have such a problem. It must worry you so much when you are going to sleep over at friends and how much it must be on your mind when you are trying to have fun at slumber parties. And I didn't see any reason for you not to have all the fun your 'fun side' wishes to have. That is why when we first got talking, I was getting perturbed to learn about this until you told me what you told me. And that gave me more than hope; it gave me confidence in you. And I guess that is what I need if I am going to make this particular tape. So I want you to know that I understand fully that when you are under 'a bit of pressure' of some kind or other, you told me you were a '97% winner'. And 97% winning to me is about as much winning as anyone would want. I don't think you have to do any more than that. There must be a little bit of room for the odd slip-up, don't you think?

And we considered how odd it was – as did your mother and your brother, Jason – how you are a winner away from home and a loser at home. So that gave me the idea of you bringing your winning home. Why not? Why not? There seems to be no reason, to my way of thinking, that you can't. If you want to . . . if you really want to get the better of this problem. You've already won a fair few times away. So, if that is your opinion too, continue to listen to this tape. If it isn't, don't listen to this tape anymore. Just turn it off. After all, sooner or later, say when you are fourteen or fifteen, you probably will stop wetting the bed naturally. It will just happen as you grow up and your body matures. So you don't really have to put pressure on yourself to put pressure on the problem if you don't want to.

However, you convinced me that you were ready and that your twelfth birthday which is just around the corner would tell you that you were ready and able. And I know you can. And you know you can. That is not to say that it doesn't require you to undergo some pressure because it does.

121

So, if you do want to go dry, keep listening. Now, Hannah, my guess is that it's dark; you've got the light out, even if you are reading with a torch under your blankets. So if you are, that's fine but if you are wishing to go to sleep, that is the very best time to do what I am going to suggest you do.

I suggest you find a really cosy place in your bed ... find a place where you feel cuddly and warm and your head fits just right into a little place in your pillow. And I hope it is a very comfortable pillow. Are you ready to head off to sleep? Well, before you do, you have something to think about ... something to put into your mind. All you have to do is put in and on your mind those things that you do when you 'win'. You are a winner. The problem loses when you are away from home or have to get away early the next morning with your family.

Now what you told me I found very, very interesting and even inspiring. That is you were able to find reasons for not wetting the bed. You have three separate reasons. One was that when you go away to friends or are at slumber parties, the second was when you have friends to stay and third, the day before you go to the cottage because you want to be thoughtful of your mum and don't want her to have to rush and wash your sheets before your departure. That is very, very thoughtful of you. But I wonder if you want to be thoughtful of your growing up. And if you do, you will use your own ideas to discipline and grow your bladder up to your age.

It's a problem, Hannah, of your bladder being a little bit undergrown ... not as grown up as you are because I found it very easy to accept that you were twelve and I could even have thought of you as 13. And I know you aren't quite twelve according to your birthday. So in every other way, you are a twelve year old twelve year old. But your bladder is undergrown and you thought more like a five-year-old twelve-year-old bladder.

So it's your job to grow it up to your age. And to do that you already have many ideas. All you have to do is try a bit harder to train it to do what you want it to do rather than what it wants to do ... to take instructions from you rather than it just going whenever it wants to go all over the place.

Now, Hannah, what you said to me when I asked – and I was very interested to learn what you had to say – is that when you are at your girl friends' places or at a slumber party, you "have it on my mind ... I think about it". And that led me to ask – "What do you think about? What are you power thoughts?" Because on these occasions, your problem does not go whenever it feels like it. And this is what you told me – "I think over and over again to myself- I can't wet the bed! I can't do it! I can't wet my bed!" and then you tell yourself your reasons – "My friends are going to think I am a baby!" Now, that is probably true because our friends don't know that just one tiny bit of you – your bladder – is a bit undergrown. But they may judge you by the age of your bladder and that would be very unfair. And what else you think that seems to help you keep it on your mind and put thoughts into your mind and makes you try harder is – "I don't want them to find out because they might tell each other and spread it!" And you know as well as I do that girls your age can be quite mean gossiping. So I can understand your concern here. And you also start wondering if 'teasing' could become a possibility if they find out.

And this is what you do and this is what you can do and this is what you do that you know works. It works 97% of the time which is as perfect as anyone wants to be. And this is what you say so listen carefully to yourself. I am only putting your words into my words but they are your ideas, your power ideas, and they work: "I tell myself to wake up just before I go to sleep" or "if I wake up in the middle of the night, I always wake up and go to the toilet because I don't want them to find out". So, Hannah, this is all you need to do but you need to do it!

When I asked if you were ready to take this on, I thought you were but who am I? I don't know you as well as some others do. So I asked your mum if she thought you were ready and this is what she had to say: "She has already started to grow up". And when I asked your mum in what ways your growing up had shown itself, she said it had to do with "a more mature attitude . . . more philosophical . . . she can think things through". Also she thought you can even "recognise feelings within herself and discuss them with me". And I thought that was a very, very good sign of maturity. And also much to my interest, your mum thought you were "starting to be original".

And when I asked what your dad would say if he were here, you thought he would say that he too had noticed that you were starting to grow up. And the proof for him would have been that you are starting to save your money instead of spending it all on sweets, like younger people often do. You had got quite serious wanting a bike and you saved up for it and then approached your parents and they matched your contribution. But wasn't that a grown up thing to do? No one could deny that. I certainly was convinced!

However, what really clinched it for me was your brother, Stuart. He's only nine but he was clear that you are certainly growing ahead of him. He said you now had a "different attitude" towards your life. And the evidence for him was that you were reading more and that when he would ask you to play a game, you would say that you would like to but you had your home-work to do. So even Stuart noticed that you are getting more serious. And when I asked Stuart, "Well, do you think she's ready?", he said: "I think she's ready! She's old enough . . . strong enough . . . she's confident!" And then your mum told me something that perhaps I could have guessed but wouldn't have dared ask. And this is what she said: "When the chips are down and she has to do it, she will." And I said, "Like what?" And your mum gave me the examples of your swimming and your ballet and your school-work. So, Hannah, it is clear to me and I hope as clear to you that when you really have to do something – and you want to do something – you will do it.

Now you don't have to solve this problem but do you want to? No-one can make you do it. But, by all accounts, you are ready and able to do this should you decide to put yourself under your own pressure to grow your bladder up to your age. And I know that everyone who knows you would be proud of you if you did, even though they are already proud of you.

When we thought of this idea of how you try harder when the chips are down, we came up with some ideas to put the chips down on you to help you but only if you want to. You don't have to do this . . . it will go away but who knows when . . . 13, 14, 15, 16 . . . the oldest person I know was 23.

Now, Stuart thought he had a "silly idea" but from my point of view, it wasn't so silly. I think you agreed with me. His idea was that the first time you wet your bed, you give 50 cents to your youngest brother, the next 50 cents to him and after that, to each of your best girlfriends. And we thought you might like to add a note such as this:

Dear friend,
Would you please accept this 50 cents to help me put myself under a bit of pressure to solve a problem I've got. I don't choose to tell you what it is but I will tell you when I solve it. Just accept this money and spend it and have a good time. Thank you very much for helping me.
Your friend, Hannah.

Now, Stuart said something which I thought showed he was a very concerned and thoughtful brother. He said he would return 50% of your 'gift money' after you go dry.

There undoubtedly will be slip-ups along the way. When you play basketball, for example, you would expect the other team to score the odd basket, wouldn't you?

In conclusion, I just want to remind you what you said near the end of our meeting. Hannah, you said this: "I saw there were more ways I could overcome it". Yes, you have enough ways to overcome it, should you strongly desire to do so. And if so, you will try as hard as you need to.

So, Hannah, it is time to go to sleep now, knowing you are ready and able to do what you need to do. You are ready to have those powerful thoughts in your mind that will tell you what to do when you need to do it. You need only listen to yourself and take your own advice. Your own advice is good advice . . . but just right now, you can let yourself go to sleep because you are ready and able to watch over your bladder during the night. You have had a lot of fun today because everyone thinks you are a 'fun-loving' person. Fun is fun but it sure can make you feel tired and sleepy. But you can feel reassured that you will try as hard as you need to. So my guess is that you can fall asleep and have a good sleep and wake up when you need to and do what you need to do. Until then, sweet dreams!

Summary

This is an approach to seemingly refractory bed-wetting problems that derives both from clinical experience and the conviction that young persons can develop knowledges of their own, even though they may well be revisions of adult advice. The approach depends on the distinction that can be drawn from the practice of this 'knowledge' when the young person is 'away' and dependence on other's knowledge(s) when 'at home'. The parental 'cover over' which has been instituted to take the pressure off the young person is replaced by the young person willingly putting pressure on themselves to put pressure on the problem (see also: Epston, 2006). Further meetings are organised, if necessary, around the predicted hazard of 'complacency' and the review of 'forgotten' knowledges. Audio-taped accounts are made available to the young person to summarise their knowledges and their motives for and intentions to employ them so that the young person can take 'their knowledge' home with them and deploy it at night or at will.

Reference
Epston, D. (2006) Putting pressure on yourself to put pressure on the problem, *Context*, 85, 2-5.

8

Rangi's story of honesty

David Epston & Rangi

Restorative justice now commands considerable interest here in New Zealand as well as elsewhere by way of mediation, conferencing, sentencing circles and community panels. The main focus here in New Zealand is on 'doing victims justice'.

This approach to shop-lifting focuses on the redeeming of one's reputation. This might be thought of as 'doing justice to one's moral identity' as an 'honest person'.

The following proceeds through 1) the avowal of honesty, 2) tests of hazard, 3) recruitment of an 'audience' to referee the moral significance of the undertaking of such tests, and 4) the preparation of the letter to the court.

Unlike many letters prepared for courts, this is not a psychological apology but rather something akin to a statement of Rangi's intentions and evidence to support it. The report is written with the clear intention that Rangi can be brought to the attention of the court for examination and cross-examination. I will review this matter in the conclusion of this chapter.

I answered the phone but no one replied to my 'Hello, David Epston speaking'. I hesitated before I hung up sensing there was someone there. 'Hello . . . hello', I repeated and then repeated myself again. In the background, on the other end, I could hear whispered encouragements that over time became strongly-worded exhortations. Finally, my caller reticently spoke aloud: 'My name is Rangi and you helped my friend, Mere, with her stealing'. 'Are you a friend of Mere?' I interjected to relieve her of the burden of the conversation. 'Yes, she is my foster sister'. I once again took the initiative: 'Well, any friend of Mere is a friend of mine!' Rangi replied, 'I didn't know there were people like you who could help people who were stealing'. 'You're right . . . they aren't too many of us around. Why don't we meet for honesty's sake! What do you say?' She agreed, but from some of the background commentary that I could overhear, her decision was not entirely voluntary.

We met soon after. Rangi was a 25-year-old Maori woman and a mother of two pre-schoolers. She was accompanied by her brother who made it quite clear that his role was merely supervisory by immediately falling asleep, or giving that appearance. 'Tell me', I asked, 'Are you all dishonest or do you have any honesty left?' She said she was 70% dishonest and 30% honest. She assured me that she could be honest 'sometimes'. 'What makes you want to go honest?' She went on to tell me that the previous week she had stolen from an auntie. 'What was different about that?' She informed me that this time she felt guilt whereas in the past, 'I felt good . . . and if I take from a shop, I feel no guilt'. 'How do you understand your guiltiness? What made it happen when it hadn't happened for some time now?' She said in reply: 'She was family and what I stole belonged to her daughter. My auntie won't trust me in her house again. They might think I am like my auntie Michelle who steals off everyone. They rubbish her. She has a no good future and is having a tough time'. 'What's different between you and your auntie Michelle?' Rangi replied: 'My mom helps me. Whenever she says not to do something, I don't
128

do it. Whenever she says anything, it seems to happen. A lot of people believe what she says'. I asked: 'What does your mother think about your stealing?' She replied, 'She's told me to stop and when she says things like that, we do it.' I then asked: 'Look before you go any further can you tell me the history of your stealing career?'

I will leave it until later for Rangi to tell her own story, but it is important to know at this point that the stealing incident mentioned in the above occurred soon after her fifth shop-lifting offence. She was given periodic detention after her fourth but had now become concerned that she would be sentenced to jail, something she had not seriously considered before. When I asked her who would be upset the most if she were to be jailed, number one on her list of thirteen relatives and friends was 'Dad'. 'He's an ex-thief who went to jail. He always told us not to do it. He doesn't know I have any offences. He'd get really angry if he did'. I enquired as to how each person listed might express their concern if she gave them the opportunity. I also learned that at one time, she had stopped stealing and although that was 'harder' than stealing, 'it's not impossible'.

'Does anything tell you that you may be ready to regain your honesty, an honesty you lost when you were 15 but regained for a period of time when you were eighteen and nineteen?' She thought long and hard and then became quite animated. 'What is it?' I enquired. 'I think everyone is watching me. The last time I got caught, someone was watching me. I got a lot more to think about now . . . my kids. I can go to jail'. We investigated this in some detail. I learned that she had formed the conviction that 'if I pinch something, it will bulge out of my jacket or bag. Before I couldn't care less, but now it's written on my face and my eyes are looking all around. I am trying hard to look innocent but looking guilty instead'. Further exploration led us to discover that she was 'sweating, feeling flushed, nervous, fidgeting hands, playing with my fingers and shaking slightly'. The investigation was so detailed, with me at times proposing these possibilities and at other times Rangi spontaneously came up with her own descriptions of her 'guiltiness'. I concluded with the question: 'Do you think your honesty is getting stronger than it was?' She assured me it had. 'Do you want to test your honesty further?' She again reassured me that she did.

She agreed to the following test, summarised in the letter I provided for her to take to the manager of the supermarket where she had recently offended. It was addressed to the manager whom she knew only too well from her apprehension.

Dear Mr Brown,
You may recall that this young woman was apprehended by you last Thursday and made a statement of her guilt at the Rochdale Police Station. As you may know, this is her fifth conviction. However, until now, she has regarded herself as invulnerable and always believed she would get off lightly. She now is becoming aware that this is no longer the case. Recently, she has been experiencing all the symptoms of guilt which is novel. She now believes that everyone is watching her. She is starting to contemplate

her future and that of her two young children if she is sentenced to jail. She now is becoming concerned that if she did steal, it would show e.g. bulge out of her jacket or bag, whereas in the past, she "didn't care". She is becoming increasingly concerned that "it's written on my face . . . I'm looking guilty, sweating, feeling flushed, nervous, my hands are fidgeting, playing with my fingers, and slightly shaking".

By my way of thinking, these are all signs of her guilt operating. She has come to me with a concern for her future and with the knowledge that I have successfully developed approaches to stealing problems. I am requesting your co-operation for this young woman to fully experience those sensations in the setting that seemed to have evoked them.

If you were willing to assist her, I would propose the following:

1) that you come to an agreement that she be allowed to shop at your store.

2) that you agree to a specified time for her to be in attendance at your store.

3) that she put up an agreed upon bond of money, which you will return to her at the end of a trial week.

4) that she will submit to being searched before leaving your premises.

5) that she agrees to pay for any stolen goods and will contribute that sum of money to your Staff Social Fund.

I believe that Rangi is really committed to break her stealing habit and I am afraid the best place to start is at the last place she offended. It is my experience that your co-operation in the above would provide some of the circumstances to allow her to challenge the direction her life is heading – a criminal career.

Feel free to phone me if the above needs further explanation.

Yours sincerely,

David Epston

We met a week later. She had phoned Mr Brown and asked if she could deliver a letter to him. He told her that 'there was no point'. Rangi then remonstrated with him: 'You've got a negative attitude towards me. Why don't you at least read the letter and see how you feel after reading it'. He then agreed to do so. Reflecting on this, she told me that 'taking the letter to the supermarket was the big thing . . . I was too ashamed . . . could I do it?. . but I just walked in'. She showed the manager the letter but he said he could not agree to it without seeking his supervisor's consent. She then rang me and we both decided against further action.

Still, Rangi told me that she 'felt better when I walked out. All the girls were staring at me. They knew about me'. She turned to them saying: 'Thank you very much!' and left. Her mother had accompanied her and Rangi turned to her outside the door concluding: 'Now, I can say I am not a thief! I am determined not to be a thief!' I asked: 'What has determined your determination to go honest?' She told me: 'Being honest to you and mum!'

However, her mother had gone even further recommending 'this is so good, let's do some more'. She then insisted she accompany Rangi to several other shops 'where I used to pinch'. Despite such tests of hazard, she told me: 'I was tempted

130

but I never touched. This is the first time in two and half years. I felt neat paying for everything. I admit to being tempted by small things though'. She had tested herself under her mother's supervision at a supermarket, a toy shop and a dairy. Summarising these tests, she proudly announced: 'The temptation is there but I think about what would happen to me. Straight to jail. That's what's stopping me'.

I asked if she was ready and able to further her honesty testing. She willingly agreed to send letters to the thirteen people concerned about her future, including her father. I provided her with a sample letter:

Dear Dad/Sister/Brother/Cousin/Auntie/Uncle, etc.:
You may not know that I have been stealing since I was fifteen years old. I have been arrested and convicted four times and recently, I was arrested for my fifth offence. For the first time in my life, I have started to seriously consider that I might get sentenced to jail and have to leave my children behind.
I have also started stealing from our very own family, much like Auntie Michelle, which told me that stealing was getting the better of me. I have decided to do something about it and have gone so far as to seek help from an anti-stealing professional.
I have started to feel guilt whereas before I thought stealing was a joke. I have been testing my honesty with my mother's help and have passed so far. There are more tests to go before I think I can say that I am an honest person and that you can return your trust to me. I will let you know when that time has come for me to declare myself an honest person in front of my whanau. (1)
Yours sincerely,
Rangi

We met a month later. We reviewed all her 'temptations' and how she had resisted them. On one occasion, she had gone so far as to 'pick up a little puzzle book and folded it and went to walk out. There was no one there. But instead I stopped. I don't know what made me do that but I stopped. I unfolded it and paid'. On another occasion there was another close call. 'I saw a little mirror at the chemists and picked it up and sort of hid it. I tucked it in my sleeve. But I just pulled it out and put it back on the shelf. When I did that, I told my girl-friend and she slapped my hand. That felt good. I don't pinch anymore. I even told one of the shop assistants – 'I almost pinched that little mirror but I put it back. I told her about coming to see you'. She said in reply: 'That was great! I just felt great. I tell everyone.'

We agreed that honesty was coming back in full force. I asked if she thought that three more months of honesty testing would be sufficient preparation for her to make her declaration. I had found out that her whanau customarily held a New Year's Eve party attended by over a hundred people. 'Would this be an appropriate occasion?' She thought so, although she would need her parents' permission. When she applied to them for their consent, they agreed that January 1st would be a good time for Rangi's announcement.

I was requested to write a court report. I submitted the following to Rangi to read and forward to her Probation Officer.

To Whom It May Concern,

I met Ms Rangi Arawa on three occasions (2/10, 10/10 and 21/11) in regard to her stealing career. It is my understanding that this is her fifth offence. I was interested to note that although Rangi thought it would be "hard" to stop stealing, she did not think it was "impossible". In fact, she reported, from my point of view, some extremely positive experiences: "I now think everyone is watching me. When I got caught, someone was watching me. I've got a lot more to think about . . . my kids . . . going to jail. Now if I pinch something, it will bulge out of my jacket or bag . . . before I didn't care. It's written on my face". She reported that she thought she was working so hard at looking innocent that she was looking guilty; she was sweating; she was flushed, fidgeting, playing with her fingers, and experiencing a slight tremor.

As is my custom, I asked her willingness to submit herself to some testing. I consider each test to have been quite demanding. Their tests were as follows: 1) she listed those people (13) who were concerned about her becoming a convicted criminal and then agreed to inform them all that she had decided to break her stealing habit; 2) She was to return to the site of her most recent offence carrying a letter I provided (see copy). I requested that a Mr Brown assist Ms Arawa in breaking her stealing habit by doing the following – i) that they make an agreement between them that she be allowed to shop at his store for one week, ii) that he agree on a specified time for her to be in attendance in his store, iii) that she put up an agreed upon bond of money which would be returned to her at the end the trial week, iv) that she would submit to his scrutiny before leaving the premises, and v) that she agreed to pay for any stolen goods plus donating the same sum of money to his Staff's Social Fund. Ms Arawa alleged that she rang him up and asked to deliver my letter to him. He finally agreed to read it. She said: "That was the big thing . . . I was too ashamed . . . could I do it?... I just walked in . . I showed him the letter . . . He said he couldn't agree to do it because he would have to go to a higher authority". She then phoned and discussed it with me and we decided to take no further action. From my point of view, the purpose of the test had been served. Ms Arawa described the experience as follows – "I felt better when I walked out . . . all the girls staring at me . . . they knew about me. I said: 'Thank you very much!' and walked out".

Such responses from a person with a stealing history are, in my experience, extremely promising. Each response indicates firstly that they may have taken responsibility for their actions and secondly, that they wish to redeem their reputation.

On the 21/11, Rangi was now able to test herself against temptation. She reported several incidents to me. She was tempted in a toy shop in Southern Park: "I saw a little book . . . a puzzle book. I picked it up and folded it and went to walk out – there was no one there. But instead I stopped . . . I don't know what made me stop but I stopped . . . I unfolded it and paid". She also was tempted at a chemist shop where she placed a prescription: "I saw a little mirror . . . I picked it up, hid it sort of . . . tucked it up my sleeve. I just pulled it out and put it back on the shelf". She reported that she felt "good" in the first incident. In regard to the second, she alleged that she told one of the shop assistants: "I almost pinched the little mirror. I put it back. I told her about coming to see you. She said: 'That was great!' I just felt great. I tell everybody".

She then agreed that it would be three months of honesty on New Year's Eve and I asked if she would be willing to make her announcement of her habit breaking to her family at their gathering. This was to be audio-taped. I had hoped this would be available for her court appearance but apparently this was accidentally erased by another family member. I believe it would be of interest to the Court to call one of those who were in attendance to testify to this.

I have worked with 50 plus stealers in my career and I base my impressions on that. It is my opinion that Ms Arawa has made a determined effort to break her stealing habit and has called upon her own and her family's resources to do so. Ms Arawa herself, however, has argued that the Court was "letting me off" in regard to her earlier offences. I would urge the Court not to be so lenient; on the other hand, I also request the Court take into account the efforts she has taken on her own behalf. To do so, she has had to face up to herself, her victims (Mr Brown and staff) and her family. If the verbatims of the meetings are sincere, which I believe them to be, it is my opinion that she has embarked upon a career of honesty although, of course, time will tell. I found Ms Arawa concerned about her future and she appears to me to have taken action(s) to ensure she has one.

Yours sincerely,
David Epston

She appeared in court and was given a sentence of Community Care for six months. To my amazement, the presiding judge sentenced her to 'do' her Community Care meeting with me. Rangi and I discussed this and decided that she write up the story of her stealing career and how she redeemed her reputation for honesty. She agreed that I would ask her questions and she would provide answers and together we would 'knit' her story out of this. It was agreed that this story could be distributed by either of us to anyone either working with those who were into stealing or stealers themselves. Rangi chose the title.

My stealing career

How did I take up my career? I watched other people do it. Gee, they got that for nothing. Then you copy. I could have done it though without copying anyone. Either way, I could have done it if I had run out of money. When I was 15, all I thought of was – "I like that . . . I'll try and steal it!". I saw a jacket I liked and got caught. I got a fine. The next time I started pinching was when things got rough for me four years later. I was separating from my husband. We were still together but he was spending all his money on drink. I had to pinch food. But I got greedy as far as clothes are concerned. But then I didn't need to do it anymore but I just kept going on. I liked nice things so I would steal them. Most times, I would make special trips to go out shop-lifting and it *got so that I was getting stuff I didn't really need. I would go out to steal anything, even it if was little. One time, I was even satisfied if I pinched a rubber from Woolworths. I was aware that it was becoming a habit but I didn't want to do anything about it because all I could think about was what I could get for nothing. I started to show off to other people, to add it all up to see what I had got away with but only to people I thieved with. When I was twenty, almost twenty-one, I was organising shop-lifting trips and doing deals with others. I used to even get baby-sitters or take the kids with me. That was what I mainly did with my life – shop-lifting. I'd go out especially to do a deal but it became greed. I thought I was neat because I got away with it or almost got caught. My attitude to shop-lifting was that it was neat to go out and do it and that you were in with everyone else and what you could make if you sold your stolen goods. When I got caught, I was scared until the Court case. But I kept getting fines and I thought I was being let off. I might have stopped sooner if I had Periodic Detention but I can't say for sure. I'm helping myself now.*

It was a big step asking Mere for David's phone number. I wasn't sure what to do or how to react. When I first came to see him, I thought I was going to lie to him. I didn't; I couldn't. It was this feeling I had. I felt relaxed – I couldn't lie. I opened up. I had big ideas of lying: "I'll lie to him that I wasn't going to pinch anymore". It was the tone of his voice – I felt relaxed. He joked and that but he was serious. He's not tense. He tells stories to help explain things better. I rang him after watching Mere. She told me how it had helped her. I didn't think there were people around who could help thieves. I didn't want to ask Mere for his phone number because I didn't want her to know about me.

I thought the tests were good. Otherwise I would not have done them. I had to face up to Mr Brown again which I didn't like doing. Not only that, the girls there wanted to tell me to get out. I thought it was a good idea because of the testing – it was only seven days after being in Court. Mr Brown couldn't do it unless he went to higher authorities. I then rang David. I think making the effort was the biggest thing.

I wrote letters to everyone – thirteen. David provided me with a sample letter. It talked about how I used to be a thief and I'm not now. The letter said would they like to come on New Year's Eve for me to announce I wasn't a thief anymore. At the party, everyone was drunk. Dan then told everyone that I had something to say. Some turned around then and said: "I didn't know you were a thief. I'm glad you don't pinch anymore. What about your kids? You'd go to jail". They kept talking about it when they were sober. Even now, I still talk about it. I don't feel embarrassed because the majority of them knew. I even told my ex-husband's family. Most of them didn't know. When I told my brother-in-law, he said: "I think that it's really good you're honest about it". They were a bit shocked but thought it was good I was being honest. I felt good telling everyone I had given up. You know how you get called up on the stage - you get shy – everyone is waiting for you to say something. It just came out; I was not telling them I was a thief but that I wasn't a thief. You feel sort of happy and excited when they say – "Good one!" "You're doing it for the kids!" You know they care about you by the remarks they make. My brother Jimmy said "Good one!" – and he's really close to me.

134

I just told Dad. He was shocked. He had not known about my stealing. He got wild and angry. He asked: "Why didn't you tell me?" "I was scared of your reaction", I told him. He was glad when he found out I was meeting David. My father had been in trouble and he didn't want me to go through all that. I was scared of getting a whack. He only talked to me about it though. He was worried about what was going to happen to my kids; he's a family-type man. But once he says things, then the subject is closed. And then you start to think about it.

I don't think I ever had any doubts about Rangi, but six months later, she referred her friend, Marama. I asked Marama if she had attended the New Year's Party when Rangi made her declaration. She told me about it in some detail: 'Everything went dead quiet. Rangi said that a light in her life had gone on and it was going to stay on. And she was going to do good for herself and her two children. She said that there were some words that really got to her and that these words had come true'. Marama also told me that Rangi had arranged to make similar claims to the identity as an honest person at a number of *maraes* (2) to which either her family or her ex-husband's family were genealogically connected.

By chance, I met Mere some many months later. She caught me up with Rangi and her new life, her remarriage and her moving to another city and she reassured me of her continuing honesty.

Conclusion

Some years later I was contacted on the same day by three agents of the Department of Criminal Justice, who had remembered Rangi and her shop-lifting. It seems that Dorothy had been shop-lifting for over 50 years but was now facing, after yet another conviction, like Rangi, a jail term. Given what this could have meant to her recent reconnection with her children and grand-children, who had severed their relationship with her for some years, she was ready to end her life. That explained the concern of the Department. The very first thing we did on meeting was read aloud Rangi's story. From that moment on, Dorothy abandoned the prospect of suicide for redeeming her reputation as an honest woman.

I am including the following 'letter to the court' by way of a conclusion to this chapter, as it perhaps is a significantly different genre for preparing such reports and needs to be highlighted. The report is admissible evidence, in this instance the moving audio-tapes with Dorothy providing a moment-by-moment account of her tests of hazard. Once again, this led to Dorothy being sentenced to community service.

To Whom It May Concern
I was referred Dorothy Dickinson by several representatives of the justice system. However, as is my practice, I insisted that Dorothy ring me and arrange her own appointment. I did not wish for her to be mandated. Admittedly, it took her some time and when she rang, she sounded very hesitant and extremely embarrassed at

disclosing her stealing to me. I was to find out that this was, in and of itself, something of a moral achievement on her part. We have met on two occasions – June 23 and July 25th; however, if you listen to the tape-recording which I have suggested her legal representative submit to the court for review, you will be aware that, in a manner of speaking, Dorothy decided "to take you shopping with me, David".

When we first met, I asked Dorothy this question (a question I was to learn later had a kind of psychological shock): "What are your thoughts and feelings about stealing?" At the time, she informed me that "I am unhappy about it…I hate it". But contrast that with "It never used to worry me..I never thought about it much. I didn't care about the consequences. It (stealing) may have started when I was about seven or eight. I can't remember. I had no fear. I had no respect".

When I enquired as to why she should start considering her stealing, and in addition worrying about it, she told me that she has been estranged from her children for the past five or six years (Nicola, now aged 36, James, now aged 35, and Rachel, now aged 33). This estrangement had to do with her leaving their father for another partner. Any reconciliation was complicated by her ex-husband's terminal illness and consequent death. It seems that Dorothy took the opportunity of the Millennium to initiate further attempts at reconciliation with each and every one of her children. She wrote them saying to the effect that "this is a new century…life goes on…I would still like to be your mother and friend". To her delight, she has been able to reconstitute her relationships with her adult children and initiate a grandmother relationship with a treasured grand-daughter.

Dorothy, it seems, now had a reason to fear for her reputation – "If they ever found out, I would lose them for good". In addition to that, what appears to be behind this 'change of heart' is Dorothy's commitment to herself "to win back my self-respect and be able to look at myself in the mirror". This recent offence and the likelihood of the disclosure of her offending to her adult children had the effect of "I've got a problem… It's something that I've got to stop...I am suicidal. If I am going to be like that, I would be better off dead".

It was at this point a probation officer contacted me to see if I was willing to meet with Dorothy. As you can see from the other document I suggested her legal representative present to the court (which is a chapter I am preparing for publication, as I have an interest in shop-lifting and stealing more generally – see Seymour, F. & Epston. D., An approach to childhood stealing with an evaluation of 45 cases in Epston, D., & White, M. (1992) Experience, Contradiction, Narrative and Imagination).

In fact, in discussion, Dorothy alleged that "I have stopped, but I'm not sure…" I could understand her uncertainty as her means to her cessation of stealing was not a very practicable one, e.g. no longer shopping. In addition, she did tell me that after our phone conversation proceeding our first meeting, she did return to a shop from which she had periodically stolen and "as soon as I saw the shop sign, I said to myself: 'danger, stay away'. My stomach started turning over. I felt like I was having palpitations. I was sweating around my hairline and my hands were fidgety". For me,

136

these are the signs of 'guilt' or in other words a 'conscience'. I asked her if she could consider the happiness she might feel if she were "to prove to yourself that you are an honest woman, honest grandmother and honest friend?" She concluded – "I have to do it or kill myself. I'd rather go to jail than worry about it (further stealing)". Recall that in the past Dorothy had no sensations that she could recall of worry, shame or guilt whatsoever. She could also recall an incident some three months ago where "I took some sweets and put them in my handbag and went to check out my groceries. I paid for it. I said to myself, 'you've got sweets in your purse – you are stealing'. I got them out and placed them with the rest of my stuff. I paid for them. I felt really good about it. I was able to take it out of my purse and walk out of the supermarket for the first time in years with everything I paid for". She acknowledged that to do so required 'conscious awareness' on her part.

I then enquired if she was prepared to take the next step. She assured me that "I am ready to do anything…I have to…I am sick of feeling sick". The next step was outlined in a letter to her and that was for her to have an 'honesty guard' (I suggested her friend, Jeanette) and she was to shop as usual and bring her 'conscious awareness' to bear and resist the by now well-engrained 50 year long temptation to steal. I suggested she take along with her photos of her granddaughter and before entering a shop to 'speak' to these photos. She should tell the photos of her granddaughter what contribution she wanted to make to her life as she grows up and that she could not do this "if I would be nervous about them finding out that I had a number of convictions for stealing, and that I had been stealing for so long that I couldn't really remember when it began and that I am unable to look at myself in the mirror".

The last paragraph of my first letter read as follows: "Dorothy, let me reassure you that I take this matter seriously and accept that it is a matter of life-or-death!"

Dorothy rang me acknowledging that she did not feel able to enlist Jeanette in this project, but requested that she metaphorically take me along and proposed the following: That she should go shopping with me as her 'security guard' and she would record her thoughts on audio-tape and bring them to me so I could listen to them. I accepted this as a reasonable alternative proposal. I guess there are grounds here for concern on the Court's part as she now wasn't having a 'friendly witness'. I will leave that up to the court to decide by listening to the audio-tape recorded during the various shopping 'trials of moral purpose'.

We met again recently (July 25th) at which time I listened to the tape. If Dorothy's accounts are reliable, she would appear to have 'broken' the stealing habit. In addition, she spoke of the significance of my enquiry – "How do you feel about your stealing?" She told me that "You were the first person who ever said that…It was a shock…I've never used the word 'stealing'.…It's a bad, bad word…shop-lifting was OK. It made me realise I'm a bad person, not just a petty shop-lifter. I've never admitted to anyone before I'm a stealer. It has to be stopped. It has to be healed. Previously I thought it was like speeding tickets. I should respect the Law".

Admittedly, the evidence you have before you has not been witnessed. However, I hope you will cross-examine her about the content of the audio-tape. Here she asserts the following: 1) *"I am now able to pick something up and put it down again",* 2) *"I have bought things I have never bought before", and 3) "I don't like stealing".* She proposes some accounts indicative of honesty: 1) *"I haven't stolen anything for three weeks…I can't remember the last time I went three weeks",* 2) *"I feel guilty…. It (honesty) now matters. I need to be able to hold my head up and look at people at eye level. I need to make some dramatic changes in my total being before I destroy myself",* 3) and most significantly, Dorothy reported that she went shopping in the company of her eldest daughter, Nicola, despite the fact that *"I feared that I would shoplift regardless",* and 4) she told of making amends by apologising to each shop saying, *"I'm sorry…I will never do that (stealing) again".*

What are we to believe here? I ask myself that question and I know that if Dorothy fabricated the tape, then in doing so she is betraying our relationship, one in which I have trusted her to tell me the truth with me as her witness. I base my trust in the conviction I have placed in Dorothy to become honest. In addition, Dorothy has discussed with me her willingness to go to jail, thinking that is what she deserves.

I leave it up to the court, which has more experience than I do to discern when the truth is being told and when it is not. If you listen to the audio-tape, I want you to know that it was specifically my request that it be entered as evidence and this was only discussed 'after' the fact of its production. I swear to that.

Yours sincerely,
David Epston

Reference
Seymour, F., & Epston, D. An approach to childhood stealing with an evaluation of 45 cases, in Epston, D. & White, M. (1992), *Experience, Contradiction, Narrative and Imagination – selected papers of David Epston & Michael White 1989-1991*, Dulwich Centre Publications

Notes
1. Whanau is a Maori word meaning 'extended family'.
2. Maraes is a Maori word meaning 'a culturally sacred space.

9

Community approaches – real and virtual – to stealing

David Epston and Fred Seymour

Genealogical source for this approach

My approach to the problem of childhood stealing owes a great deal to the intriguing ingenuity of my father and how he contrived the means for me to substantiate my claim as an honest young person. In addition, I had the added bonus of a conviction that endures to this day that I have a talent for finding lost objects.

I stole fifty cents from my father one day when I was about eight. Not too long afterwards, he came to me and said: 'Son, I've lost fifty cents. Would you help me find it?' I said nervously: 'Oh, yeh, yeh, I'll help you but how?' He advised me: 'Right, well, you go into the laundry room and look there and I'll go into my work shop and look there and then we will meet back in the kitchen and see if either of us has found the lost fifty cents.' So I followed his advice – of course unsuccessful in my search for the lost money – and returning from his quest, he asked: 'Did you find it?' I replied: 'No! Did you find it?' I was really hoping he would turn up some fifty cents or other and save me from admitting my theft. 'No,' he said and before I could confess, he eagerly proposed the next step: 'Right, okay, well you go and look around the back yard and I'll go and look in the front yard and we'll meet back in the kitchen.' Perhaps he noticed my dismay because he added: 'Don't worry. One of us has to find it somewhere!' So I went out to the back yard, dutifully searched and he went to the front and we met back in the kitchen with no better results than last time. He said: 'Right, well, you go to your bedroom and I'll go look in your mother's and mine and we'll meet back in the kitchen.' There nestled dead centre on my pillow was what looked like the very same coins adding up to the fifty cents that I had stolen. I was bewildered but immediately returned to the kitchen. He came back and asked: 'Did you find it?' I said with relief: 'Yeh, I did!' He accepted it appreciatively and thanked me more than once for finding the lost money.

The very next day, he came up to me and said: 'Hey, you won't believe this! I've done it again. I've lost some more money. Would you help me find it?' We went through the same sequence until finally he searched his bedroom and I was directed to my bedroom. Again fifty cents lay on my pillow. Returning to our meeting place, I proudly proclaimed: 'Look, I've found it!' He kindly replied: 'Look, you are getting so good at finding lost things, why don't you keep the money?' I replied: 'Well, thanks ... thanks.' This happened every day for the rest of the week as he seemed more and more upset with himself for his carelessness at the same time as more appreciative of me for my new-found talent at finding things. (1)

Perhaps what follows lacks some of the benefits of my father's approach to my childhood stealing, in that many who undergo it never gain the sense that I did that I was good at finding things. However, it did provide me with a prototype from which to fashion a 'community approach' that would not require from the parents concerned my father's humility and generosity of spirit. Many had run out of such sentiments by the time we met, having been 'robbed' on many occasions despite the chastisements, humiliations, recriminations, etc. they had instigated in order to have their children desist from stealing from them and others.

What I was searching for was some form of a 'ritual of re-grading' (2), by which a young person could undertake a purposeful act of moral redefinition that would repair the damage done to his/her identity by their stealing. Most families find it morally reprehensible to be robbed by their own children or to be known in their neighbourhood or school community as the parent of a 'stealer'. I was unconcerned with any kind of 'ritual of degradation' (Garfinkel, 1956), the purpose of which would be to first establish the young person's blameworthiness, to define him as the 'guilty party' and alter one's identity as a 'lower type or grade' of person. A judicial trial would be the prototype for such a ritual. On the other hand, I was unconvinced by the then prevalent psychoanalytic view that young people were 'stealing love'. If one followed the logic of such a premise, one would necessarily be required to respond by loving their stealer. I considered this far too much to ask those parents who had been robbed by their children.

In addition, I was concerned that this should take place before members of his/her community who had been convened for such a moral purpose. Here these young people could seek by specified means to re-identify themselves as competent members of their moral community. Recalling my father's 'finding tests', I conceived of 'honesty tests' as the means for the young person to publicly lay claim to a moral decision between two available identities e.g. an honest or a dishonest/stealing person. Secondly, as a result of asserting such a claim, the young person volunteers to engage in 'honesty tests' fully aware that they are putting themselves in moral jeopardy but not knowing exactly how.

The volunteering of the young person is premised on what I think of as 'understandings' that are agreed upon by all the parties to it before we proceed any further. Firstly, how the young person contends with such trials and tribulations e.g. honesty tests, constitutes a durable statement of who s/he is and can be e.g. an honest person. Secondly, the publication of the results of the 'tests' stands at the same time as a disavowal of his 'reputation' as a stealer, thief, or more generally, a dishonest and untrustworthy person.

This approach does not formally concern itself with the establishment of stealing or not although, in many instances, that had been established by the young person being 'caught red handed' either by the family, shop keeper, neighbour, school teacher, etc. Rather it settles for a far different concern: whether you are stealing or not, do people believe you are a stealer? Whether you are stealing or not, have you now got a reputation as a stealer? This by-passes at this point any requirement the young person might feel to defend their innocence and any requirement others/the therapist might feel to establish the young person's guilt. A community-wide moral dilemma is substituted for any quasi-legal concern for his/her guilt or innocence.

This approach as described in the following was contrived for referrals from the Youth Aid section of the New Zealand Police and as such these young people had 'long' records of stealing and had come to the notice of the police. An abridged approach was then developed for young people referred by their families for stealing which was often restricted (as far as the family knew) to themselves.

The moral dilemma

Are you interested in providing evidence to one and all that you not only can be but are an honest person or would you rather become known as a stealer?

The effects of both proposed moral statuses can now be surveyed without getting caught up in a debate of 'you did it' versus 'no, I didn't' nor any kind of pastoral (moral) care e.g. preaching. The effects on other relationships can be surveyed, especially those who allege they have been robbed by the stealer e.g. parents, siblings, grandparents, aunts, uncles, siblings, friends, class-mates, team-mates, neighbours, shop keepers, etc. Such questions can be addressed to absentees either indirectly or by means of internalised other enquiries (3).

Direct enquiries

- *If you become known as a stealer, do you see that having any effect on your son-father relationship? Son-mother relationship?*
- *Do you now find your mother watching out for you more than loving you?*
- *Have you found that your father no longer turns his back on you?*
- *Have your parents started keeping their valuables under lock and key in their own home?*
- *Do you think they have lost their sense of security when you are around?*
- *If you bankrupt your mother, are you concerned that you might bankrupt your son-mother relationship?*

Indirect or internalised other enquiries

- *(Indirect) Do you think Mr Jones (next door neighbour) still welcomes you to watch rugby at his place now that you robbed him of his DVD player?*
- *(Internalised Other) If Mr Jones were here today and I asked him this question: 'Is Johnny still welcome to watch rugby at your place now that he robbed you of your dvd player?', what do you guess he might say?*
- *(Indirect) Do you think your granny and grandpa are as willing to have you around and sleep over at their place as much now that they believe you are a stealer?*
- *(Internalised Other) If your granny was sitting right there (pointing to an untenanted chair) and I asked her this question: 'Is your grandson still welcome to sleep over at your and his grandpa's since you became convinced he is a stealer?', what do you guess she might say?*

The injustice of being known as a stealer

Inserted into this set of enquiries is what has turned out to be a very significant question, one which almost all stealers have answered strongly in the affirmative, even if they have seemed indifferent to any of the above mentioned.

- *Have you ever been accused of stealing something you hadn't even seen or thought about stealing?*

142

- *Does the fact that people believe you are a stealer give you a bad reputation? Stain your reputation?*
- *Are you finding that people don't want you to play with their kids, believing that about you?*
- *Do the neighbourhood shopkeepers not allow you on their premises, knowing your bad reputation?*

Similar enquiries can now forecast the 'injustice' of being known as a stealer for the young person's future:

- *Do you think it will be easy as a well known thief to get the kind of girlfriend you want?*
- *Do you think as a well known robber you will be able to get any other job than either in a gang or in a prison?*

The creation of compassion all round

Parents are most often and very obviously aggrieved, humiliated or outraged by public concern over their children's activities that have involved them with the police (Youth Aid) and a referral to a government or non-governmental agency. Such outrage is in addition to the insult they have often experienced to the moral integrity of their family by their child's stealing from them and others. It is hoped that the 'relative influence questions' structured around the effects of the problem (stealing) on the young person and the members of their family may have reunited them as sufferers rather than as perpetrator (stealer) and the victims (those who have been robbed). In a manner of speaking, they are on the 'same page'.

- *Ruth (mother), Jim (father) and Johnny, did you all find that it was hard to hold your head high at the Parent Teacher's Meeting?*
- *Ruth, Jim and Johnny, is it a concern to you at church that people will find out, if they haven't already, that your family is known as one that has a stealer within it?*
- *Ruth, Jim and Johnny, does it matter to you all what has happened to your family's reputation in the community?*

Another round of questions can further assist with this. These questions highlight the lure of ready cash and what it can be turned into and how this is a temptation for everyone, even if historically in the case of the parents.

To young person
- *Do you find the temptation of money sitting around just too hard to resist?*
- *Do you find that you can readily turn money into all the sweets you want? All the music downloads you can possibly listen to on your Ipod?*
- *Do you find that when you share out the stuff that the money buys you get the impression you have a lot more friends than you thought you had?*

143

• *Can money buy friends for very long? Or will you have to keep stealing to buy them? By the way, how much does a friend cost these days?*

To parents
• *When you were ten or eleven, did you ever give into the temptation to steal money from your parents, especially as it was just sitting there in your mother's purse or your father's pant's pockets?*

If either parent is willing to disclose any episodes of childhood stealing (after all, how many of us didn't steal something as a young child), this can lead to discussions around their histories of the moral evolution of their 'honesty'.
• *What made you turn away from the temptations of stealing – after all wasn't robbing your granny easy money?*
• *What did it matter to you that you and your parents were called into the headmaster's office and you owned up to having stolen Sally's lunch money, and not only returned that to her but went around to her home with your mum holding one hand and your dad holding the other and apologised to her and her parents?*

Another tactic I often follow in any instance of a parent or parents minimising the stealing e.g. 'it was only coins!', 'what does it matter, we share everything in our family', 'it was only twenty dollars! What's twenty dollars?' etc. I try to introduce the fiduciary advantages of the young person's thefts. How I go about this is to enquire as to the young person's allowance or weekly income. And then I ask an estimate of the family's weekly income. Say the young person receives $5.00 per week in an allowance and his family's weekly income $1,000.00 per week, I then suggest the real income of their child's thefts might well be considered as a factor of 200x. Here in the instance of the above mentioned $20.00, the child would have realised a relative weekly income of $4,000.00. When the parents consider the relativity of their incomes and their child's 'income', they often appreciate how significant such a theft might be to the financial well-being of such a young person.

The proposal for restoration of a moral reputation: a good versus a bad reputation:
I have an idea that has worked 60 or 70 times before today ... after I tell you about it, your mother and father might like to ring up some other parents of young people who 'turned honest' so they can check this 'honesty approach' out in case they have any concerns or doubts about it.

I regularly recruit family members, after their child's reputation as an honest person has been restored, as consultants (Epston and White, 1992) to other parents 'who will come after you and perhaps feel as desperate as you did four or five months ago about Billy's future'. I have never known a family who did not willingly offer their services in anticipation to another family.

144

To the young person:

I can't give you the phone numbers of people your age yet. Why? They undoubtedly will tell you about the 'honesty tests' that you will have to pass to prove beyond a shadow of a doubt that you not only can be but are an honest person. That would mean you weren't being tested. A bit like a test at school where the teacher gives you the test questions a week before. That wouldn't prove anything, would it? Now if you are still interested, I will provide you with some names and phone numbers after your honesty party celebration if you want to compare notes with them.

But let me assure you of this – I have a way that will prove beyond a shadow of a doubt that either you are a stealer or that you now have proved to one and all that you can be and are an honest person.

Here, if the interview has avoided so far the contentiousness of an adversarial discussion premised on parental blame and young person denial and at the same time created some compassion for all concerned, the next stage flows naturally.

Do you trust me on that one? If you do, please indicate that in front of everyone by shaking my hand and giving me consent to go on.

I then formally have the young person say after me, breaking the 'consent' up into easily remembered sections:

I, Johnny Hopewell, hereby give consent to David Epston to provide my parents with information as to how they might 'honesty test' me. I do not expect to know how they will test me; otherwise, it wouldn't be a test and it wouldn't prove anything to anybody.

I offer a last minute confession but without any concern if the young person demurs.

Now that you have decided to prove to one and all that you can be and are honest, are there any accusations of your stealing that you would like to admit to so you can get it off your chest?

Often at this point, the young person will take advantage of this opportunity to admit to contested incidents. This is always very encouraging of a very favourable outcome.

Community honesty meetings

The first matter of concern is who should be invited. A guest list is reached by interviewing parents, siblings, or anyone else in attendance e.g. police officer, along with the honesty candidate around this enquiry:

145

- *Who cares whether you become a stealer or an honest person?* (to the young person)
- *Who cares whether your son/this young man proves to them he is a stealer or an honest person?* (to parents, siblings or Youth Aid police officer)

The most obvious candidates are as follows:
(1) Siblings, grand parents, aunts/uncles, cousins, and other extended family;
(2) Neighbours and family friends;
(3) School-teachers/class mate;
(4) Soccer coach/team-mates; and
(5) Boy scout leader/girl guide leader/fellow guides/cubs/scouts;

The least likely candidates but equally significant are as follows: victims of the young person's thefts, which of course could be any of the above, but in particular shop keepers. Often here, the young person or family members are reluctant to issue such invitations to shop keepers e.g. 'I am too embarrassed...I wouldn't know what to say', that I will offer to issue invitations to such people on their behalf. I secure a pretty good attendance from aggrieved shop keepers, who often relish such an opportunity to confront those who have robbed them under such circumstances.

The meeting place is a matter for discussion e.g. family home, grand parent's home, church or community centre hall or agency depending on the number of attendees and the family's preferences.

Invitations

Invitations are collectively prepared and written but most typically I interview the young person and write down his/her responses. Obviously I will change the pronouns. For example, Johnny replies to my enquiry: 'Johnny, are you sick and tired of having a reputation of being a stealer?' Johnny replied: 'Yah, I am sick and tired of having a reputation as a stealer.' I write down his words while uttering them aloud. I would revise that to: 'John is sick and tired of having a reputation as a stealer'. If I have a computer nearby, I type this up and read it back to Johnny asking – 'Do you confirm that, Johnny? Or do you want me to change anything to suit you better?'

Here is a facsimile invitation (I have inserted in brackets the questions that produced the text of the letter):

As you may well know (Do you think many people know about your stealing reputation, John?) *I have got a very bad reputation* (What is your reputation, John?) *over the last year* (How long has it taken for you to receive such a reputation?) *as a stealer.* (Do you know what people call you? Has anyone said it out loud to your face?)

Now people are even accusing me of things I have never done which isn't fair. (John, you mentioned that people are accusing you of stealing things you haven't stolen.

146

Do you think that is fair or not?). *But when I think about it, I don't blame you.* (John, if you were to think about it, would you blame them for having the idea that you are a stealer?) *Also I am sad that I cannot play at some of my friends' homes.* (John, your mother mentioned that your friends' parents won't allow you to sleep over there or play there any more. Do you care about that or would you rather not have friends like Jimmy any more?) *Grandpa, I am sorry that you won't take me out fishing with you on your boat anymore after I robbed your wallet.* (John, is it a good thing or a bad thing from your point of view that your granddad won't take you out fishing anymore? Why is it a bad thing?)

David Epston, a family therapist, has told me that it is possible for me to prove to you I am and can be honest. (How does that sound to you, John? Do you want to add anything or take anything away from that?) *I do not expect you to believe me if I just say I will not steal anymore.* (John, have you found that most people don't believe what you say anymore?) *I am willing to go through the 'honesty tests' that my parents will set for me with David's help.* (John, are you willing for your parents to honesty test you? Do you give me consent to tell them how to do it?)

I and my parents wish to invite you to join us at (time/place) *for my honesty meeting. I know some of you still care and love me, even though I have robbed you.* (John, of those who you have robbed, who do you guess still love you and care about your future?) *Those of you I have robbed that don't know me so well, I want to prove to you that I deserve to get my reputation as an honest person back.* (What do you want to prove to those whom you robbed but who don't really know you that well as a person?) *I am hoping that then I can buy stuff in your shops again?* (Why do you want them to know you are an honest person?)

This document is then produced and the young person signs the following postscript:

All the words in this letter are mine and they were the answers to questions David asked me. And he typed them up into this letter.
Signed by:
Witnessed by: Both parents formally sign
at The Family Therapy Centre on the day of 2007 in Auckland, New Zealand....

In some cases, I request that the parents take this document to a lawyer and have Johnny swear it as an oath and sign an Affidavit to indicate the seriousness of the matter and its legal significance.

Although his parents go along with him to the Post Office, he is expected to post all the letters himself. If it is more convenient, contact is made by telephone or email, although here parents closely supervise the phone calls or emails. It is commonplace for such young people to quite quickly receive encouraging and congratulatory replies from family and family friends.

From an older brother and sister:

We would like to come to your Honesty Party. It is nice to see that you are grown up enough to be able to determine which is right and wrong, as a lot of people find this very hard to do. We both think that if you try hard enough, you will be able to pass your honesty tests with ease, but remember, you still have to work hard. (Epston, 1989, p. 106)

From a family friend:

Thank you for your letter. It is really good to hear of someone like you, trying to make a big step forward in their life. Some people seem to have it easy – they never seem to get into trouble, and everyone likes them, and they seem happy with themselves. Other people go through big struggles within themselves, and feel that nobody likes them – but when they win the struggle they turn out to be the best people of all. So I'm pleased to hear that you're sensible enough and grown-up enough to struggle with dishonesty. I look forward to hearing how you get on; and hope to be able to come to your Honesty Party (Ibid, p.106)

Honesty Community Meetings: Real or Virtual

a) Real Community Meetings

Seating arrangements:

The young person and I sit at the centre of a circle and we merely rotate in our chairs to face each of the attendees as they speak.

Two rounds of enquiries

Starting with his most intimate relationships, e.g. parents, grandparents, caretakers and then passing from person to person who are encircling us, this question is asked in some form or other:

What will you feel/think/do if John keeps stealing? If his stealing is contested? What will you feel/think/do if John keeps his reputation as a stealer?

John, is requested to face each speaker, although admittedly it is difficult at times for him to look the speaker in the eye. In this round, the tone of voice of the speakers is often gloomy and their comments are dismal as you might expect. The young person is often visibly upset and will cry. There is no attempt to console him at this point.

Straightaway, the next round is initiated following the same route around the circle.

What will you do/think/feel if John passes his honesty tests with flying colours and proves to one and all that not only can he be honest but that he is honest?

Not surprisingly, the mood lifts as those most concerned people e.g parents, grandparents, uncles and aunts, etc. prophesy about how they will respond to him after he substantiates his claim to be an honest person. It is often the case that some of the victims of the young person's stealing spontaneously propose some 'restorative justice' projects. For example, a neighbour as well as close family friends might suggest:

Johnny, if you pass all those honesty tests, you might like to give me a hand on some concreting work and some other jobs I've got planned. And since the dvd you stole was worth about $200.00 and I think you are well worth $10.00 an hour, if you work twenty hours, I figure you and I are quits. And then you can come over and watch All Black Tests at my place like you used to with your dad. How does that sound to you, son?

Honesty Tests and Testing

I explain only in principle the honesty tests to this young man's moral community informing them why I cannot tell them the specific details, *e.g.. If he knew any more than merely agreeing to risk being honesty tested, it couldn't or wouldn't be a test at all. For example, if a young person at school knew all the answers to tests at school and passed with an A average, it wouldn't prove anything at all about how much they had learned so far.*

Re-performance of the Consent Procedure

John and I stand before his moral community and re-perform the consent procedure:

We keep a firm handshake *(John, do you trust me enough to tell your parents how to set the tests which will prove beyond a shadow of a doubt whether you are a stealer or an honest person?)*

If he consents to this, I ask him to repeat after me:

I, John Hopewell, give David Epston consent to tell my parents how to set honesty tests without me knowing how they are going to do it. If I knew when and how I was going to be tested, it wouldn't be a test at all and you wouldn't believe I deserve to be known as an honest person when I pass them.

Before I and his parents go off together in order to inform them how to set the tests, all the attendees are advised of the following:

Each and every one of you will be informed either by letter, email or telephone call immediately after each test. If it is a letter/email or phone call, it will read or Johnny will inform you that – 'I passed or failed my honesty test today . . . Johnny'.

The meeting is then ended by my assisting Johnny to thank everyone for coming along 'to help me prove to myself and to you that I not only can be but I am an honest person'. The parents reiterate their thanks to the attendees as they see fit.

Chairs are left vacant for those unable to attend, but who would have wished to have been there if their circumstances were different e.g. siblings overseas, grandparents out of city or on some occasions, if this is considered

149

appropriate protocol, the deceased. We would have contacted these people ahead of time with the same two rounds of enquiries and Johnny's mother or father would be asked to be their proxy and read out their answers to the two enquiries. Still, John would be asked to 'face' the chair left for them. Or I would have interviewed the deceased in an internalised other format ahead of time (3):

If Johnny's grandfather knew all about what has been going on over the last three years regarding how John has lost his reputation as an honest person, but on the other hand, he knew too that Johnny now wishes to regain it and is willing to undergo honesty testing, what do you guess Johnny's grandfather would say if we asked him the following questions?

And here I would go through the two enquiries and record his putative answers in writing and have, say, his daughter/Johnny's mother elaborate on his reasons for his opinions. I would then ask Johnny's mother if she would like to read his (her deceased father's) thoughts 'from beyond the grave' aloud or would she like someone else to do it for her.

Post-meeting Meeting with Parents
Parents are provided with careful instructions immediately after the real community meeting regarding the setting of the tests. Specific examples are provided. And they are advised to set tests at as many sites of stealing as they can judiciously arrange. I would have got some information as to who believed Johnny had stolen from there and where. Most of the young people who warranted such a community approach had stolen from almost everyone they possibly could have e.g. parents, siblings, uncles and aunts, family friends, school teachers and class-mates, shops and by breaking and entering neighbourhood homes.

Car and Groceries
Here is an example I might use:
Say you just got home from going to the supermarket and you had a car-full of bags of groceries. Count out a specific sum of change and leave it in that depression by the gear shift, knowing Johnny would have to see the money if he were to get the groceries. Lock the car so only Johnny and no one else possibly could have taken the money. Then give him the car keys requesting he bring in the groceries. The moment you observe all the groceries have been brought in, say: 'Johnny, you have been honesty tested! Let's go to the car and see if you passed or failed.'

Staying Over at Grandmothers
Here is another example:
Can you arrange with your mother when Johnny stays over at her place to phone you at a convenient time. Tell her to leave a five dollar note right beside the telephone. Then tell her you will phone back in a few minutes. Your mother answers the phone and

then goes to find Johnny to tell him you wish to speak with him. You talk to him about picking him up for a few minutes, knowing all the time he will be tempted by the five dollar note which is conspicuously right in front of him. When your mother hears the phone call end, she enters the room saying: 'Johnny, you have been honesty tested. Let's see if you passed or failed?' Then she is to phone you and put Johnny on to let you know the results of the honesty test. Any number of other examples are provided if the parents suspect they need detailed advice. However, most parents soon get the gist of an 'honesty test' and can contrive their own.

When they learn how scrupulously the tests are set and how rigorous they are, their opinion is sought as to the 'limits of the tests':

(1) How many tests do you think Johnny would need to pass before you could be convinced of his honesty?
(2) And over what period of time?'

The usual conclusion of such discussions is ten tests over a three to six week period. Others then call for a kind of moral cease-fire for several more months to be sure and seek the right to spontaneously honesty test if they have any suspicions that their young person has reverted to stealing. All this is negotiable but the important thing is that their decisions are communicated clearly and fairly to Johnny (3). Accordingly, they now can propose a date for the honesty celebration/party and attendees are asked to put this into their social calendars in Johnny's first communication (e.g. phone, letter, email) to them announcing his pass/failure on his first test.

It is important that the moral jeopardy that the 'testing' implicates is fairly conducted. Care should also be taken that Johnny could be the only one to be tempted. That means that considerable care is taken in planning the test and that the test is decided almost immediately. In one family in whom I did not place full responsibility for administering the tests, when I rang to find out the results of a test, having gone over the setting of that particular test with them, they replied that they couldn't say as their daughter hadn't stolen the test yet. It seemed they were determined to leave it there long enough so she did. In some families, other siblings have either joined in the stealing or are stealing under the cover of their well known stealing sibling. This must be guarded against.

Parents have my phone number for emergency discussions if they run out of ideas for tests. This has rarely been called upon. People don't have too much trouble getting the idea and implementing it to their satisfaction.

Honesty Party/Celebration

When the time comes as agreed with the family, this is organised with John at its centre. Once again, I assist Johnny in writing the invitations. This is done in a very similar fashion to the invitation letter to the honesty meeting.

Dear x:

Although I want you to know that I was tempted to steal on two or three occasions, I didn't. I was honest instead and left the money where it was. Mum and Dad say that I can now start thinking of myself as an honest person but that I still have to prove it to you because you weren't there at the tests.

I want you to hear my honesty speech at my honesty party at (time and place) and have a piece of my honesty cake that mum said she would teach me to bake. If you are interested, it will have chocolate icing and 'honesty is the best policy' ('honest as the day is long' or 'Johnny ... an honest person') on the top of it in silver balls.

There will be food and drinks so don't bring anything but yourself. This is my way and my parents' way to say thank you for helping me to prove I am honest to you. And for the fact that you were willing to give me a chance, even though I had robbed some of you.

Yours for Honesty,

Signed by:

Witnessed by: parents

The Honesty Party is convened as a pleasant social gathering with its highlight the young person's honesty speech. Those who cannot attend often send letters that are read aloud by Johnny or other family members. At the appropriate time, all the party goers are called together for Johnny to read his honesty speech aloud. Once again, we (his parents and I) often get together to help him with this ahead of time, if he requests such assistance. But as often as not, although offered, this is turned down by the young person. The young person is happy to assume full responsibility for his/her speech-writing. Afterwards, many of the attendees pass their congratulations on to him through hugs or hand-shaking. Attending such meetings have been some of my most pleasant memories.

Here is a transcript of twelve year old Jimmy's honesty speech, which due to the fact that his revered grandparents were unable to attend, it was audio-taped so they could have their own copy:

"You are all aware of what I did earlier in the year. I now realise what I did was not only stupid but selfish. And I am sorry for that. Since the incident occurred, my mum, dad, John (sibling) and I went to see Mr Epston, a family therapist who suggested I go on a programme of honesty testing which you all know about. I did this to prove to myself and my family that I could withstand the temptation of taking things that did not belong to me. I have now successfully completed the tests which have led to this gathering. I'd like to thank you all for your support which has certainly made me realise what I did was wrong. And in the future, I will be earning my money and not taking it." (Freeman et al., 1997, p. 142)

b) Virtual Community Meeting

I regularly convene virtual meetings in instances of minor stealing, especially where the stealing has remained within the family – as far as they know. In fact, the vast majority of the meetings, apart from referrals from Youth Aid/Auckland Police where the incidence of stealing was widespread and had come to the notice of the Police, are virtual. The real community meetings are rare and exceptional. The meeting is still conducted as in the above but with family members in attendance only, much like a typical family therapy meeting. As you can imagine, it would be impossible to ensure attendances at community meetings if people knew that the parents' eight year old daughter had stolen ten dollars from her mother's purse or her father's pants' pockets. In virtual meetings, we still make up the list of 'all those who care if you become a stealer or an honest person' and may proceed through the same set of enquiries but here by way of internalised other enquiry.

If Mrs Staples, your school teacher who said in your last school report that you she loves teaching you, were with us now and I asked her this question (insert question such as – 'What would you think if you knew Julie was stealing money from her mum and dad?' What do guess she would say? If your sister, who is at University in Dunedin, were here and I asked her this question............, what do you guess she would say, etc.).

In chapter one I describe in far less detail than in the above how I proceeded 'virtually' with Hayden's restoration of his moral identity as an honest person through the virtuality of his 'community' e.g. those people who loved him and cared about him so they were concerned whether he regained his reputation as an 'honest person' at the same time as disavowing his reputation as a stealer.

Failure
I have had remarkable success with this approach and can recall only one young man, aged fifteen with very limited intellectual abilities, who ever failed a test. And I might add he successfully completed the rest of the nine tests. I suspect being required to contact each and every member of his virtual community to report his failure on his inaugural honesty test was a very salutary experience. However, in two notable instances, this approach was not taken up by the young person. Both were in their mid to late teens and were running professional stealing-on-commission rings. For example, you would apply with a request say for a certain brand of Ipod and an 'agent' on a commission would be assigned to steal it for you. Both young men were particularly brazen about their criminal prowess. They were running very successful financial operations with many part-time agents. In fact, they were more than satisfied with the reputation they had acquired in their school communities. Some parents have been unable to co-operate because of their illegal activities and for the fact that their young people were more or less black-mailing them. In either case, they felt too morally compromised to seek a moral community to oversee the honesty testing of their young person. However, in one instance, I was required to do a home visit early one evening by a family to find myself in a most unusual set of circumstances. The

young person, aged thirteen, who had been caught 'red handed' stealing from his mother's purse sat between his parents in their living room. In every corner of the room stood a very sinister, brawny man with his arms crossed across his chest with the most intimidating demeanor. Strangely, they were never introduced to me but they remained on guard throughout our meeting. I proceeded as normally as did the young man and his family. He passed his honesty tests with flying colours. I always wondered about this and my curiosity was only satisfied some years later when I was teaching a workshop on this approach to stealing to a special training day for Youth Aid/Police people. In conversation, I was to learn that this family was a notorious criminal family and had been so for several generations. Nonetheless, they obviously could not countenance a young person stealing from his family.

Research

In the mid to late 1980s, this approach, or discrete elements of it, were researched, providing evaluation support for its efficacy. Certainly at the time, there were surprisingly few studies of clinical procedures reported in the literature. The two research studies were developed and conducted at The Leslie Centre, then a family counselling agency sponsored by the Presbyterian Social Services Association in Auckland, New Zealand. In 1984, almost 5% of the families seen had nominated stealing among the presenting problems. Indeed, the incidence of stealing, as discovered in community surveys, is surprisingly high – between 4% and 10% (MacFarlane, Allen & Hozick, 1962). A further concern, according to Patterson (1982) was that the parents of stealers were the most difficult to engage in treatment, seldom carried out their assignments and furthermore, had a high drop out rate.

The Leslie Centre approach, an evaluation of 45 cases of reported stealing over a three year period, was based on many of the ideas in this chapter, most significantly the 'regrading' to an honest person with a good reputation (p. 188). For almost half the children, stealing was the sole presenting problem. For others, presenting problems typically included oppositional behaviours such as aggression and non-compliance with family rules. For half, parents reported the stealing having persisted for two years or longer. Parents' detection of stealing was estimated as being daily for a small number, and for 42% detection occurred at least weekly. 80% of the young people were under the age of 13.

Therapist reports indicated that the vast majority of families (84%) were successfully engaged in therapy, which lasted an average of 3.3 sessions, which would have also included therapeutic letters and progress phone calls. At follow-up telephone calls six to twelve months later, 81% of the 45 children were reported by parents to not be stealing at all, or that stealing was 'substantially reduced'. We believe that this re-grading approach as substantiated by 'honesty testing' led to a very high rate of engagement compared to researchers at the Oregon Social Learning Center (Patterson, 1982).

Fred Seymour supervised and was the therapist for Michael Hamilton's MA thesis (Auckland University), once again at Leslie Centre, in which the then Department of Social Welfare was approached for young people who were considered to be intractable stealers, several of whom were in care of the Department. A rigorous single case design involving four families, with more sophisticated and detailed measurement procedures, revealed similarly strong positive results. The follow-up measurements were as incontrovertible as could be imagined. Six months after the completion of the honesty testing, sums of money were displayed in the surrounds of the young person and rejected by him/her.

Conclusion

This community approach to stealing, in both forms – complete and abridged – has been very successful in at least 40 occasions other than the 45 cases reviewed at Leslie Centre over the years. As far as I know, the only failures were those mentioned above. For a notoriously difficult problem to 'treat', the results, both researched and anecdotal, highly recommend such an approach.

Footnotes
1. This is slightly altered from Epston, 1989, p. 117.
2. Ibid, p. 115.
3. Internalised other questioning is a format for enquiry developed in the first instance by David Epston and developed by Karl Tomm (Department of Psychiatry, University of Calgary). See references below.

References
Burnham, J. (2000) Internalised other interviewing: evaluating and enhancing empathy, in *Clinical Psychology Forum*, Volume 140, 16-20, (published by the British Psychological Society, Special Edition – Working with Adults and Children.)

Epston, D. (1989), Guest Address: Australian Family Therapy Conference, Brisbane, Sept. 24, 1983, in *Collected Papers*, Dulwich Centre Publications, Adelaide, South Australia.

Epston, D. & White, M. (1992), Consulting Your Consultants: The documentation of alternative knowledges, in *Experience, Contradiction, Narrative and Imagination*, Dulwich Centre Publications, Adelaide, 11-26.

Epston, D. (1993) Internalised Other Questioning with Couples: the New Zealand Version, in *Catching Up with David Epston, A Collection of Narrative Practice-based Papers, 1991-1996*, Dulwich Centre Publications, Adelaide, 61-68.

Freeman, J., Epston, D. & Lobovits, D. (1997), *Playful Approaches to Serious Problems: Narrative Therapy With Children and Their Families*, W.W. Norton, New York.

Garfinkel, H. (1956), Conditions of successful degradation ceremonies, *American Journal of Sociology*, 61: 420-424.

Hamilton, M.G. (1984) *Evaluation of a treatment for stealing in young people*, Masters Thesis in Psychology, Auckland University.

Hurley, D. (2006) Internalised other interviewing of children exposed to violence, *Journal of Systemic Therapies*, Vol. 25, No. 2, 50-63.

Lysack, M. & Bakhtin, M. (2002) From monologue to dialogue in families: Internalised other interviewing, in *Sciences Pastorales/Pastoral Sciences* 21 (2) 219-244.

McFarlane, J.W., Allen, L. & Honzik, M (1962) *A Developmental Study of Behavior Problems of Normal Children Between 21 Months and 14 Years*, Berkeley: University of California Press.

Nylund, D. & Corsiglia, V. (1993) Internalised other questioning with men who are violent,

Dulwich Centre Newsletter 2, 29-34.

Paré, D. (2001) Crossing the divide: the therapeutic use of internalised other interviewing, Journal of Activities in Psychotherapy Practice Vol. 1(4) 21-28.

Patterson, G (1982) A Social Learning Approach to Family Intervention: Coercive Family Process, Castalia, Eugene, Oregon.

Seymour, F.W. & Epston, D. (1992), An approach to childhood stealing with evaluation of 45 Cases, in Epston, D. & White, M., Experience, Contradiction, Narrative and Imagination, Dulwich Centre Publications, Adelaide, 189-206.

Tomm, K., Hoyt, M. & Madigan, S. (1998) Honoring our internalised others and the ethics of caring: A conversation with Karl Tomm. Chapter in The Handbook of Constructive Therapies, edited by Michael Hoyt, 198-218, (republished in Interviews with Brief Therapy Experts, 2001, Brunner-Rutledge, Philadelphia, 245-264)

10

Your brother's/sister's keeper: an approach to intractable sibling conflicts

David Epston

I had been meeting with Judy, aged 35, over several months relating to an important career decision. Just before she had reached her conclusion, she asked if she could bring in to our conversations a matter of great concern to her – the disputatious and violent relationship between her sons, Justin, aged 13, and Adam, aged ten. Judy was parenting them on her own. She said her sons fought over absolutely everything and the fighting alternated between verbal abuse and physical violence. Absolutely everything was contested. The front seat of the car was one such bone of contention and most proposed outings had to be called off. Both sons resented the air the other breathed. I asked – 'Do you suspect each would prefer the other to stop breathing altogether?' She replied with horror – 'Yes, I think you are right!' I asked – 'How do you experience witnessing your sons violate and abuse each other?' Her reply was painful to hear: 'It is like a knife being driven into my chest!' She estimated that on a school day, they were spending approximately an hour a day strangling one another and that weekends were 'far worse'.

In a vain attempt to initiate a discussion of any alternative ways of their relating, I asked if she could ever recall times of co-operation, play or even distant respect. If there was such a history, Judy's despair blinded her to it. She could not remember them ever being in each other's company without it leading to an inevitable fracas. To pursue such enquiries at this time could have seemed disrespectful, given Judy's sobbing. She had consulted relatives, friends and professionals and the summary of their advice was that 'brothers will be brothers!' or 'they will grow out of it!'. Such reassurances were now wearing very thin.

When I asked about her current approach, she told me she felt helpless to intervene and suspected that any attempts on her part to adjudicate their competing claims and accusations only made matters worse for everyone. I then asked Judy two pertinent questions: 'If you learned that Adam or Justin was being subjected to the selfsame violation or verbal abuse at the hands of a class-mate, what would your reaction be?' 'If you chose to call a spade a spade, would what passes for their brotherhood more aptly be called hatred?' She rallied from her despair in reaction to my first question, saying she would in no way permit this and would demand an urgent remedy. To my next question, she ruefully acknowledged that hatred was certainly a more apt description of their relationship than brotherhood.

She then requested I meet them the first chance I had. I suggested the following as a prelude to such a meeting where we could all discuss the kind of brotherhood her sons might prefer. I then asked if she was able to predict when her sons were warming up to blatant screaming or hitting. She laughed and assured me that that would be no problem whatsoever. I then asked if her sons had ever included weaponry in their disputes. She said this was not the case.

I then proposed the following 'experiment in brotherhood' and discussed it at length with Judy. In my own mind, I was thinking – how could either son choose any alternative way of relating without any experience of it? Wouldn't it be folly to propose 'good brotherhood' to combatants? Couldn't I assume that many others had made a case for the moral virtue of brotherhood? After talking the 'experiment in brotherhood' through, Judy came to the conclusion that, if nothing else, it offered her some relief from refereeing their disputes and offered Adam and Justin a chance to 'try out' their brotherhood, admittedly under contrived and unusual circumstances.

By rendering this through an externalising conversation, the practice of the relationship ('the brotherhood') becomes elevated as an 'object' for everyone's consideration and metaphorically, 'pulls' all the participants (Judy, Adam, and Justin) back to a reflexive position. From here, each of them could reflect on the ways of practicing their relationship of 'brotherhood'. At the same time, it calls into question her sons' adversarial practices and her refereeing and replaces it with a dilemma – to salvage their brotherhood from hatred or knowingly practice hatred and violence against each other.

The 'experiment' was as follows. However, it is important to note that this is not issued prescriptively but constructed through conversation and questions, e.g. Does such an idea fit with what you consider right and proper? Would you feel comfortable undertaking this? etc. The intervention would probably more aptly be termed an invitation to intervene rather than an intervention proper.

'Go home tonight and tell your sons that you are sick and tired of refereeing their fights and no matter how hard you try, it only seems to make matters worse for them as well as for you. Instead, you have decided to retire from refereeing and substitute a 'family noise level' for that. Tell them that you will let them know when they are approaching the 'family noise level' by saying – 'Look, you guys, you are getting close to the 'family noise level' and leave them. Should they desist, which you tell me is unlikely, congratulate them for starting to win back their brotherhood from violence and hatred. However, if they persist as you expect they will, return and say only – 'You are now 'next' to the 'family noise level' and once again depart. But, if they keep it up as you expect, return and conclude: 'You have broken the 'family noise level' and I insist that you leave this house immediately by the side door'. I would imagine they will ask how or when they might regain entry. Say something to the effect – 'After you practise your brotherhood rather than hatefulness'. Undoubtedly, they will be curious as to how they might achieve this. Tell them that when both of them finds something to appreciate about the other and convinces you that they have done so 'sincerely', they can return home. You will probably have to suggest some ways of appreciating their brother. 'Look, you guys, I doubt if you will have any idea as to how to go about this, given hatred has featured so largely in your relationship for as long as I can remember. So let me give you an example or two. 'Adam, you might ask Justin what he did at school today that he is proud of and then you can try to convince me that you sincerely appreciate him for whatever it is he tells you about'. You might say something like this: 'Mum, Justin scored his team's first goal and he deserves to be proud of himself for that. And I am proud of him too because I am his brother!' Judy, you may like to use this opportunity to give them

159

extra practice by saying: 'Why should you be proud of him for that? Why couldn't you say that even though he scored a goal, he is still a loser!' Then close the door, saying: 'You are getting closer to brother-appreciation!' When they knock on the door again, say: 'Well?' If Adam were to say something like – 'Justin should be proud of himself because he plays on defence and defensive players don't score many goals', acknowledge Adam for his appreciation of his brother. Judy, both sons must convince you of their appreciation of the other before they both can bring 'their brotherhood' back under your roof. If either complains, which is very likely, say: 'How can Justin learn to appreciate you if he cannot ask you appreciating questions. This is a matter for your brotherhood, not for you or for him alone!' And certainly not for me! So see you guys later! You are getting warm!' Wish them – 'Good brotherhood!' and close the door behind you. When you are convinced of the sincerity of their mutual appreciation, thank them for starting to win back their relationship from violence and hatefulness and that you will no longer referee, except to save a limb or a life.

Several weeks later when we met for the first time, both the physical and verbal violence had abated and brother-appreciation was on the increase, thanks to the 'experiment in brotherhood'. In fact, Judy had not had any occasion to send them out of doors, although she had been prepared to do so rain or shine. Perhaps, the improvement was merely due to the parent/referee's reduced involvement in the 'life' of the problem. Adam and Justin could no longer press their charges against their brother without anyone to hear them and adjudicate. If only the parent experienced some temporary relief, that in and of itself would have been a satisfactory outcome. Here, however, Adam and Justin were relieved and this permitted me to ask them questions about their preferences in terms of hatred versus brotherhood and the practices associated with each of those competing versions. It also allows for the therapist to be excluded from a senior adjudicator role and to stand alongside the concerned parties comparing and contrasting different ways of relating and their respective effects.

The following is a summary faithful to the 'flow' of the interview. The sequence of therapist queries/family member replies will become very obvious to you. For example, 'It seems that your brotherhood has gotten pretty hateful and hurtful over the years' summarises their answers to questions relating to the history of a violent and hateful brotherhood and when it got 'pretty hateful and hurtful'. You will also notice that the therapist does not advocate for 'niceness' at this point or moralise. I was guessing that that had been tried 'ad nauseum'.

Dear Justin and Adam:
I really enjoyed meeting you guys the other day. Here is the letter I promised to send you.
It seems that your brotherhood had gotten pretty hateful and hurtful over the years. Your mum described your brotherhood as if each of you was fighting to get more than your half of her. She talked about how she had to divide herself down the middle with each of you having 50% and forbidding the other to get 1% more.

However, you both thought you might like to improve your brotherhood and here you two were for the very first time in history in strong agreement. Each of you thought you might like a 50% improvement in brotherhood. As of the other day, Justin, you thought you had a 15% good brotherhood and an 85% bad brotherhood; Adam, you thought you had a 20-ish % good brotherhood and an 80-ish% bad brotherhood. Your mum had this to say: "They are now getting along 30% of the time – 20% tolerance and 50% fighting".

When I asked you what the highlights of your brotherhood had been, Justin, you thought when you were living overseas. And that had something to do with separate bedrooms. Adam, you thought it was when you were younger: "I looked up to Justin when I was younger. He started leaving me out of things so I started hating him".

Both of you were of the opinion that when your mother no longer refereed your fights but instead, sent you outside to appreciate each other and not let you back in until you had proven to her satisfaction that you could appreciate each other was a good idea. Justin, when I asked what effects this was having on you, your mother and your brother, this is what you had to say:

"I was getting more attention from mum of a good kind. I am borrowing things from Adam. I get help from Adam with my spelling and he is good at solving some kinds of problems. And he is now shrieking less."

Adam, this is what you had to say:

"There is less thumping, shouting and abuse. I can play with his gameboy. We play together more and are starting to respect each other. We share things more. We can now be in the same room and not fight or shout."

I started wondering to myself that all this must be leading to something or other. And that either or both of you must be practising your brotherhood differently. And sure enough I was right! Justin, you said that "instead of giving Adam an order", you hit upon the idea of saying: "I think you might do something" instead of saying "you should do it". To my surprise, you found this quite easy to do, even though you had been doing the other for so long now. And Adam, you said that you don't "take orders from bossy people", although you said you could accept them from "caring people".

Justin and Adam, your brotherhood seems to be heading in a good brotherhood direction after all these years. And due to that, there is quite a bit of room for improvement. You each agreed on a 50% improvement.

Justin and Adam, do you think you have gone as far as you want to go with your 'brotherhood'?

Adam and Justin, do you think you will keep going in a good 'brotherhood' direction? Or do you think your mum should referee and have you fight over her?

Do you imagine a loving mother would appreciate being her sons' battleground?

I look forward to meeting you both again with your mum so I can learn what you have done to your brotherhood: pushed it in a good direction or let it slip back into hatred.

Yours sincerely,
David

We met two months later after the summer vacation. They had pursued the 'good direction' and increased the 'good brotherhood ' by 20% at the expense of hatred. Justin had come up with the idea of 'nice weeks' and Adam had decided to go along with it, although it took him five days of careful consideration before he agreed to the plan. The former 'bone of contention' – sitting in the front seat – was resolved by her sons even before a car trip was planned. Judy had not known about this scheme until the meeting but considered it a 'nice surprise'. This assisted Judy to comprehend an incident earlier that week: 'When your cousin hit you, Adam, Justin hit him back to protect you. In the old days, Justin may have encouraged his cousin to thrash him.' Judy summed up the new state of affairs as 'a dramatic improvement – the fighting has gone way down . . . it's now 50% good stuff and only 20% fighting . . .'

Out of the generative excitement of this conversation, Judy came up with a new twist on the 'experiment': 'If you start fighting at McDonalds, I will walk off and leave you to it and say – 'Come over here when you have finished the game!' - or I will walk out of sight and tell you where to find me. That would mean I wouldn't get involved or embarrassed.' Adam thought that his mother would no longer 'feel like a referee or a battleground'. They both agreed to pursue this direction, concluding that 'life is better in general!'

I have used such 'experiments in brother/sisterhood' numerous times over the years with continuing success. It has never failed to make an appreciable difference. Most recently, a 12-year-old brother refused to allow his two younger brothers to speak in his presence because such 'noise gives me a headache'. His parents had accommodated to this until they rented a cottage over summer and invited many of their family friends to join them on site. However, each and every visitor decamped after a day or two because they could not bear the relationships between their friends' children. This gave the parents cause for reconsideration of the 'boys will be boys' conclusion they had reached. Of course, the eldest brother had to tolerate his brothers' speaking if he was to learn how to appreciate them. The parents were so concerned that they bought three camp-stretchers and a portable toilet for the garage as they expected their sons would spend a great deal of time outside the house. Once again, the portable toilet was returned unused to its vendor.

On only one occasion, the older of two sisters, aged 12, continued to declare a strong preference for hatred and her conviction that her ten-year-old sister should commit suicide. This was in spite of the cessation of bickering and taunting after the 'experiment' was instituted. However, now the parents refused to concede to this and came up with a range of ways to intervene.

Genealogy

This approach owes everything to meeting early in my career with Jean and her two sons, Dean, aged 13 and Ronny, aged 15. Jean had first attended National Women's Hospital after her general practitioner had observed 'anorexia' or a dramatic but sustained weight loss. The hospital then referred her family to me for reasons that were obvious as soon as I met everyone. From what Jean told me, her marriage to the boys' father had been 'a nightmare' because of his drinking. It had reached such a state that she had initiated a divorce six months earlier. Apparently Ronny's father had promised he would take him with him when he left as they had always had a very strong bond. Although this may have been his intention, he rarely showed up again and if he did, he was too inebriated for Ronny to wish to travel in his car. Ronny, however, was so disappointed that he went to the garage where his father sometimes worked as a panel beater and took a five pound hammer to his car such that it was beyond anyone's panel beating. In addition, the school had become concerned about Ronny's seemingly inexplicable rages that on one occasion led him to pull a door off its hinges, despite the staff's attempts to restrain him.

As Jean told me of the above, it fleshed out the skeleton of the tableau I saw before me. Dean sat up close to his mother, preening himself like a prince and chuckling at any mention of Ronny's misdemeanours. Ronny sat as far away as he could get from Dean with his legs astride with his head dropping towards his knees as if his team had just lost a major sporting event. The 'anorexia' got explained quickly. Apparently, Jean spent every night running from Ronny's room to which he was confined back to Dean's room where he had to be confined. These confinements were the only way she could contain the potential violence between them. Whenever she reached one son's room, the screaming from the other side of the house recalled her there and she would have to sprint from room to room until her sons' bedtimes gave her some relief. I had never witnessed two siblings so at odds with each other. I was young in my career and I was simply at a loss as to what to say or recommend. I am convinced that whatever I did do was utterly inconsequential to what happened.

I was hardly looking forward to meeting these two young men and their harried mother. To my amazement, the brothers entered the room alongside each other and Jean followed them beaming with pride. I wondered what in the world had happened and immediately set about finding out. And what I found out was the germ of an idea for the 'brothering intervention' I proposed in the above.

Although Jean didn't have a theory she was putting into practice, she did have a very cogent idea. If she could find a way to have them depend on each other (and not her and her father), they might find out that they could count on each other when the chips were down. Jean finally came up with an idea. She knew her sons wanted to go to the zoo, which was a good eight mile or so walk from their home. She suggested they do so but when the day arrived, she feigned illness but provided them with the time to catch the bus there and the time to catch it home. Purposefully, the time she gave them for the return ride was a half hour late for the last bus of the day from the zoo. However, she did give them a city map just in case they got lost. Well, apparently, they had to co-operate over the map-reading or they would have not been able to find their way home. It took some hours and to her delight, through their 'trials and tribulations', her sons had forged some sort of co-operative brotherhood. I can recall to this day the amazement I experienced hearing about this.

It was not long after that Bartholomew (Bart), aged 16, strode ahead of everyone else into my room. He had a large black eye. Aeneas, aged 17, followed in his footsteps with a matching black eye. Their parents, George and May, arrived a few moments later. They spoke of the constant fighting between their sons which was becoming violent. Bart then took the floor and looking towards his parents and away from Aeneas, declared that he was disowning his brother. Aeneas looked bewildered and wondered out loud: 'Why is he like this? I don't understand. I don't understand. I want to understand him'. May became sad and said all this must have to do with the fact that she hadn't been able to hold either of her sons when they were young. When I asked her how that had come about, she spoke of the needs of her eldest daughter, aged 23, who lived in a wheelchair and the demands of nursing their second son who died of leukaemia when he was ten. We talked at some length of these sad and difficult times.

Aeneas came alive when George and May spoke of their disappointments that Bart wished to leave school. Bart asserted his rights to lead his own life. Aeneas became visibly upset every time his parents and his brother reached an impasse in this heated debate and would reproach his brother. By the same token, the parents expressed concern that Aeneas was so driven to achieve at school that he 'was becoming a nervous wreck' and 'does nothing but study from morning to night'.

We discussed Aeneas' retirement from what everyone agreed was a 'loving mistake' he had made – the need he felt to 'parent' Bart at the same time as causing them no concern by being 'so good'. His parents discharged him from any further responsibility but in respect for his care and concern, that they hadn't quite realised, they proposed a two month winding down period before making his retirement official. Everyone felt it would take that long for Bart to be comfortable with Aeneas as his brother and the same was expected to be the case for Aeneas.

This was the first attempt at re-working Jean's great idea. I proposed a 'family noise level' and a similar set of warnings (see above). But what followed was a far more literal rendering of Jean's ingenious scheme.

'If they persist, order them out of your home in separate directions. Inform them that they need some brothering practice. When it is convenient to you as parents, provide them with this golden opportunity to rediscover their brothering. You can do this by taking them blindfolded by car to a place some distance away that they don't know. Provide them with a map. Divide their route back home or to a designated pick up point in half and give one half to each son. This means they will have to co-operate if they are to find there way back/or to the pick up point. During this journey, Bart, you will have plenty of opportunity to find out if Aneas is your father or your brother. Aeneas, you will have plenty

164

of opportunity to find out who your brother really is and what he wants for his future.

We met a month later. George and May were not required to provide Bart and Aeneas with any brothering practice. In fact, there had not been any incidents whatsoever. Aeneas said they 'had words' on two occasions but he had 'just walked away'. Bart and his parents had negotiated a settlement for his future that satisfied everyone, i.e. an accountancy cadetship. Aeneas too had decided on future, i.e. surveying. Bart had been taking Aeneas out and 'showing me how to have a good time'. He was discovering that Bart was 'a very good brother to me'.

Sibling Crisis Intervention

Meeting the Crummer family was to leave an indelible impression on me relating to siblings. I suppose if you were to think about it, the circumstances leading to the addition of children to their family were so unusual as to almost predict the dire outcome. The circumstances were as follows – Jill and Jim were in their late and early thirties. They had discovered their infertility soon after they were married some nine years previously. They decided to pursue adoption along with fertility treatments. They had to wait five very long years before they were able to adopt Nathan several days after his birth. From their accounts, Nathan was a 'beautiful baby' and had certainly retained that winsomeness when I met him, aged three and a half. He had such an appealing look that only the hard-hearted could turn down a request from him. Although they had put in an application for another adoption, they had been warned that this was very, very unlikely. For that reason, they had put their application out of their minds accepting Nathan as their only child.

However, two-and-a-half years after they had lodged their application, they were taken aback by a phone call from the then Department of Social Welfare advising them that an adoption had broken down after two months and if they wished, they could have another son. The only catch was that they had to make up their minds within seven days. According to Jill and Jim, they were confused by the offer but on the sixth day, they came to the conclusion to adopt. They wondered about the consequences for their relationship with Nathan at the time but felt that if they turned down this opportunity, they would never have another.

They breathed a sigh of relief when Nathan took little notice of his newly adopted brother. But that was not to last for long. When Jason started to make his way beyond his cradle or his parents' arms, Nathan would attack him – hitting, scratching and biting. He showed no restraint whatsoever. When Jason started to walk and was very unsteady on his feet, Nathan now posed the gravest risk to him, charging him on every occasion and knocking him over. Jill had to mount constant surveillance of her two sons and despite this, the only safe place for Jason was behind closed doors. They hoped time would heal but Nathan's fury increased the more Jason was making his impression on the 'world'. Despite her admonitions never to touch Jason while she was bathing him, on one occasion when Jill left momentarily to get some safety pins, she returned to find Nathan holding his brother's head under water. This was more than she could bear and she consulted her family doctor who prescribed tranquilisers. She now really had to struggle to be as vigilant as was required by the risk to Jason's well-being.

I remember meeting Jim and Jill. Jim was apologetic he couldn't make a stronger contribution to Nathan's surveillance but he had just started up as an electrical contractor and had to work long hours to make ends meet. The summer holidays were coming up with the the Crummers planning to join their extended family camping at a beach. Jill's desperation was palpable. I had to come up with something to tide them over. They considered the matter to be if not life-threatening at least limb-threatening for Jason. Having observed Nathan's unconcealable hatred, I couldn't help but agree with them.

This is the letter I wrote them prior to their departure for their month-long summer holidays. What I tried to do in the following was firstly to develop a set of alternative descriptions (big boy(s) in contrast to little boy(s)) and the behaviours that distinguished one from the other and secondly, to assist Nathan to describe himself as 'big boy', thirdly, to distinguish himself from Jason by enacting 'big boyness' and fourthly, to contrive circumstances for 'big boyness' to be exhibited alongside the display of 'little boyness' and fifthly, to signify 'big boyness' as the absence of competitive displays followed by 'scaffolded' exhibitions of Nathan's helping, caring, or mentoring of Jason. By 'scaffolded' exhibitions, the parents were required to actively shape and coach such activities.

Here is the sequence I provided for the Crummer family just before my/their holidays.

Sequence

1) *Jim and Jill, can you sit down together and decide on and define 'what big boys do'. For example, 'big boys play outside ... big boys play with their friends'. Stress either what concerns you about Nathan or what defines Jason's behaviour as 'what little boys do'. For example, 'big boys run outside and play: little boys like Jason have to stay inside and crawl'.*

2) *Educate Nathan by defining, if he is not presently doing so, how you are seeking for him to behave or better yet, acknowledging his current behaviours as 'big boy'. Do so in contrast to Jason's actions. Encourage him to repeat 'what big boys do' and have him distinguish that from 'what little boys like Jason do'. Every time he identifies what he has done as 'big boyness', give him a star to affix to his 'big boy's chart'. Place this chart on the refrigerator. Jim, on returning home from your work, ask Jill and Nathan – 'Have you been a big boy today? Jill, has Nathan been a big boy today?' After which, you all retire to scrutinise his 'big boy" chart which should decide the matter. Jim, you might like to encourage Nathan to describe to you any instances of 'big boyness', once again contrasting them to 'little boyness = Jason'. Be generous in your approbation of his 'big boyness'. Feel free to make a fuss over Nathan's 'bigness'. For the first few days, you may have to help him get some stars*

to provide him with a 'taste' for 'big boyness'. Jill: 'Jim, Nathan just about played by himself when I had to feed Jason. He really is getting 'big'. I think he should get a star. What do you think?' Jim: 'Well, how 'big' do you think you were Nathan?' Seek for Nathan to advocate for his own 'bigness'.

3) Be on the lookout for any signs of 'big boyness'. Every time, you notice such a sign, state as clearly as you can how your description of 'big boyness' was related to an action he took (or refrained from taking). Before he affixes the star to his chart, have him reiterate his claim to 'big boyness'. For example, what did you do again that makes you a 'big boy'? Was giving Jason some cake 'big boy' or 'little boy'? Do you like being a 'big boy'? Do you think Jason likes being a 'little boy'?

4) After two weeks, initiate separate playtimes. For example, Jill, announce you are planning a 'little boy's playtime' with Jason, say for five minutes. Jim, draw this to Nathan's attention just before you take him off for some rewarding 'big boy' pursuit, e.g. going to the shops, playing ball outside. Later on in the day, reverse with Jill engaging in a 'big boy's playtime' with Jim taking Jason off so he cannot intrude. Jim and Jill, do everything you can to draw Nathan's attention to the reverse.

5) After another week, add a 'family playtime'. Monitor Nathan's behaviour in relation to Justin closely, approving what you consider to distinguish him as 'being a big boy' and what doesn't as 'not being a big boy'. Feel free to make a fuss over any instances of what you perceive to be 'big boyness'.

6) After another week, time out (two minutes in the bathroom) for any aggressive act against Jason. Say: 'you are having a time out. Hitting Jason is not 'being a big boy'. We like it when you are a 'big boy' and he is a 'little boy'. You might expect a struggle here.

This could succeed much quicker if you can enlist the co-operation of your extended family. Try to explain to them the problem and your 'programme' of distinguishing 'big boyness' from 'little boyness'. Please don't shield them from your concerns. Although Nathan's problem is very common, it has certainly been aggravated by Jason's unanticipated arrival which provided no time for anyone to prepare for it, least of all, Nathan.

Yours sincerely,

David

We met soon after we all returned from our summer holidays. With Nathan standing by, Jill considered the results 'amazing really because even before the Christmas holidays, it had started to get better. 'Nathan's really a big boy now; he helps little boys now; he even plays nicely with them outside. He lets Jason play with his blocks sometimes, don't you? And some of your toys.' He plays really nicely now. That 'big boy' idea took about a month, but it really worked. It took away the competition. And it wasn't hard to do; it was a lot easier to do than other things we had been trying to do. It wasn't only him, we, especially me, had to take a really hard look at ourselves. Then it was hard for me to realise that I had been giving in to him. I've only just been able to admit that to myself but he had twisted me round his little finger and I can see that now. However, to start with, it was really hard because the problem was still really bad but as things went on and as we did more things, it sort of came all of a sudden'.

This was just in the nick of time because over Christmas Jim and Jill learned they were pregnant. I thought I might hear from them again in some months time but I didn't. I phoned them about the time they were expecting the birth and everyone was very excited and ready for a newcomer to their family. In fact, Nathan was so excited about this prospect that he had taken to asking if he could look down his mother's throat to see the baby.

Summary

I have used this intervention on many occasions over the years with immediate and positive results. In saying that, I am not proposing that all rancour immediately abates. Rather, an alternative to sibling-hatred is established as a prospect for everyone's consideration. Of course, there may have to be special considerations when arms or implements are taken up in course of these disputes. The hatred engendered by such disputes can be very dangerous.

11

Anti-anorexia/anti-bulimia: bearing witness

David Epston

Based on the Plenary Address to the Australian & New Zealand Academy of Eating Disorders, Adelaide, 20th October 2006

Let me begin by telling the most remarkable anti-anorexic story I have ever heard, although I have heard my fair share.

I first met Larissa after anorexia had denied her the capacity to read while in early secondary school. This of course baffled her family and the professional specialists they consulted. This finally meant that she had no other option but to leave school behind when she turned 15. Given her seeming inability to read, beauty college seemed a career option where that might go unnoticed.

I first met her around this time and when we got talking, it seemed anorexia had entered her life when she was merely six, at the time her father abandoned her mother for another partner with three children and her soon to be born brother in a foreign country. Their circumstances were such that her mother had to apply for welfare for them to survive. Sophie was determined to be good, which soon turned into being Perfect as good never seemed good enough.

On graduation from beauty college, Larissa went overseas herself and to her surprise, she became very distinguished in her craft while still in her teens. In fact, she was even assisting making up such luminaries as super-model Naomi Campbell. She emailed me with a revelation – that she has seen through Perfection because she, in fact, was the very agent of its fabrication. And because of this knowledge, she found it hard to believe in Perfection any longer. I replied with considerable interest and enquired if she had ever met a happy model. In fact, aside from one whom she had met on her very first day 'at work', she spoke of their despair and wretchedness.

She fled back to New Zealand determined to abandon such a life, but had to turn away the blandishments and financial inducements of agents from movie productions flown out to lure her back overseas. Instead she decided to lead a life of her own design, earning her living waitressing.

I can't recall how long it was before she travelled to Europe, but this time with quite a different mission than her first overseas trip. She had determined to become a pilgrim and walk the two thousand kilometres long 'camino' to Santiago de Compostella in north west Spain. Pilgrims from all over Europe had walked this route, from France over the Pyrenees, since the ninth century to the tomb of St. James at the church there. In fact, by the tenth century, 25% of the then population of Europe would have made this pilgrimage at least once in their life-time.

Larissa proposed to be such a wayfarer, like so many before her, travelling on her own with only that which she could carry for the necessary two to three months. As not too long before anorexia had tried to take her life, I am sure her loved ones were concerned for her well-being as she passed along the camino to her destination.

Now twenty-two, Larissa sent me this email some time after she returned to New Zealand, after first circulating it around the Anti-Anorexia League. (1)

Yes, I had many interesting experiences on the Santiago de Compostella pilgrimage. It is as if one lives a whole life in two thousand kilometres. One day, about a week to the end, I decided to take a detour. I went into the Valley of 'Silencio' (silence). It was a very lonely and difficult route, but incredibly beautiful involving lots of mountains and very unclear paths. So I spent almost two days in silence.

It was when I was climbing the last big ascent for the day that anorexia appeared. It has always felt like a voice within me but this time it wasn't. It was the same voice but this time it was outside of me, so completely foreign. At first, I felt afraid. I remember stopping, sitting down and thinking: "My gosh, what's going on?" But anorexia was talking such complete nonsense that it actually made me laugh.

It was as if along the road, I had faced so much and seen so much beauty and kindness. Indeed, I had seen all aspects – the wonderful and not so wonderful things about myself and others that somehow I had changed. There was a deep sense of peace about who I am and was. So when anorexia tried the usual one-sided conversation, I couldn't quite understand it. It was as if it were speaking a foreign language. It was as if all its support had been stripped away. Surrounded by no one and miles of nature, I could see it for what it is. It really looked ridiculous out there on a mountain top surrounded by scenery that stops you for its sheer beauty! I think I finally had evidence from my own experiences of the pilgrimage that had made any claim by anorexia discountable. To be free of the world, especially the one that anorexia inhabits, helps one to see clearly. It was as if I was actually was seeing for the first time!

You will recall how anorexia had denied Larissa her ability to read which had obliged her to leave high school when she turned fifteen. Now she applied for a provisional admission to a BSc programme at a New Zealand university, was accepted and completed her first year with a straight A average. At that time, I enquired:

'Larissa, do you have any idea how your pilgrimage turned anorexia, in a manner of speaking, from the inside out?' She replied: 'I think the pilgrimage didn't so much turn anorexia from the inside out; more I think I had filled myself up with me so that anorexia's echo couldn't make it seem that it came from inside me. I feel as though the world is so full of noise and confusion that we miss the original voice of anorexia and are just unlucky that we are empty enough to hear that echo reverberate inside us as if it were part of us.'

I couldn't refrain from asking: 'Has anorexia ever tried to reinstitute itself inside your life and disrupt what you refer to as your 'deep sense of peace'?' She answered: 'Yes, being in the world means that there are always times when anorexia reappears. I guess over time I have just grown more and more aware of that and now know what works for me to move past such moments.'

Several months ago (2007), Larissa emailed to inform me she had graduated on an accelerated academic programme with such distinction that she had been offered the very generous national scholarship for two years' study towards her further studies.

Does this make you wonder as much it intrigued me ever since? How a young woman, almost at the end of such a venerable moral ordeal, should confront anorexia, which had demoralised her and 'caused me to feel that I wanted to die' for so long, and find that it spoke a foreign language? Or had Larissa taught herself another language of the self by which 'I was fully, intensely and whole-heartedly engaging in my life'? What relevance did reading her story and then enquiring about it have on me? It told me where I should stand – as a witness. I will have a great deal more to say about that as this chapter unfolds.

Introduction

When I was first informed of the grievous suffering exacted by anorexia on the lives of insiders (2) through their own utterances, I committed myself to find ways to adequately recognise and acknowledge this. And by the same token, how could I find ways for them to speak the unspeakable as a 'knowledge' that there suffering had endowed them with? And that in the same breath could testify as a kind of 'witnessing text'?

Let me explain 'witnessing text' with reference to the writing of an Australian literary scholar, Ross Chambers: Untimely Interventions: Aids Writing, Testimonial and the Rhetoric of Haunting' (2004). The title had caught my eye for its juxtaposition of 'testimonial' and 'haunting'. Why you might ask? For so long, I have felt myself to be a haunted man, haunted by the suffering through torture and other degradations I have been informed of by insiders.

Here are some comments of Rachel, aged 19, to my colleague, Rick Maisel, in Berkeley, California in 1994:

It's like a concentration camp and you kind of stumble in to it and you don't know and all of a sudden you're in there. It's hard. When you realise you're really there and when you actually realise you don't want to be in there and you want to get out, you don't need someone telling you – 'Rachel, you are too skinny...you can't dance!' It makes you feel worse. It just takes so much to finally try and get out of something like that. (Maisel, 1994)

I have heard time and time again statements from eleven and twelve-year-old school girls referencing anorexia as evil or the devil himself. You will agree, I'm sure, that neither are commonplace terms of reference in school girl culture.

Back to Rachel and Rick:

Rick: *One thing that would be helpful to me would be to know what role, if any, I played in facilitating your fightback against anorexia?*

Rachel: *You played a big role. Before, I kept thinking about it as my problem. It was my fault. It was something I did. But the way you talk about it as it being something outside my body, like almost another being that kind of comes over you and takes control of your life. It's a lot easier to deal with that way because you can then stop blaming yourself...*

Rick: *When you stop blaming yourself, what do you start doing?*

172

Rachel: *You can see it. Everything kind of gets clearer. You can actually look at it for what it really is.*
Rick: *What is your understanding of what anorexia is?*
Rachel: *It's like the devil...it's this controlling...murdering thing. It just wants to kill.*

In the same way, Rachel stumbled in to the concentration camp of anorexia, I stumbled upon so many others who had similarly stumbled in to the same abominable predicament.

As far as I know, the first known insider account of the experience of anorexia was that of the pseudononymous Ellen West, some of whose comments were included in Ludwig Binswanger's clinical treatise first published in 1944 in Berlin, Germany (Binswanger, 1944). Let us listen carefully to her words:

I don't understand myself at all. It is terrible not to understand yourself. I confront myself as a strange person. I am afraid of myself; I am afraid of the feelings to which I am defencelessly delivered over to every minute. That is the horrible part of my life; I am filled with dread. Existence is only torture. Life has become a prison camp. I long to be violated. And indeed I do violence to myself every hour of the day.

If she could have spoken anti-anorexically, she may well have proclaimed her conscientious objection to anorexia rather than such a confession of her supposed offences:

Anorexia, would I regain understanding myself – and those feelings of fear and dread – if I could link you and the anti-semitism of the emerging Third Reich? Are you inciting my torture with its violations and violence as a prelude to my genocide in the Holocaust which is to come? If I were to do so, would I be risking my life in your regime?

Naomi Wolf, another Jewish insider, writes without any apparent reference to Ellen West's disparaging testimony fifty years or more later. But in *The Beauty Myth* (Wolf, 1991) she locates the cultural circumstances that foster anorexia:

Anorexia is a prison camp. One fifth of well-educated American young women are inmates. To be anorexic or bulimic is to be a political prisoner. Women must claim anorexia as political damage done to us by a social order that considers our destruction insignificant because of what we are – less. We should identify it as Jews identify the Death Camps, as homosexuals identify AIDS, as a disgrace that is not our own but that of an inhumane social order.

Let's go back to Ross Chambers:

In responding to what he refers to as 'cultural obscenities' (p. 32), he asks the very serious question which resonated with my concerns over the past fifteen years or more:

How can one 'point' to an X that the culture's conventional means of representation are powerless, or at least inadequate, to reference, precisely because it lies at a point of supposedly distant extremity with respect to what the culture regards as its normal concerns (xv).

He replies to his own query:
Witnessing is an ethical practice that seeks to inculcate a sense of shared responsibility that it is only too easy – for other cultural reasons – to deny (xix).

He makes the case for a 'discourse of extremity' (viii) which will speak in what he refers to as 'a voice that awakens and falls to the bottom of our spirit....that comes from regions remote from everyday experience. And it is for this reason it penetrates and persists.' (xx)
I conspired to turn my anti-anorexic practice into a kind of 'witnessing text' that would make us all consider 'that we had been transported there to the scene of the extremity, when we had not" (xix) and for those who were already there to know the moral injustice of their circumstances, perhaps for the very first time. Why? Perhaps up until then anorexia has co-opted the existing discourses (professional and lay) and successfully either deceived or blinded them in part through these means.

Julie, aged 45, writes:
I experienced a pressure (from anorexia) that I was meant to relinquish the living of my life as the best apology and therefore any signs of (my continuing to live my) life could be seen as a punishable deviation. It (anorexia) tried to convince me that my own execution was the only moral act of which I was capable and that this was inevitable even though I had managed to evade it to some extent until that time ... It had me believe that I would be relieving the world of a significant quantity of 'badness'.
Everything I tried seemed so inadequate to counter or question anorexia's moral judgement ... I didn't really question anorexia's monopoly on moral judgement until a day only a few years ago when it struck me suddenly (and I remember exactly where I was when it happened) that I had a dictator inside my mind. At first it horrified me but then I was mobilised to do something ... When I had the realisation of the 'dictator', I did wonder how it had happened but I STILL had no answers. I just knew I couldn't trust my own thought processes, as if they weren't entirely my own; in some ways a disconcerting concept, although I came to discover it was also a liberating concept ... I remember at the time I was studying Hamlet at university and also had a brief introduction to some of the ideas of Foucault. I ended up writing an essay about Hamlet. I was quite affected by the death of Ophelia in the play, who had apparently gone 'mad' and drowned. I remember her obligatory obedience to her father and the State. I think subjects at that time were considered part of the actual body of the State. When asked what she thought, she responded: "I do not know, my Lord. What should I
174

think?" And "I shall obey, my Lord." Viewing her voice as somehow being appropriated by the voice of a higher authority helped me think about thinking in relation to authorities which direct our lives, which allowed me to question anorexia's moral authority. (3)

I have turned to the papers of Arthur Kleinman, the Harvard psychiatrist/anthropologist such as 'Pain and Resistance: The Legitimation and Delegitimation of Local Worlds" (Kleinman, 1995). He speaks especially in reference to post traumatic stress disorder but also more generally 'how the clinician reworks the patient's perspective into disease categories which distort the moral world of the patient and community'. And how this 'ends up delegitimating the patient's suffering's moral commentary and political performance'. That this 're-creates human suffering as inhuman disease'.

But he casts his concerned gaze over my first profession – anthropology. This meant I was unable to breathe a sigh of relief and exempt myself from such a critique. And perhaps this is why I would return so often to these papers.

Let Kleinman speak for himself:

She or he (the anthropologist) can engage in professional discourse every bit as dehumanising as that of colleagues who unreflectively draw upon the tropes of biomedicine or behaviourism to create their subject matter ... an experience – rich and near-human subject can be converted into a dehumanised object, a caricature of experience (97).

He concludes:
1) *We, each of us, injure the humanity of our fellow sufferers each time we fail to privilege their voices, their experiences.*
2) *The professionalisation of human problems as psychiatric disorders causes sufferers (and their communities) to lose a world, the local context that organises experience through moral reverberation and reinforcement of popular cultural categories about what life means and what is at stake in living ... Experts are far along in the process of inauthenticating social worlds, of making illegitimate the defeats and victories, the desperation and aspiration of individuals and groups that could perhaps be more humanly rendered, not as representation of some other reality (one that we a experts possess special power over) but rather as the evocation of experience that stands for itself* (117).

Early on, Judy, then 30, explained matters by appeal to Bob Dylan's 'Just Like Tom Thumb's Blues' – She (anorexia) *takes your voice and leaves you howling at the moon.* I determined as best I could to find the means to allow these women to regain their moral voice and speak through that to the sources of their suffering. And that I was justified in joining as a chorus, as a co-league – that they would never be alone again.

Morality and Counter-Morality

In a manner of speaking (4), anorexia claims that it possesses the moral authority to decide the fate of a person – whether they are a 'somebody' or a 'no body'; whether they are in fact 'worthy' or 'unworthy' of life itself. Anorexia, then amongst other matters, is a distinctly perverse morality of personhood, intending to deceive and catch people up in their benevolent intentions, their aspirations and their vulnerabilities. Often anorexia appropriates both the secular and the sacred in its moralising by promising these young woman what Liz Eckermann refers to as a 'secular sainthood'. (Eckermann, 1997).

Although anorexia represents itself as a forum for moral reflection on the 'goodness' or 'badness' of absolutely every aspect of one's conduct, it soon blurs the distinction between right and wrong with normative measures – e.g. grades, scores, marks, weights and any other form of the assessments and objectifications of a person our culture has so far contrived. These norms by no means transcend the culture but rather are mirror-like reflections of it. How moralities of personhood and measures of the good have merged cannot be discussed here as it would take us into a long excursion into the theorising of Michel Foucault and the feminist scholars who have appropriated it for their own scholarly and political purposes. (5) Suffice to say, such considerations are critical to an anti-anorexic practice.

But more to our point, how does anorexia authorise itself to 'pass' or 'fail' a candidate for a contemporary personhood? Who or what has warranted it to do so? If it has arrogated to itself such momentous powers, what are its grounds for determining a successful candidate? And if one considers such tests and their criteria insupportable, how does one appeal and to whom?

Why the right of appeal is so important to consider is that when anorexia fails a candidate, such a person is rejected from the human fold and exiled into such obscurity that their own death is often preferred to such a 'living death' as some have referred to it. The 'living deaths' are dedicated to a purgatory to measure up to measures that continually shift out of their reach. They are not told that this is merely the antechamber of Hell.

It seems that once a candidate is taken in by anorexia, anorexia assesses them relentlessly as 'bad', 'unworthy', 'undeserving' and the only way out is their death. Anorexia sets a myriad of tests of perfection and ironically, only their death can now ensure their success e.g. 'the perfect failure'. A family reported the cry of their daughter – Perfection or Death! – as she attempted to jump from their roof to her death.

Anorexia turns any of our conventional moralities on their heads. Here 'bad' becomes 'good and 'good' becomes 'bad'. Here junk food is transformed into all food is junk and then converts a young woman into being junk. How else can we comprehend how young women, still in the thrall of anorexia, often refer to their zealous pursuit of anorexia's onerous requirements of them as a form of 'goodening'. Anyone else looking on would consider this a kind of enslavement these women are labouring under. What criteria does anorexia use to 'measure' a person 'up' for the very status of a person? And how does anorexia conceal from a candidate this immorality- and its fundamentalist distinctions between good/bad and right/wrong and instead dress them up as moral virtues? Why do these young people so rarely doubt or even quibble about its moral authority over them? And how does this morality operate so that once the candidate accepts its promises and devotes herself to meeting it prerequisites, she experiences herself in a maze and loses her hold on her moral agency. Getting out of this maze is like extricating oneself from quicksand – the more effort you put into your escape, the deeper down you sink.

How does anorexia purport to improve the morals of its candidates? What remains so sinister to an observer is that it appeals to the very high-mindedness of such women and before they know it, they find themselves accused by anorexia of crimes, convicted without knowing the specific nature of their wrong-doing or having any defence. Soon after, they are found guilty and beyond redemption. By what sleight of cunning does anorexia transform itself into censure, then criminal charges and finally a conviction for which punishment and torture immediately commence?

From now on, all their rights as citizens are stripped from them. All joys and pleasures, including smiling save fake smiling, are forbidden. The 'concentration camp' of everyday life is now instituted and they enter it, utterly convinced unlike on those on their admission to Auschwitz, that 'arbeit mach frie' (work, or here perfection, will set you free).

Judy wrote:
I told you I felt all these years like a silent Jew, forsaken by God, everyone and everything. You asked if I regarded anorexia and bulimia as sinister forms of power comparable to the naked tyranny that destroyed the Jewry in the Holocaust. Whereas they knew evil was being done to them – and they didn't deserve it, anorexia gets people to go to the torture chamber smiling; grateful even. I became grateful to my abuser. (Judy, 1994)

Anti-anorexia seeks to undo the cunning by which anorexia distills from this culture what Chambers might call one of the most compelling and lethal 'obscenities' of our time. Anorexia turns cultural images of a person, especially of a woman, to its own ends. Despite these images being contradictory, anorexia denies those very contradictions for a 'good and successful woman'. Moral measures e.g. selflessness, niceness, being a relief to others, self-abnegation, etc are merged with the requirements of a 'ruthless individualism' determined by scores, marks, weights and other objective assessments of those norms which promise entry into the world of a 'successful person', especially that of men. Such contradictions form the cross to which anorexia fixes these young women.

Because anorexia's prosecution takes place within the domain of its own moral jurisdiction, a viable defence can only be mounted within the domain of a counter-morality. Such a rival morality often takes shape by way of controverting anorexia or building bridges back to local moral orders that have been overridden by anorexia, such as various spiritualities that help women clarify and adhere to such values/virtues. Anti-anorexia as a style of living is not fixed to any particular pre-existing psychological code.

Such a rival or counter-morality allows anorexia's declarations of what is good or bad and who is a good or bad person to be first interrogated and then disputed. In the absence of such a rival, breaches of anorexia's dogma can only be interpreted within the very terms of anorexia's perverse morality as heresy or sin. Such a sin cannot be redeemed through penance but only expiated through torture and recantation. Without a counter-morality, freedom from anorexia's moral jurisdiction is virtually impossible.

Anti-anorexia provides the grounds for a counter-morality to rival that of anorexia's hegemony. It attempts to do so by turning anorexia against itself. Anorexia's arguments are found, under such scrutiny, to intend to deceive rather than uplift. Its reasoning is unveiled as misleading or fallacious. Furthermore, under such inspection, anorexia doesn't merely fail to improve their morals but manifests the very evil to which these young women are so opposed.

This moral disputation asks such questions as:

Is good done by evil? Would you grant evil to distinguish between who is 'good' and who is 'bad'? What is 'right' or what is 'wrong'? Should anti-anorexia convene with you and others to decide this matter? If so, would it make available a counter-morality in which one's benevolent intentions can be acted upon to serve benevolent ends? Is this something you might consider taking up with your goodness? Should such a counter-morality turn anorexia's sinister deceit on its head? Might an anti-anorexic counter-morality generate love of self and others, goodwill towards oneself and others and confirm the innocence and tragedy of those seduced, betrayed and murdered by anorexia?

Do You Think There Is Some Injustice Here?

This video-taped interview took place in the mid-90s in the peadiatric wards of a hospital in an unspecified country in Europe. I had been leading a workshop not surprisingly to do with anti-anorexia/anti-bulimia. Over the course of the day, I observed my colleague and director of an eating disorders ward becoming more and more distressed, answering what seemed to be persistent phone calls. She approached me at afternoon coffee break and told me of an emergency in her ward. It seemed that the nursing staff intended to go on strike the next day if she did not order Monica (6), aged 18, out of the children's hospital into an adult psychiatric unit. It seemed that for some time now Monica had been screaming in anguish for much of any day while hitting her head against brick walls and tearing her hair out by the roots. Her life had been in peril for many months now. The nursing staff referred to this as 'tantrumming'. They could not tolerate this any longer, so concerned were they about the effect this was having on younger in-patients. What could I do under the circumstances? I agreed to meet Monica several hours later after the day's teaching was over. My colleague was able to invite along her mother, Franziska, who lived nearby. By the time we met, Monica looked kempt and had obviously recovered some of her equanimity. This is no way diminished in my mind the nursing staff's concerns.

The following is a somewhat abbreviated version of the first half hour of this interview:

David: *How does anorexia talk you into torturing yourself? What does it tell you that gets you to violate your body and pull out your hair and make you seem a lot younger than you really are? What is it telling you?*

Monica: *That I don't have the right to be happy.*

David: *Why do you think anorexia has forbidden you to have life, liberty, freedom and happiness? Do you know the Declaration of Independence in the United States? Liberty and the pursuit of happiness. It's denying you your human rights. Why do you think it's doing this? Have you committed some crimes?*

Monica: *I don't know.*

David: *Have you murdered anyone?*

Monica: *No.*

David: *On what grounds is it denying you your freedom?*

Monica: *I don't know. I can't figure it out.*

David: *Say you were walking down the street in your city and the police came and threw you in jail and said: "You can't have any freedoms!" What would you do? Would you say: "What are the charges against me?" Would you say you wanted a lawyer? Do you believe justice should operate in your country?*

Monica: *Yes!*

David: *Do you think this is just? You are being punished and tortured and you don't know what you've done wrong. To me that doesn't sound like a democracy. Do you believe in democracy?*

Monica: *Yes, I do! But anorexia says I've done something wrong but I don't know what it is.*

David: *Where do you think anorexia got that idea from?*

Monica: *I don't know.*

David: *Do you think you've had a fair trial? In my country, and I think in your country, you're told what you did wrong. Then there is a judge or jury. And then you defend yourself?*

Monica: *She (anorexia) never tells me. I ask but she won't say.*

David: *This is even worse. This could drive anyone crazy.*

Monica: *Yes, I feel like that sometimes.*

David: *Why do you think she (anorexia) would play such an insidious and cunning trick on a young woman? What purpose would she have in doing this? (to her mother) Would you consider Monica a nice daughter or a nice person?*

Mother: *She has been nice to me .... too nice to me.*
David: *Why do you think anorexia would take advantage of a very nice young woman?*
Monica: *I don't know.*
David: *I don't think the answer is easy. I'm wondering why?*
Monica: *I've asked myself that question many times and I haven't found the answer.*
David: *Maybe there isn't a simple answer. If you ask yourself why is there injustice, you may never find the answer but you may find a revolution to put things right.*
Monica: *Mmm.*
David: *Do you think there is some injustice here?*
Monica: *(with emphasis) Yes, I do!*
David: *Well, I've got to tell you – so do I! Why do you think there is some injustice being done to you by anorexia? What's the nature of it? When did you realise anorexia was immoral? Did she tell you she was good or serving a good cause?*
Monica: *Yes.............*

In this abstract from an interview, anorexia's morality was called into question rather than allowing it to condemn Monica. Conversations that inspect anorexia's morality from the perspective of a counter-morality can challenge anorexia/bulimia as the arbiter of the 'good'. Moreover, in time, these inquiries often reveal the perversity and malevolence not only of the judgements but the principles upon which these judgements are based. Under such anti-anorexic/anti-bulimic scrutiny, anorexia/bulimia is defrocked. It is no longer viewed as the only means to improve a person's morals but, rather, as a manifestation of the evil and one of the very violences these women oppose" (Maisel, Epston & Borden (2004) pp. 151-2).

David Bears Witness
David, aged 12, fulminated against anorexia, demanding reparation by writing an apology on anorexia's behalf.

Apology from Anorexia to Myself
I am writing this apology to myself because I know that even though I may dream about it. Even though I thoroughly deserve it. Even though you have stolen every pleasure that I had in my life. I know that you are so heartless, so shallow and so ruthless that you would never have the compassion or decency to ever make the apology that you have for so long owed me.

Here it is:
I am sorry that I have stolen your life away from you. I am sorry for turning every pleasure you once had in your joyful life into an unbearable torture, from your

pleasure in eating to your pleasure in good company and sport. I made you hate yourself and see fault in everything that you were and did. I took away all your happiness and turned everything you found into a horrible ordeal. I sapped all your strength, turning you into a lifeless body without a soul. I deprived you of all the tastes you enjoyed and stole from you x kilograms, turning you into an unhappy skeleton. I lied to you, telling you that I would make you happy and an overall better person. When you did what I said, I was ruthless and pushed your face into the mud, making you hate yourself and blame yourself for things that I had forced and tortured you into doing.

It is obvious that it would be impossible to fix what I have done. There is no way that I can take back what I have done because I terribly scarred and mutilated you. All I can do is apologise and leave you and your family alone forever. I know I cannot make up for what I have done to you but I will do all I can to fix what I have done. I am sorry for what I have done and you deserve this apology and more.

Yours truly sorry,
Anorexia (March 26, 2006)

Judy Bears Witness

Judy, aged 30, by identifying anorexia as 'evil' secures her own innocence. She is no longer wrong but wronged:

For some reason, I couldn't listen to the audio-tapes of our meetings at all, no matter how hard I tried or well-intentioned I was. When eventually I got to hear them, I felt cheated, realising patently that it was anorexia which had prevented me all along. All sorts of indications from the feeling someone was using my body to speak to you from the chair I sat. While you took the side of hope, frustrating her designs, anorexia insisted on being well-practiced in taking the side of despair. You said at one point that anorexia might not come in to your office but if it did, we would get rid of it quickly.

Listening to our conversation, I felt I could see it attempting to come in, or be there dominant, at every point. With some incredulity, I listened to a tortured, twisted logic. A voice through which my experience was being structured and through which it developed – degraded. I did feel the whole force of The League behind your attempts to evict it from my body or the room. But at the same time, even such a force of resistance did not make me feel entirely comfortable. In fact, I became scared for you and maybe me, when I realised what you were confronting there.

As I listened another time – nothing! No bulimia, not able to seduce me away. When I heard anorexia speaking to you from my chair, I was reminded of everything I had witnessed. Everything that was anti-life condensed into this voice. I could see and even sympathise with my own weaknesses, that it was the coils of a serpent that suffocated me, that had its hold on me and wouldn't let go. I realised then what was being done to me WAS EVIL! That first you and then me were up against evil. This was a revelation to me – to confront evil was immediately to detach from it.

You asked me if I thought anorexia rendered a person heartless? Does it take control of your mind and erase your heart and soul? The short answer is 'Yes' but it also produces resistance to it. In a way, the first time I self-consciously took the side of outrage and perhaps self-consciously did anything at all was when I listened to the audio-tapes and in some way, anorexia was exposed.

Since then anorexia has become an object of amazement to me. Amazement because it feels as I have been lived by something unbelievably bad and ridiculous. It made me uncomfortable as I learned more about her because I had never imagined anything quite so bad. I would say now, I never really knew existence of evil. That is ironic coming from someone almost consumed by guilt, but it is true. I don't share the same moral universe as this thing anorexia. It's hatred of me and life generally is beyond comprehension. (31/6/1993)

David Bears Witness on behalf of The League

Mary, aged 17, had pulled herself out of the quicksands of anorexia over 1997 and 1998 for the time being. It was painstaking for her parents, Warren and Sharon, as well as myself. However, faced with her final secondary school examinations late that year, we all feared that every freedom she had reclaimed would be forfeited and she would perish. Warren, usually a strong contributor to any anti-anorexic discussion, sat with his head bowed, tears running down his cheeks and pooling on his shirt collar. Sharon, also a thoughtful commentator, seemed frozen into a glacial silence. It seemed as if Mary had come to say her final farewell to me. I found this unbearable and wrote from the very 'heart' of the archives.

Dear Mary:

I wanted to write you after our meeting on Thursday. I strongly felt anorexia, once again, pulling you away from us and down, insinuating that there was no other 'world' for you than his Hell, where he promises you will sit beside him as his Queen. It was unnerving for me and judging from Warren's helpless tears of frustration, it is for us all. Before I had time to put my fingers to my keyboard, your mother rang to reassure me that you were able to come back to us a bit. That was a great relief to me and I know it was to Sharon and Warren. However, it did delay my response.

Mary, I am writing to you in defiance of anorexia and all that it stands for. I swear to you – and all those murdered by anorexia are my witnesses – that nothing will prevent the League from keeping a 'place' open for you – a place to stand and take a stand for your life and entitlements to happiness, peace and fulfillment. Admittedly, such a Resistance must at times go into hiding underground and at other times strike fiercely. And we do sustain losses. But such losses are trivial compared to the suffering at anorexia's hands. After all it will even "eat your smile for dessert!" What kind of life is it that anorexia promises? To be a well-dressed Barbie-puppet, looking pretty? What do you make of Barbie smiling as she goes about measuring herself up to Perfection and torture?

What does Anti-Anorexia promise? Nothing but a place to stand and hold up a mirror for you to see anorexia without its mask of benevolent solicitude. It is a longstanding tradition in the annals of punishment and torture that the executioner keeps his face well hidden, is it not? From an anti-anorexic point of view, anorexia can no longer blindfold you or keep you in the dark. Now can you see what there is to see? Can you speak out against anorexia because you now have the language to do so? Can anorexia conceal its intentions from you any longer? Are its promises turning to dusty betrayals?

If my experience in the League over the past ten years is anything to go by, there will be a struggle but I suspect in and out of these very struggles, you will forge your 'self' for yourself. I can assure you there will be fun and celebration along the way. And one day you will decide for yourself to put your arms down. However, will you ever set your vigilance aside? After all, anorexia is nowhere and everywhere; anti-anorexia is merely somewhere.

Mary, we remain your sisters, your brothers, your comrades and your friends. We remain where we are, even if sometimes we go underground but we never surrender. If I am any judge of Sharon and Warren, I believe that they would never surrender either. Never!!!! To be one of us, there are no measurements, no examination and no assessments. Your suffering, which is so evident to all of us, is your welcome.

Welcome back even if you have to jump the hurdle of your examination. We want you to know we abhor examinations. You are more than enough for Anti-Anorexia.

I look forward to catching up with you next week.

David Epston

On behalf of the Anti-Anorexia/Anti-Bulimia League. (7)

Ann Bears Witness

Ann Epston writes to Emma, aged 13 and her parents Sandra and Brian after their first meeting together. Emma's life is in peril and a hospitalisation is imminent:

Dear Emma, Sandra, and Brian,

It was good to meet you all last night and make a start on getting to know you. Thank you, Emma, for your frankness and bravery in talking and in answering so many questions asked by a stranger.

I woke up at midnight and couldn't get back to sleep for hours; my mind was boiling with a furious anger against anorexia. I thought, "Here we go again, anorexia! So you've sneaked into the life of yet another innocent young girl, pretending to befriend her at a time of big changes. How cunning of you to detect Emma's uneasiness with her developing body, and how unscrupulous of you to offer her an 'easy' solution – dieting! How neatly you insinuated yourself into her uncertainty, her longing for friends and boyfriends, promising her that thinness would ensure attractiveness and popularity, would win her admiration and make her the envy of all who know her. Anorexia, did you tell her the price she'd have to pay? Did you warn her you'd eventually steal even her soul in exchange? I heard you actually convinced Emma she's your only victim, in a school of 1200 girls!

You vampire, anorexia, haven't you taken enough already? Aren't you satisfied with the stream of young girls you've preyed upon, stealing their fat, then their flesh, their strength, their energy, their enthusiasm, their sparkle, their humour, opinions, sports, games, friendships, social times, confidence, trust, creativity, originality, individuality – their very lives?

I suppose Emma was an attractive choice: intelligent, friendly, humorous, a lover of animals, responsible, ambitious, prepared to study hard and train to be a vet. What a delightful tall poppy to cut down at the threshold of adolescence! What pleasure you must be taking in draining her energy, blurring her concentration, and alienating her from her own body.

How did you do it, anorexia? How did you train Emma to criticise and reject her body instead of loving herself? How did you make her believe that some imaginary schoolboy's opinion was worth starvation? What vulnerabilities did you seize upon to convince her that thin weak conformists are more desirable than strong individuals?

I suppose you have lots of help: the movies, magazines, TV soaps, advertising, schoolgirl culture – they all tell the same story, that less is best for girls' bodies and minds. Did you use your usual trick of comparing? Making Emma compare herself against friends and declare herself the loser, then offer your services in consolation, the perfect solution? Did you use the old drug dealers' trick of just a little bit at first? Did you slip smoothly from the oh-so-reasonable 'no junk food' to gradually defining all food as junk? Did you use secrecy and the pretence of 'specialness' to isolate Emma in subtle ways from the loving concern of family and friends? And of course I know you used fear, that despicable technique favoured by tyrants and bullies the world over. Yes, you terrorised this 13-year-old into accepting your lie – that you offer 'control' and without you, Emma will lose all control and her hunger will be insatiable.

If it weren't so vicious and evil it would be laughable, your threat that a healthy, active young woman will become the size of a whale just by the simple fact of eating ordinary nourishing food. This fear has tormented and tortured countless thousands upon thousands of young women into submitting to your hateful rule.

But, anorexia, we will not stand for it. Emma has wise and loving parents who will not allow you to prey upon their beloved daughter. They have chosen me as their anti-anorexic therapist, and with the help of Dr_____ and her dietitian and everyone who cares about Emma, we will fight anorexia and fear and drive you out of this family's life. We do this because we are perfectly clear about what is right and what is wrong. Take notice, anorexia, we will do everything in our power to free Emma from the spell you have cast over her. We are guided by two principles: unwavering support and love for Emma and unwavering hatred for anorexia and the harm it does."

Yours anti-anorexically,
Ann Epston (8)

Conclusion

I have come to consider 'anti-anorexia/anti-bulimia' as much as anything else a moral endeavour. How could it be otherwise if we reach the conclusion that anorexia is a perverse morality or worse yet, an immorality tricked up as an assemblage of moral virtues? I have known of so many disheartened and disheartening treatments. I am asking us to consider remoralising (Frank, 2004) our vision of our practice in order to assist these young people to remoralise the living of their lives. To do so may have us seriously question how we might conduct ourselves with that in mind. For me, to do otherwise would now make me wittingly complicit with anorexia – a bystander pretending not much is going on here but whatever it is it should be rendered solely through the extant professional discourses. I do not consider them adequate to such a moral task. After all, I have been told time and time again that 'I became anorexic for the hospital' or even on behalf of a particular professional person. Here I am reminded of Michel Foucault's quote: People know what they do; they frequently know why they do what they do; but what they don't know is what what they do does (8) (Foucault cited in Dreyfus & Rabinow, 1983, 187).

I believe that as much as anything else we are in need of counter-moralities to those anorexia would have these young women pay homage to and tell their lives accordingly. Here I am thinking of some of the most enduring and moral political rhetorics we have at our disposal:

1) Fighting for your life and the lives of your 'sisters' and against your murdered and the murderer of your 'sisters',
2) Fighting for justice to be done in your life and the lives of your sisters and in principle and against injustice in your life and the lives of your sisters and in principle.

This is in line with Helen Gremillions' metaphor for such women – 'the canaries in the mines'. (10) Canaries were kept in mines until not so long ago to detect the odourless and invisible toxic gases that aside from mine cave-ins were the greatest risk to miners' lives. For when a canary, who stood guard in their cages on behalf of the miners and did so by their indefatigable singing vigils, fell silent through their own asphyxiation, miners immediately would flee to safety. To this day in many mines, their empty cages remain as testament to the innocent songbirds that perished on the miner's behalf. Shouldn't we listen to the innocent songs of these young women which brings to my mind such sorrowfulness and seek that they along with us become worldly-wise. And that they be reindentified as competent members of their moral communities and in doing so enable the further expression of their goodness.

Addendum

During the conference, I met Warren Ward, Director of the Eating Disorders Service at the Royal Brisbane and Women's Hospital. He told me of Kylie, aged nineteen, who had been declared a 'hopeless case' following numerous hospitalisations and out-patient care since she was eleven years old. But on her mother and herself reading Biting the Hand that Starves You (Maisel, Epston & Borden, 2004) she was subsequently declared in recovery. He agreed to ask her if I might be in email contact with her to discuss this matter. She happily consented and the following is the entire email record of our conversations, except for the removal of my queries for her document, headed 'Dear David and Rick'. This conversation took place between October, 2006 and January, 2007.

Dear David
In Adelaide I spoke to you about Kylie, one of our 'hopeless cases', who really turned around thanks to she and her mother reading your book. I had my last appointment with her last week as she is moving interstate. She is now well and truly in recovery. I told her you had expressed an interest in contacting her and she would really like that.
Regards
Warren

Warren Ward
Director
Eating Disorders Service
Royal Brisbane and Women's Hospital

Dear Kylie:
Thank you for allowing Warren to pass on your email address to me. As you may know, I met him very recently in Adelaide at the Australian and New Zealand Academy of Eating Disorders Conference. He attended the pre-conference day long workshop I did which gave me a chance to have some discussions with him. He mentioned in confidence how 'Biting the Hand that Starves You' had played some part in you proceeding to recovery. As you may realise from having read the book that this work – anti-anorexia/anti-bulimia – has been very central to the 'work' of my life for over fifteen years now. And the book itself was the culmination of an eight-year-long collaboration with Rick Maisel (in Berkeley, California). Thank God for computers and email!

I know it was a hope of both Rick and myself that this book might 'reach out' beyond a professional readership to both 'insiders' and their families/partners/ friends. In fact, although we may have started out with the intention to inform our professional colleagues, as the book progressed, we gave more and more significance to our other hoped for readerships e.g. insiders/families/etc. For this reason, I am taking every opportunity that comes my way (e.g. through colleagues or through the website) to discuss how 'Biting the Hand' works. Obviously with regard to professionals, you can read book reviews that tell you how your colleagues view the book and 'anti-anorexia/anti-bulimia'.

Would you (and perhaps your mum) be willing to have an email conversation with me so I could find out if Rick's and my hopes have been realised, if only with
186

one insider and one family? I would be really grateful if you would join me in such a conversation. And don't worry as you probably know from the book, I am 'full' of questions and curiosity.

Yours anti-anorexically,
David

Hi David and Rick:
Thank you so much for your email. It is really exciting to be talking to the person who has written 'Biting the Hand'. And if it is of any interest, it all started when I borrowed the book from the library while I was looking for weight loss books. So yes, you can speak to me and my mum if you would like. I stumbled on to it in the 'health and diet' section. It stood out amongst the books on depression and other eating disorder books. It wasn't the cover that stood out but the title. And it was that it was bigger than the others, which were very brief and this book seemed more in depth. What caught my interest about the title was because 'Biting the Hand That Starves You' is like something is doing it to you; you are not doing it to yourself!

When I first looked at it, I thought it was your typical symptoms and basic eating disorder book. But when I started reading it, it was different altogether. It was as though I was writing it word for word myself. What the book was saying was what I was (and still) think. But now it was as if my mind was written on paper. At first, I felt I was ... well ... being made fun of ... rather like this book was trying to make out it 'knows'. After all, I thought this was my secret and at first I was angry that this book had got into my life.

I had borrowed many such books before and had never been able to read them. When I borrowed 'Biting the Hand', I just did it because it was an eating disorder book and I could flip through and that would be that. You asked me if anorexia tried to have me put 'Biting the Hand' down. I think so but I am not really sure for I was in a daze. I couldn't really read it. The words stood out on the page and this time I wanted to read them. So I got my mum to read a bit to me. But then my mum started reading it and began to treat me differently. She began to read some of it to me and I began to feel differently. Mum started talking to the anorexia and getting it angry. For example, she would ask – "Is the anorexia stopping you from eating that?" She told me what she was doing but we did fight a lot over it. My mother is amazing. She is real; she tells it how it is. I have told her every thought that goes on in my head. She knows me and anorexia very well. She is great and knows how to talk to 'me'. But at first, I felt like mum didn't get it. But what she said would sit in my mind and later I would keep thinking about it. Then slowly it was – "Why am I eating that? Why can't I eat that etc.?" It took ages and I still go back to it now and again.

But I have been telling everyone about 'Biting the Hand'. I still want to be thin and they ask me why. And I don't really know. So I am starting to question that. The fighting continued. It was about my mum not leaving anorexia alone. And her thinking she knew what I was going through. But really at that stage, my mum probably knew more than I did about anorexia. She certainly knew anorexia wasn't me.

187

Kylie's mum: *My first reaction from flipping through 'Biting the Hand' was the girls'
stories catching my eye. They sounded so similar to what my daughter
had been telling me, both through her words and feelings. Those girls in
the book were saying exactly the same things!*

Kylie: *What thoughts ran through my mind? I was scared. I had never been
scared like this before. I was scared that the whole 'you have an illness
– anorexia' could be true. I was afraid that others and this book might be
right and that I was really sick.*

*But, this was when for the first time I was out of my self . . . that might sound weird . . .
I was in a book. I felt separate from myself. At the same time, I felt I had betrayed myself.
I still didn't think anorexia was entirely separate from me. I had always thought that
anorexia was me! When I first got the idea it was anorexia, I denied it. I still wouldn't really
let myself believe it. Then I felt very angry for quite a while and then (and I am still) a bit
hurt.*

*I had believed I did deserve the torturing anorexia was doing to me. I wasn't good
enough and I thought I should be in pain. I was (and still am a bit) very hurt and feel
so back stabbed by my so-called 'friend' who was supposed to be looking after and
protecting me from bad things. It took me months to realise this. My mind had been so
taken over by anorexia that it took a while to start to hear myself. But I did take my anger
out on anorexia by trying to take control away from it and do what it would not want me
to do.*

*Yes, I am still very, very angry! You asked what would have come of me if I hadn't
chanced on to 'Biting the Hand'. Ahhhhhh I don't want to even think about that. This book
was my turning point. I think to be honest I would be dead by now. Anorexia would have
taken my life. To be truly honest, the saving of my life was this book. Without 'Biting the
Hand', I am convinced that I would not be here alive. I have had this illness for eight years
and had a lot of therapy. But not once had anything every hit me like the words in 'Biting
the Hand'. It pulled me out of Hell. I'm still a work in progress but I have come so far.*

*Finding myself in a book between two covers, I realised that finally someone
understood. I had never ever felt understood before. Thank God for this book! Almost
all of the many professionals I had met didn't really know anything. They just didn't
understand. But reading the book felt good. It was like anorexia was diagnosed and it had
symptoms and it was not just a matter of me losing my mind.*

*Nothing like this had had ever happened before in my life. And it remains unique to this
day.*

*David, this is what happened to me last week. I went to my cousin's wedding and had
a three course meal of baked ricotta, potato mash with pesto oil dressing and cashews,
then mousse and cream with strawberries in syrup for dessert plus two dinner rolls with
butter. And you know what? For the first time in forever, there was nothing – silence, not
a voice to be heard except the happy chatter of my family and friends. Anorexia was
nowhere to be seen or heard. I had the best time.*

*To me this doesn't happen very often but such days are happening more and more
– even on an average day. Well, yes anorexia speaks to me but the words are now*

spoken, not yelling or coercive but spoken in a small, timid and unsure voice. I have to go back a long way in my life to remember when anorexia didn't scream or rant at me. David, it felt so good to hear nothing but my family speak and my own thoughts thinking the food was lovely and nothing else. And that's when my voice is bigger and louder. I win a lot of the time. I am eating well. I am resting when I feel like it. I am thinking about other things. Deep down I do love myself and like what I am. I'm not quite all me yet but anorexia is getting smaller and weaker by the day. And it is a dream come true! I just wanted to share this with you!

David, if I can help in any way please let me know. You have helped me so much. Thank you. And I would like to help other girls in any way I can. 'Biting the Hand' really did save my life. Mum wants to thank you too. She is of the firm belief that this book saved my life above all else.

Footnotes
1. When I first began to learn of the desperate solitariness of these young women, I investigated how it was that they had become so confined, standing so alone in their 'cells', crying out but no one seeming to be able to understand their torment. At times, their cries were read as 'acts of control' or 'manipulation' and they were regarded as prima donnas at best and spoiled brats at worst. I heard desperate silences, only relieved by self-accusations, self-condemnations and confessions of the guilty. The clinical wisdom at the time was that 'anorexics shouldn't speak to each other' which justified even more solitary confinements. I viewed these young women, much like Gremillion, as 'canaries in the mine', but who would care to listen once they had been confined to psychiatric versions of themselves. My first thought was –'other canaries' which led to next query – how might they inform each other of their impending fate to which anorexia had doomed them?

    I immediately began to contrive any form of association I could think of, many of which were contrary to the orthodoxy of professional-client relationships, so that concerned parties could 'convene'. I circulated, with careful consent, forms of documentation e.g. 'letters', stories, transcripts of interviews, the interviews themselves recorded on audio or video-tape, and consultations in which 'insider knowledges' were both constructed and shared. I began to develop ad hoc 'communities of concern', although soon learned how anorexia could both inform and pervert their very 'community'. Anorexia would have league members compete against each other to be the 'best' anorexic ('Look at Bridget ... now she is a real anorexic and you're not even in her league!) or failing that, the 'best' anti-anorexic (Look at Rhonda ... now she is a real anti-anorexic person and you're not even in her league!). I realised how important it was for me to mediate these relationships to anorexia-proof them to the extent that we were able to do so. There was also a risk of such women selflessly dedicating themselves to the anti-anorexic causes of others, almost as if they were bequeathing what remained of their short lives to inspirit their survivors.

    I conceived of a 'community' that was flexible and fleet enough to side-step such anorexic coups. Perhaps the name 'league' itself came from my notion of 'being in league' with others against anorexia and 'its effects on you, on another league member and women in general'. Or was it a taking apart of co-league to stand for how we all might stand together in solidarity. A league then merely became a kind of compact to prosecute common concerns e.g. the unmasking of anorexia and the development of counter-practices, and I have always imagined leagues as taking any number of associational forms. The most modest being an association between two young women and their families to something as elaborate as the Vancouver Anti-anorexia, anti-bulimia League, a non-taxable charity (Grieves, 1997). Obviously the latter had a much larger programme and more considered purposes than the 'ad hoc' arrangements I was regularly instituting through my practice. These ad hoc arrangements and the circulation of documentation soon reached the point of an extensive archive that I administered for some years by means of xeroxing copies and posting them off to their recipients. However, the scale of such an anti-anorexic operation was circumscribed by its very means. The Archives of Resistance: Anti-Anorexia/Anti-Bulimia were put up on *www.narrativeapproaches. com* which now allows for much more ready access to these materials (go to *www. narrativeapproaches.com/anti_anorexia_index.htm*).

2. I use the term 'insider' to stand for those who have suffered and have become knowledged (10) through their suffering. The composite – 'insider knowledges' is intended to distinguish 'insider knowledges' from the far more prestigious and established 'outsider knowledges' associated with the disciplines and the professions. Reading the literature of narrative therapy, 'insider knowledges' can be considered as synonymous with previous usages as 'alternative' or 'local knowledges. (White& Epston, 1990).
3. Julie King. 2007. From unpublished correspondence.
4. See *Manners of Speaking*. In Maisel, R., Epston, D. & Borden, A. 2004. W.W. Norton, New York. pp. 75-89.
5. See Lock *et al.*, Relevant Works on Anorexia, Feminism and Foucault, in Maisel *et al.* pp. 303-304.
6. Monica is a professional practitioner and has requested her anonymity and that of her country be protected.
7. See Epston, 1999, (pp. 137-157)
8. See A. Epston in Maisel *et al.*, 2004, (pp. 160-162).
9. See Dreyfus, H.L. & Rabinow, P. 1983, (p. 187).
10. Gremillion, H. 2003.
11. This is a neologism of Michael White which I recall first hearing him use around 2000.

References

Binswanger, L. (1944) Der Fall Ellen West, *Schweizer Archiv fur Neurologie und Psychiatrie*, 53, pp. 256-277.

Chambers, R. (2004) *Untimely Interventions: AIDS Writing, Testimonial, and The Rhetoric of Haunting*, Ann Arbor: University of Michigan Press.

Dreyfus, J.L. & Rabinow, P. (1983) *Michel Foucault: Beyond Structuralism and Hermeneutics*, 2nd Ed, Chicago. University of Chicago Press.

Eckerman, L. (1997) Foucault, embodiment and gendered subjectivities: The case of voluntary self-starvation, In A. Petersen, and R. Bunton (Eds.), *Foucault, Health and Medicine*, London: Routlege.

Epston, D. (1999) Co-research: The making of an alternative knowledge, in *Narrative Therapy and Community Work: A Conference Collections*. Dulwich Centre Publications, Adelaide, Australia. An extended version can be found at *http://www.narrativeapproaches.com/ antianorexia%20folder/AAcoresearch.htm*

Frank, A.W. (2004) Moral Non-Fiction: Life Writing and Children's Disability. In *The Ethics of Life Writing*, P.J. Eakin (Ed). Ithaca. Cornell University Press.

Gremillion, H. (2001) A canary in the mine: An anthropological perspective. In *Working with stories of Women's Lives* (pp. 133-150). Dulwich Centre Press, Adelaide, Australia.

Grieves, L. (1997) From beginning to start: The Vancouver anti-anorexia, anti-bulimia league, *Gecko: A Journal of Deconstruction and Narrative Ideas in Therapeutic Practice*, 2, 78-88.

Kleinman, A. (1995) Suffering and its professional transformation: Toward an ethnography of interpersonal experience (with Joan Kleinman). In *Writing at the Margin: Discourse between Anthropology and Medicine* (pp. 95-119), Berkeley: University of California.

Kleinman, A. (1995) Pain and resistance: The deligitmation and religitimation of local worlds. *Ibid* (pp. 120-146.)

Lock, A., Epston, D., Maisel, R. & de Faria, N. (2005) Resisting anorexia/bulimia: Foucauldian perspectives in Narrative Therapy, *British Journal of Guidance and Counselling*, Vol. 33-3, August, pp. 315-332.

Maisel, R. & Rachel (1994) Unpublished transcript.

Maisel, R., Epston, D. & Borden, A. (2004) *Biting the Hand that Starves You: Inspiring Resistance to Anorexia Bulimia*, W.W. Norton & Co, New York

White, M. & Epston, D. (1990) Narrative Means to Therapeutic Ends, W.W. Norton. New York.

Wolf, N. (1991) *The Beauty Myth: How Images of Beauty Are Used Against Women*. Vintage, London.

Afterword

I would like to thank all my co-authors, co-leagues and co-researchers for the very obvious parts they played in thinking up much of what got into text in this book and more importantly, living it out. For it has been the ways in which any of the inventions have been lived out by those who subscribed to them that substantiated such innovations as practice.

I would also like to thank Barry Bowen for thinking up this project in the first place. And then he took the idea up with the Association for Family Therapy (United Kingdom) and after some time, this book has come about. It is as much his as mine in that he has played a far greater role than an editor. He was an intimate partner in the project from the beginning and I know for a fact that if it wasn't for him, it could easily have been dropped by my wayside. Despite my disappearances for months at a time from the project, he calmly just took the lead and waited for me to catch up to him. I am extremely grateful to Barry for this book.

David Epston
(2008)